BUSINESS
CYCLES
AND THEIR
CAUSES

D0060724

WESLEY CLAIR MITCHELL

BUSINESS CYCLES AND THEIR CAUSES

UNIVERSITY OF CALIFORNIA PRESS
BERKELEY AND LOS ANGELES: 1963

University of California Press
Berkeley and Los Angeles, California

Cambridge University Press
London, England

BIBLIOGRAPHICAL NOTE

BUSINESS CYCLES, *Part III of which is here reprinted, was published by the University of California Press in 1913 as a quarto of some six hundred pages. In the early 1920's, when all the copies printed had been sold, the Press invited me to prepare a revised edition. I declined on the ground that I could not tell what was wrong, what was doubtful, and what was sound in my first version until I had studied cyclical movements more thoroughly. By that time the National Bureau of Economic Research had begun cultivating the field, and I was eager to take full advantage of the counsel and assistance it put at my disposal, as well as of later materials, in a fresh attack upon the problem.*

Now that the University of California Press has renewed its invitation, I can see no justification for reissuing the earlier parts of the 1913 volume. Part I contained a summary of the leading theories of business cycles then current, a sketch of economic organization, and a year-to-year account of cyclical fluctuations in the United States, England, France, and Germany from 1890 to 1911. Business Cycles: The Problem and Its Setting, *published by the National Bureau in 1927, and kept in print, treats these topics more searchingly on the basis of more recent investigations. And the National Bureau is in process of superseding the statistical data and analyses of Part II. A much larger collection of time series, mainly in monthly form, is being analyzed by greatly improved methods, and worked up by specialists who can interpret the findings in the light of fuller knowledge than I have. Their results will appear as a series of* Studies in Cyclical Behavior, *of which the first is nearly ready for the press. Why reprint business annals and statistics that end in 1911, or a review of business-cycle theories as they stood in 1912?*

Perhaps a better case can be made for reprinting Part III of the quarto. While the Studies in Cyclical Behavior *are being written, I am trying to piece their findings together in a volume to be called* The Rhythm of Business Activity. *At best, this effort will take several years, and there is no assurance that my working capacity will last long enough to let me be in at the finish. Nor would the immediate assumption of the task by others assure prompt completion. Thus there is no prospect that Part III of the quarto will soon be replaced by a more thorough version, as Part I has been and Part II is in process of being.*

A contribution to economic theory does not pass out of date so automatically as do business annals and business statistics. Friends tell me, and I like to believe them, that Part III still has value as a realistic account of what goes on within a business cycle. The economic organization of which it treats has changed in many ways since war disrupted the world in 1914, but the fundamental institutions of private property, money economy, and free enterprise in search of profits persist in the countries that concern Americans most. Certainly the changes have not diminished the violence of business cycles or the need of understanding how they come about. The interrelations among economic activities, out of which I framed my explanation in 1913, have not been abrogated. No one writing now would distribute his emphasis as I did then, or make all the statements I thought warranted. But I am reluctant to attempt revisions suggested by an incomplete assimilation of the observations gathered by the National Bureau or hypotheses offered by theoretical writers. So this reprint is issued with no changes beyond betterments in wording and the correction of an arithmetical blunder. The many references to Parts I and II of the quarto are retained primarily as reminders that Part III was woven out of observations, not excogitated from postulates. Also they will aid critical readers who may wish to look up in the quarto the evidence that shaped the conclusions.

Arthur F. Burns and Joseph Dorfman are morally responsible for the appearance of this volume, though they do not approve of omitting Parts I and II. For that I claim the merit. Martha Anderson edited the original text with characteristic care. My warm thanks go to these friends; also to Samuel T. Farquhar and Harold A. Small of the University of California Press, who have made reprinting an easy task for me.

WESLEY C. MITCHELL

April 21, 1941

PREFACE

THE REVIEW *of theories in Part I of my* Business Cycles[1] *and the statistical study of the phenomena of cycles in Part II had a common purpose—to provide suggestions and materials for framing an account of the rhythmical alternations of prosperity, crisis, depression, and revival in the modern business world.*

Now the recurrent phases presented by economic activity, wherever it is dominated by the quest of profits, grow out of and grow into each other. An incipient revival of activity, for example, develops into full prosperity, prosperity gradually breeds a crisis, the crisis merges into depression, depression becomes deeper for a while, but ultimately engenders a fresh revival of activity, which is the beginning of another cycle. A theory of business cycles must therefore be a descriptive analysis of the cumulative changes by which one set of business conditions transforms itself into another set.

The deepest-seated difficulty in the way of framing such a theory is that while business cycles recur decade after decade each new cycle present idiosyncrasies. Business history repeats itself, but always with a difference. This is part of what is implied by saying that the process of economic activity within which business cycles occur is a process of cumulative change.

A thoroughly adequate theory of business cycles, applicable to all cycles, is consequently unattainable. Even if some one

---

[1] *Memoirs of the University of California, Vol. 3, 1913; now out of print.*

*cycle could be fully accounted for, the account would neces-
sarily be inaccurate for cycles that were the outgrowth of earlier
or of later conditions. Nor are all the differences between the
successive cycles of one country and between the contemporary
cycles of several countries minor. Even such an elementary
matter as the order in which the phases of a business cycle succeed one another is not invariable. A revival of business activity does not always develop into prosperity—sometimes it
relapses into depression. Such deviations from the usual course
of events occurred in the United States in 1892, 1895, and 1910.
A situation of intense strain, presenting the phenomena of
crises, sometimes occurs in a period of depression, instead of
following a period of prosperity; for example, the American
stringency of 1896. It is needless to elaborate, however, for the
points of difference between any two periods of prosperity, of
crisis, or of depression are scarcely less numerous than the
points of similarity. Every business cycle, strictly speaking, is
a unique series of events and has a unique explanation, because
it is the outgrowth of a preceding series of events, likewise
unique.*[2]

*The theory of business cycles, however, need not be given
up in despair because it cannot satisfy ideal requirements. The
purposes scientific theory serves are met by explanations that
stop far short of radical thoroughness. Much would be gained
for the conduct of individual affairs and the guidance of legislation could we single out from the maze of sequences among
business phenomena a few that are substantially uniform. For,
with a degree of confidence that depends upon the regularity
with which they recur, these sequences could be used as guides*

---

[2] If theory is to be taken seriously as seeking to give really adequate understanding, it must be admitted that even this unique explanation of any single
cycle cannot be completely worked out. For, obviously, analysis can never be
carried back to the beginning of the chain of events in any cycle, and concerning
even the proximate events it is obviously impossible to collect all the relevant
information. Further, the intellectual instruments of analysis are unequal to the
complex problem of handling simultaneous variations among many interrelated
functions.

in forecasting the immediate business future. They could serve also as centers for organizing our knowledge concerning the variable sequences, and as beginnings in the search for new uniformities. Such regular sequences would help us to organize the tangled mass of facts presented by direct observation into coherent clusters. The latter would stimulate the imagination to unravel various lines of causal connection that are jumbled together in the annals of business and in the tables of statistics. Then it might be found that the irregularity of other sequences arises from varying combinations among sequences themselves regular.

The first aim of the descriptive analysis of business cycles, then, must be to look for the sequences that occur in every revival, prosperous period, crisis, and depression. The various lines of thought suggested by what lies on the surface may be followed boldly in the hope of discovering further uniformities that are obscured by the dissimilarities of the combinations in which they appear. These speculations, however, must be submitted to the pragmatic test. That is, they must be used in attempting to interpret the known phenomena of business cycles, and judged by the aid they render the mind in its effort to create order amidst the confusion of observations.

The sketch of economic organization in the second chapter of the first edition provided the framework into which the statistical chapters of Part II were fitted, and also the framework for a descriptive analysis of business cycles in Part III.

Since the quest of money profits by business enterprises is the controlling factor among the economic activities of men who live in a money economy, the whole discussion must center about the prospects of profits. On occasion, indeed, this central interest is eclipsed by a yet more vital issue—the avoidance of bankruptcy. But to make profits and to avoid bankruptcy are merely two sides of a single issue—one side concerns the well-being of business enterprises under ordinary circum-

*stances, the other side concerns the life or death of the same
enterprises under circumstances of acute strain.*

*Whatever affects profits and solvency, then, comes within
the sweep of the analysis. And we already know the factors of
chief significance: the prices that constitute business receipts
and the prices that constitute business expenses, the volume
of sales effected at the prevailing margins of profit, the need of
having currency to make payments and of obtaining loans in
adequate amount from banks and investors. But to know what
these factors are, and even to know what fluctuations they un-
dergo in severalty, is only half the battle. The other and the
harder half is to follow the interactions of these factors through
all the permutations that brighten or darken the prospects of
profits and make easy or difficult the maintenance of solvency.*

*Since the processes of a nation's business life never cease
or begin afresh, no natural starting point for the descriptive
analysis to which we are committed exists. It is necessary to
plunge in medias res by breaking into the unceasing processes
at some arbitrarily chosen point. The grave disadvantage of
this procedure is that the whole situation from which we start
must be taken for granted. But, by following the interlacing
processes forward through their successive phases we can work
round again to our point of departure, and account for our
original assumptions in the only way in which we can account
for any of the intermediate phenomena—that is, by tracing the
processes of cumulative change through which one set of business conditions gradually evolves into quite a different set.*

*The starting point chosen is that stage of the business cycle
in which activity begins to quicken after a period of depression. How the characteristic features of this stage are evolved
by the depression itself will be treated last of all.*

                                                            W. C. M.

CONTENTS

CHAPTER 1

THE CUMULATION OF PROSPERITY

I. Beginnings of Revivals in Business Activity

BETWEEN 1890 and 1910 the United States had five seasons of business revival following upon periods of business depression: midsummer 1891, spring 1895, midsummer 1897, autumn 1904, and winter 1908–09.[1] In England, France, and Germany similar revivals occurred in 1895, 1904–05, and 1909.[2]

The conspicuous agent in rousing business from its partial lethargy has often been some propitious event. For example, highly profitable crops of grain served as occasions for the American revivals of 1891 and 1897; President Cleveland's contract with the Morgan-Belmont syndicate for the defense of the gold reserve started the revival of 1895; an increase in the export demand for British commodities stimulated English trade in 1905 and 1909; and the extraordinary development of the electro-technical and chemical industries led the way in the German revival of 1895.[3]

But, with one striking exception, these propitious events did no more than accelerate a process of business recuperation already begun. To show how the very conditions of business depression beget a revival of activity is a task reserved for Chapter 4; but certain results of this later investigation may be anticipated. Among the ultimate effects of a period of hard times, then, are: a reduction in the prime and supplementary

---

[1] Numbered references are to notes on pages 193–218.

costs of manufacturing commodities and in the stocks of goods held by wholesale and retail merchants, a liquidation of business debts, low rates of interest, a banking position that favors an increase in loans, and an increasing demand among investors for corporate securities. Now all these conditions are conducive to a resumption of business activity, either because (like the settling of old accounts) they remove obstacles, or because (like the reduction of mercantile stocks) they promise a larger demand for wares, or because (like low interest and low manufacturing costs) they widen the margin of profit, or because (like the position of the banks and the attitude of investors) they facilitate the borrowing of capital. Fundamentally, the revivals of business must be ascribed to the processes that initiate these favorable conditions.

The one exception in the history of our four countries within more than twenty years is afforded by the harvest episode of 1891. Unusually large American crops of grain, sold at exceptionally high prices, cut short what was promising to be an extended period of liquidation after the crisis of 1890 and suddenly set the tide of business rising. But in this single instance the revival proved both partial in scope and brief in duration, partly at least because the stresses that had led to the crisis were not relaxed during the depression.' Over against this single instance are set several instances in which revival began quietly without the occurrence of any propitious event sufficiently striking to impress itself upon the attention of contemporary chroniclers; for example, the German revival in 1904–05 and all French revivals since 1890. The attempt to account for business revivals as the result of happy accidents therefore deserves no more credence than the abandoned theory that crises are "pathological" phenomena due to some "abnormal" cause. The quiet processes of business recuperation during dull times are quite competent to develop into revival without the adventitious help of any "disturbing circumstance."

II. The Diffusion of Business Activity

I. INCREASE IN DEMAND FOR COMMODITIES

Once started, a revival of activity spreads rapidly over a large part, if not all, of the field of business. For, even when the first impulse toward expansion is sharply confined to a single industry or a single locality, its effects in the restricted field stimulate activity elsewhere.

In part this diffusion of activity proceeds along the lines of interconnection among business enterprises traced in the sketch of economic organization in Part I. One line leads back from the industries first stimulated to the industries that provide raw materials and supplementary supplies. Another line leads forward to the chain of enterprises that handle the increased output of commodities. Still other lines, of less importance for the transmission of the stimulus, radiate to the industries that deal in complementary goods or substitutes. Of course the particular trades that receive an early share in the revival are those which stand in the most intimate relations with the trade that happens to be the first center of business expansion. But, since every important industry requires transportation and bank accommodation, the railways and the banks that serve the locality affected are always among the early beneficiaries. Among other trades coal mining has the best chance of profiting promptly.

As the industries that cater to the business needs of the enterprises from which activity radiates receive a stimulus, so also do the industries that cater to the personal needs of the families interested in the flourishing enterprises. Larger earnings for the employees and higher profits for the proprietors enable both classes to pay such debit accounts as they may have run up during the period of depression and to enlarge their current purchases. The statistics of consumption are too fragmentary to give much aid in following this process;[5] but current trade reports justify the belief that even the staple articles of food find a somewhat larger sale when business improves, and that better qualities are freely substituted for the poorer which were bought so long as severe economy was compulsory. The demands for clothing, furniture, amusements, and luxuries of all kinds are doubtless affected in larger degree than the demand for food, because purchases of such goods can be diminished or deferred in seasons of depression with less discomfort.

While retail shopkeepers are the first beneficiaries of increasing consumer demand, they are forced to place fresh orders promptly with wholesale merchants, because they have let their stocks run low during the dull times. Since the wholesale merchants have pursued the same policy, they are likewise prompt in placing fresh orders with the manufacturers. Thus the whole chain of trades engaged in furnishing consumers' goods soon feels the stimulating effect of a revival of business, no matter in what locality or industry it starts. And each enterprise that finds its own trade increasing becomes an agency in extending activity to still other enterprises—those from which it buys producers' goods, and those which supply consumers' goods to its own personnel.

At first the impetus toward business expansion grows weaker as it spreads from its original center to the branches of business that furnish it with producers' and consumers' goods. For the latter classes of enterprises have customers engaged in several or in many industries, or customers living in many sections of the country, so that an increase of say 5 per cent in the sales to one set of customers means an increase of much less than 5 per cent in total sales. On the other hand, the impetus is cumulative. If the steel trade makes more business for the railway, the railway presently increases its orders for steel, and thus sets the process working afresh at a higher pitch of intensity. Thus the revival gathers momentum as the industries that receive a mild stimulus one after the other begin to react upon those in which the movement started.

2. THE DEVELOPMENT OF BUSINESS OPTIMISM

The diffusion of activity is not confined to these definite lines of interconnection among business enterprises. It proceeds also by engendering an optimistic bias in the calculations of all persons concerned with the active direction of business enterprises and with providing loans.

Virtually all business problems involve elements that are not precisely known, but must be approximately estimated even for the present, and forecast still more roughly for the future. Probabilities take the place of certainties, both among the data upon which reasoning proceeds and among the conclusions at which it arrives. This fact gives hopeful or despondent moods a large share in shaping business decisions. A mathematician's mood exercises no influence upon his solution of an algebraic equation; but it does affect his opinion about the advisability of buying the bonds offered him.

While these emotional states are largely the product of strictly individual conditions—such as the state of digestion—they are also in part the product of suggestions received from the demeanor, the talk, and the actions of associates. Most men find their spirits raised by being in optimistic company. Therefore, when the first beneficiaries of a trade revival develop a cheerful frame of mind about the business outlook, they become centers of infection, and start an epidemic of optimism. Perhaps the buoyancy of a grocer gives a lumber dealer no adequate reason for altering his conservative attitude toward the business projects upon which he must pass. Yet, in despite of logic, he will be the readier to buy if his acquaintances in any line of trade have become aggressively confident of the future. The fundamental conditions affecting his own business may remain the same; but his conduct is altered because he sees the old facts in a new emotional perspective.

As it spreads, the epidemic of optimism helps to produce conditions that both justify and intensify it. The mere fact that a growing number of businessmen are gaining confidence in the outlook becomes a valid reason why each member of the group and outsiders also should feel confident. For the hopeful mood means greater readiness to make new purchases, enter into new contracts, etc.—in fine, means that the incipient revival of activity will be supported and extended. There is the stronger reason for relying upon the feeling in that its growth—like the growth in the volume of goods ordered—is cumulative. As new groups of businessmen become infected with optimism, their demeanor, talk, and actions confirm the faith of those who converted them. Thus the feeling of confidence becomes stronger as it spreads; that is, it becomes an increasingly powerful factor in supporting the movement out of which it grew, and in justifying itself.

3. LAGGARDS IN BUSINESS REVIVALS

Just as certain industries or localities often stand out as conspicuous leaders in a revival of activity, so other industries or localities often stand out as conspicuous laggards. Bad weather, tariff changes, technical inventions, the discovery of new sources of supply, the development of new trade routes, alterations in popular taste, and the like, may prevent particular enterprises from sharing the general improvement. Every industry or locality that languishes from any cause retards the growth of activity and of confidence among other industries or localities. But such cases seem more and more exceptional, and count for less and less as the revival progresses. For the cumulative character of the processes makes the general movement toward prosperity more dominant as it progresses.

Quite apart from the victims of special misfortunes, however, certain trades and localities have a late or a minor share in the benefits of a business revival; for example, the agricultural and grazing sections, on the whole, in contrast to the centers of industry, commerce, and finance.° Even in those notable instances when revival has begun with profitable crops

for the farmers in certain sections, it has reached the other
farming sections and the world of handicraft, small trade, and
the professions, not by direct transmission, but indirectly by
its effect upon the more highly organized world of business.
Not until the lumber companies, mines, and quarries are working full time, the factories buying materials and employing
men freely, the railways reporting few idle cars, and the mercantile houses are busy—not until this stage has been reached is
the impetus toward activity carried out from the centers to all
corners of the land. And not until this time are all the classes
that form the fringe of modern industry in cities and towns
alike swept into the movement.

4. STATISTICAL SIGNS OF BUSINESS REVIVALS

A business revival is a composite of many elements. It is not
to be defined in terms of any single change for the better, and
not to be sharply marked off from the state of depression out
of which it emerges. Indeed, the only safe way of dating a revival is to accept the consensus of opinion among men intimately familiar with business conditions at the time.

Among all the 'business barometers' not one always rises or
falls when these skilled observers agree that revivals occurred.
Because of their bearing on the practical problem of forecasting, these lapses from consistency merit attention.

#1. An increase in the physical volume of business, indeed,
seems to be an invariable concomitant of revivals, but it usually sets in months, even a year or more, before depression has
relaxed. A prophet who pinned his faith to this sign would
therefore publish cheerful bulletins prematurely. The course #2.
of wholesale prices is an even less reliable guide. For, contrary
to a widely accepted opinion, prices do not always rise in the
early stages of revival, and they do sometimes turn upward during depression. As for the money market, its changes during #3.
business revivals are in part irregular and in part indistinguish-
able continuations of changes already in progress before the

revival began.)For example, discount rates sometimes rise and sometimes fall when the change for the better occurs; bank loans expand, but the expansion antedates the revival; the ratio of reserves to deposits may move in either direction; the ratio of loans to deposits usually, but not invariably, rises; applications for investment loans may increase before the revival or not until it has come; the purchases of bonds and stocks are similarly erratic in their behavior, etc. Statistics of unemployment, monetary circulation, savings, profits, and bankruptcies are no safer guides.)

Thus there is no certain way of predicting when business will begin to recover from a prevailing depression. Only by compiling a composite record of numerous factors, and endeavoring to establish their general trend, can an intelligent guess be made. The whole business situation is so full of crosscurrents and uncertainties at this stage of the cycle that forecasts are subject to a much wider margin of error than after the cumulation of prosperity has begun.

III. The Rise in Prices

1. COMMODITY PRICES

A. Why Prices Rise

(While the level of wholesale prices often remains substantially unchanged or even recedes a trifle in the early stages of a business revival, it nearly always advances in the later stages.)

This advance is not the simple matter of course it is often assumed to be. True, the growing activity of business means an increasing demand for commodities; but it means also an increasing supply. On this basis there is as much reason for expecting prices to fall as for expecting them to rise. The readiness of businessmen both to pay progressively higher prices for goods and to buy progressively larger quantities therefore constitutes a problem.

This problem is the more difficult because several business

conditions prevailing when a revival begins are distinctly unfavorable to a rise of prices. The effect of depression in reducing the costs of doing business has already been pointed out as
among the factors that favor resumption of activity.[10] But it
does not favor an advance in the price level. On the contrary, it
means that profits can be made without restoring prices to the
level that prevailed before the depression set in. Second, at this
stage of the business cycle, business enterprises are anxiously
soliciting orders. The advantage in strategic position as bar-
gainers is on the side of the buyers—much more so than later,
when factories, railways, and shops already have all the business they can readily handle. Third, a prolonged depression
often wracks to pieces certain combinations to maintain prices,
and leaves the field over which free competition rules wider
at its close than at its beginning. Fourth, every increase in
business obtained in the early stages of revival makes a more
than proportionate addition to profits, even though it be taken
at unchanged prices. For until the existing equipment of standard efficiency for handling business is already busy, new orders
can be filled without an increase in prime costs, and at a reduction of supplementary costs per unit of output.

These conditions explain why prices often fail to rise
promptly at the beginning of a trade revival, and why in other
cases the initial rise is slow. But presently these conditions are
turned into their opposites and become incentives for raising
prices.

The magic that works this transformation is the further expansion in the physical volume of business. Beginning sometimes several months or a year before the revival, this expansion is accompanied at first by falling and then by nearly
stationary prices. But there is a critical point beyond which the
expansion cannot go without producing an advance of prices,
even in keenly competitive trades. This critical point is reached
in the affairs of any enterprise when it has already booked sufficient orders to keep busy its standard equipment and its regu-

lar staff of employees. To execute additional orders then requires overtime work, the hiring of new and presumably less efficient hands, the starting of old-fashioned machines, the installation of new equipment, or some similar change. Such measures involve higher prime costs, and often new supplementary charges as well. Hence additional orders no longer make a more than proportionate addition to profits, and may well make a less than proportionate addition—unless higher prices are asked. Fear of checking the revival of trade may make enterprises slow in putting up prices; but every delay encourages a further expansion in business and strengthens the conditions favoring an ultimate advance of the price level.

At the same time, the expansion of trade facilitates the reestablishment of those combinations to maintain or advance prices that have broken down during the preceding depression and encourages the formation of new combinations. It also reduces the strategic advantage that buyers recently enjoyed over sellers in bargaining. As sellers become less eager to accept orders at the old level of prices, buyers generally become more eager to place orders. But this statement requires further analysis.

B. How the Rise of Prices Reacts upon the Demand for Commodities

There is always danger that sellers may overreach themselves by advancing prices more rapidly than market conditions will support. For the expansion in business, upon which rests the whole movement toward prosperity, may be checked by an ill-timed or excessive advance. Frequently one or more branches of trade receive a setback while others are reviving, because mistakes of this kind are made by leading enterprises. More rarely, the whole revival is retarded or even stopped by an overrapid rise of the price level. There is evidence, for example, that this cause helped to blight the promising American revival of 1909.[11]

(But when the advance of prices is gradual and well balanced as among different goods it promotes rather than retards the growing demand for commodities.) For nothing stimulates present orders more powerfully than a moderate increase of quotations, which is thought to be the earnest of further increases in the near future. Provided they are not charged more for goods than their competitors, buyers count on being able to raise their own selling prices at least enough to defend their margins of profit. And they become eager to lay in large stocks or to make long contracts while quotations are still moderate and terms are still easy. Thus the anticipation of future advances in prices not only prevents present advances from reducing demand, but actually makes demand grow in the face of a rising level of prices.

C. How the Rise of Prices Spreads and Cumulates

Once set going, the rise of prices rapidly spreads throughout the system of prices in much the same manner as the activity of trade out of which it grew spreads over the field of business. When the price of a commodity has been advanced at any stage of its journey from original producer to ultimate consumer, that advance represents an increase of cost to every subsequent purchaser, and becomes a reason for increasing its price at later stages. At the same time, those who first put up the price have a stronger business incentive for obtaining larger supplies to sell at their wider margins of profit.) Their eager bidding offers the persons from whom they buy an opportunity to exact higher prices. Thus the advance travels backward to antecedent prices, as well as forward to subsequent prices. In less measure, the impulse toward higher prices is imparted to complementary and to competing goods. From the latter it extends to their materials, products, complements, and competitors, and so on from one class of commodities to the next. The great raw staples of commerce, which are sure to be touched relatively early in this process, play an especially prominent rôle in spreading the rise; because an advance in their prices, caused by an increasing demand from any quarter, is promptly felt in all the hundreds of uses to which they are put and becomes a reason for advancing the prices of all their manifold products.

The rise of prices resembles the increasing activity of trade also in that it is cumulative. If the advance is begun, for example, in the textile trades and spreads thence to other lines, it will flow back again in the form of higher prices for all the things textile mills buy. Then these mills must raise their selling prices once more or submit to a reduced margin of profit. And if the textile mills, as is likely, do raise their selling prices further, that step starts the whole process over again on a higher level.

Since the successive sets of businessmen who handle a given commodity are usually successful in their endeavor to pass on the increase of prices from one to another, the onus of the advance finally falls upon the ultimate consumers. For present purposes, the latter belong to one of two classes—individuals who buy consumers' goods for personal use, or investors who buy equipment for business use. Both classes pay the increased prices, not only without diminishing, but while actually augmenting their purchases. For the growing activity of business, which leads to the rise of prices, also provides the mass of families with larger money incomes to spend, and makes investors, whether acting singly or through business enterprises, eager to get the equipment necessary for participation in the high profits prosperity promises.

D. Why Different Groups of Commodity Prices Rise in Dissimilar Degrees

Of course the advance of prices is far from uniform. A few prices fall, a few remain constant, and of the many that rise some advance one or two, some one hundred or more per cent. Our concern, however, is not with the idiosyncrasies in the

price movements of single commodities, but with their average variations. That there is a distinct trend in the fluctuations
even of those relative prices which lie far above or below the
median is shown by the table of decils.[12] Evidence that this
trend has been measured with substantial accuracy is the close
agreement among index numbers compiled by different authorities from quotations obtained from different sources and
including dissimilar lists of commodities.[13]

But, as already indicated, this trend is not the same in all
parts of the system of prices. While all parts of the system feel
the influence of a business revival, they respond with varying
degrees of promptness to the stimulus. One regular characteristic of the advances in prices brought on by a cyclical revival
in business is a marked divergence in the movements of certain
classes of quotations—a divergence much wider than occurs
among the fluctuations of general index numbers made by
different hands.[14]

Of such dissimilarities in the average price variations of
groups of commodities, the following have been established:
(1) retail prices rise less promptly and less considerably than
the wholesale prices of the same commodities; (2) the wholesale prices of finished products lag behind the wholesale prices
of the same commodities in a partly manufactured state, and
the latter prices in turn lag behind the prices of the corresponding raw materials; (3) the wholesale prices of manufactured
consumers' goods rise perhaps more promptly, but certainly
less considerably than the wholesale prices of manufactured
producers' goods; and (4) the wholesale prices of raw mineral
products respond to changes in business conditions with
greater certainty and greater accuracy than the wholesale
prices of raw farm, animal, or forest products.[15]

Differences between the average variations in the retail and
wholesale prices of the same goods are due chiefly to the steadiness of certain important items of expense in conducting a
retail shop. A shopkeeper's rent, wages, losses on bad debts, in-

terest on fixed investment, depreciation charges, and the like
do not rise promptly with the wholesale prices of his wares.
Consequently he can maintain or even increase his profits on
the business as a whole while raising his selling prices less than
his buying prices have been raised. Therefore the more rigor-
ously competition constrains shopkeepers to defend their
reputations for reasonable prices and fair dealing, the more
certainly will retail prices lag behind wholesale prices.[16]

Similar is the explanation of the differences between the
average variations in the wholesale prices of the same goods
at successive stages of their progress from the state of raw materials to that of finished products. Manufacturing expenses
like retailing expenses include important items that do not rise
rapidly on the return of prosperity. Hence the more accurately
selling prices are adjusted to total expenses of production, the
more certainly will finished products lag behind partly finished
products and the latter behind raw materials when the price
level is advancing.

Even the manufacturing enterprise with a complete monopoly finds it advantageous to keep selling prices more stable
than the prices of raw materials. For if the monopoly charges
the maximum net revenue price before the price level advances it runs danger of losing profits by putting up its selling
prices faster than is necessary to meet the increase of expenses,
and total expenses increase much less rapidly than the prices
of raw materials. In fact, the large and ably managed combinations that control a considerable proportion of their industries have usually held their selling prices more stable than
prices were formerly under competitive conditions.[17]

The dissimilarities among the average price variations of
consumers' and producers' goods in their finished state have a
different source. In both classes, the goods for which we have
data are mainly important staples. Now, the consumer demand
for articles that enter into the budget of the great mass of families is fairly constant. Families economize or expand their

expenditures chiefly by cutting off or adding luxuries, amusements, savings, and the like. Moreover, population grows at a steady rate which is little affected by business cycles.[18] On the contrary, producers' demand for business supplies other than raw materials—particularly the demand for commodities that constitute part of the equipment for production—becomes much more brisk as the prospects of profits become brighter. At the same time the establishing of new business enterprises and the enlarging of old enterprises become more common. This superior stability of consumers' as compared with producers' demand is confined, however, to demand for staples. Had we price data for consumers' luxuries we should probably find them exhibiting average variations equal to or greater than those of staple producers' goods.

Finally, the difference in the accuracy with which the prices of raw minerals and of other raw products reflect changes in business conditions arises chiefly from technical circumstances affecting current supply. The production of coal, iron, copper, zinc, and so forth, is more completely under man's control than is the production of beef, pork, mutton, and wool, or of wheat, cotton, sugar, and corn. The influence of increasing demand upon the prices of the latter groups of products is often offset by favorable seasons for the farmers, or exaggerated by bad seasons, while the prices of mineral products respond regularly to changes in market conditions. Forest products belong with minerals rather than with animal and farm products, so far as concerns their conditions of production in very brief periods. But, in the United States at least, the exhaustion of the better sources of supply—better both in quality of timber and in location—has recently proceeded faster in the lumbering than in the mining business. Hence the prices of forest products have been moving upward rather steadily, and the influence of business conditions has been limited to retarding this advance during depressions and accelerating it during prosperity.[19]

2. PRICES OF LABOR

Into the sweep of changes that follow hard upon one another when business revives, even the least businesslike section of the community is presently drawn—the wageworkers whom we habitually think of not as making money but as making a living. For reasons of peculiar interest the changes in their rates of pay do not parallel changes in the prices fixed for commodities by dealings among business enterprises. The effects of this inaccurate adjustment in their turn become new factors of great weight in determining not only the material well-being of large numbers of men—a matter with which business as such is not concerned—but also the market for consumers' goods and the margins of profit between the selling prices of all sorts of commodities and the labor costs of providing them.

Both the American and the British statistics in Part II, Chapter IV, confirm the prevailing opinion that during business revivals prices of labor rise less than prices of commodities at wholesale. The American figures are confined to wages in manufacturing industries, but the British figures indicate that wages in agriculture are even more sluggish in their movements.

It is less well known that the advance sometimes begins sooner in labor than in commodity markets. Yet in both the United States and Great Britain wages began to rise after the depression of the middle 'nineties before wholesale prices had touched their lowest point. The evidence for the second decade is less conclusive. The crisis of 1903–04 was not sufficiently severe in America to cause a reduction of wages, and the Bureau of Labor has not yet published data for the years after the panic of 1907. In Great Britain the crisis of 1900 was followed by wage reductions, and in the later revival wholesale prices advanced not only farther but also earlier than the prices of labor.

The reason why wages rise less than wholesale prices lies principally in the unlike organization of the labor and commodity markets. Where trade-unions are nonexistent or weak the individual laborers have neither the prompt knowledge of changes in business conditions necessary to determine what employers can afford to pay for labor, nor the power to enforce such demands as are not readily conceded. As an organization for collective bargaining, the trade-union improves the wage earners' position in these respects. But many unions seek to make wage contracts running for a considerable time and binding the men not to ask for fresh advances until the contracts have expired. Most important of all, the individual working-man, the trade-union, and the employer are much more under the dominion of the idea of a just price than are the business-men dealing in commodities. This survival from the relatively stable economic life of the middle ages has almost ceased to influence the prices men offer or accept for cotton, wheat, or iron—such commodities are 'worth what they will bring.' But in the minds of all parties in the labor market certain notions still persist of what is a proper wage for a day's labor. When the employer offers much less than the customary price, he arouses stubborn resistance which is reinforced by the whole community's common sense that the work is worth more, or that a man cannot support his family decently on such a sum. On the other hand, when laborers ask much more than the cus-tomary prices, their pretensions strike others as absurd. Of course, such feelings impede the free working of supply and demand in the labor market—or rather constitute an impor-tant feature of both supply price and demand price—and tend to keep wages more stable than are prices in markets where pecuniary motives have unrestricted sway.

If these conditions obstruct the rapid rise of wages when business revives, they also facilitate the restoration of wages to the customary levels when a depression accompanied by wage reductions is passing away. Such is the explanation of the celerity with which wages rose after the hard times in the 'nineties. Early in the movement toward increase of activity, in the United States before a revival could fairly be spoken of, employers conceded a slight increase of pay. That English employers did not follow the same course in the revival of 1904–06 may be because the unprecedentedly high rates the men had obtained before the crisis of 1900 had not been paid long enough to become fairly entrenched in the minds of masters and men as the fit and proper prices to be charged. Hence wage rates yielded with unaccustomed ease to the pressure of hard times after the crisis and were restored in the subsequent period of prosperity with unaccustomed difficulty.

Furthermore, the economic pressure that drives the great mass of wage earners to sustain their arduous struggles for higher wages relaxes just at the moment rapid increases might be wrung from employers. The relatively moderate rate at which retail prices rise in the earlier stages of revival prevents the cost of living from going up fast. On the other hand, the economic position of workingmen is being improved by the greater regularity of employment and the abolition of 'short time.' Even without any increase in their customary rates of pay the wage earning class is better off. They hesitate to demand an increase of their customary wages until the feeling of this relative prosperity is dulled by familiarity, until the cost of living has advanced seriously, and until personal savings or trade-union accumulations have put them in position to fight with vigor.

3. PRICES OF LOANS

Wage earners may not be thorough businessmen, but bankers most emphatically are. Nevertheless, discount rates usually average less in the first year of business revival than in the last year of business depression.[20] Invariably, however, these rates move upward before the revival has been long in progress. Sometimes, as in the European money markets in the middle 'nineties, the advance precedes the rise of wholesale prices; sometimes it follows, as in the same markets ten years later;

sometimes the two movements are nearly simultaneous, as in New York in 1898 and again in 1905.

The cause of this advance in discount rates is not far to seek; what requires explanation is the slowness with which the rise starts. As has been said more than once, bank loans, like transportation, are among the goods required by nearly every business enterprise. The volume of loans demanded, however, increases, not with the physical, but with the pecuniary volume of business, and the latter type of expansion may be deferred by a continued fall of commodity prices for some time after conditions have bettered. Moreover, the banks have such liberal reserves at this stage of the business cycle that they are able to meet an increasing demand for some time without weakening their position unduly.[21] Still further, as shown in Part II, Chapter VII, during recovery from a depression that has been both long and severe, the ratio of capital liabilities to total liabilities among the banks is reduced by funds coming from depositors.[22] This inflow of money increases the lending power of the banks without increasing the investment upon which profits are reckoned, and therefore retards the advance of discount rates. But, when banks have attained tolerably full employment for their resources available for lending, they exact higher prices for additional advances, in the same way that manufacturers raise their selling prices when they have obtained substantial 'backbone' orders.

Call-loan rates usually advance more promptly than discount rates,[23] partly because the demand, which comes almost wholly from the stock exchange, expands as soon as speculative interest revives, and partly because the supply of funds for lending on call contracts as soon as favorable opportunities open for employing money in other ways. For "the call-loan market is really the storage place for the nation's surplus credit, and consequently has to take up all the stress resulting from changes of stress in other parts of the credit system."[24]

On the contrary, interest upon long loans as represented by

the net yields of investments in railway and government bonds at current prices lags decidedly behind discount rates upon the rise.[25] One cause is the increase of confidence among investors, with its consequent reduction in the premium charged for the assumption of risks. Another cause may be an increase in the current rate of savings, with its consequent growth in the sums coming forward for investment. But our knowledge of savings is too indefinite to admit of assured statements.[26] A third cause will be revealed presently when we examine into the demand for long loans on the part of business enterprises (sec. v).

IV. Increase in Profits

1. WHY PROFITS INCREASE

Since the quest of profits is the great driving force of the money economy, the significance of all the processes sketched culminates in their bearing upon the amount of money business enterprises can make.

The net resultant of these processes is to increase profits. Of chief importance is the fact that supplementary costs rise slowly in comparison with the physical volume of business. So long as this marked difference in the rate of increase is maintained, prime costs may keep up with or even outstrip the advance in selling prices, and still net profits will grow larger with each successive increment to the turnover. But in many instances prime costs also lag behind selling prices on the rise. Discount rates often and prices of raw materials regularly rise faster than prices of finished products. Rates of wages, however, lag. While the number of well-trained hands remains equal to requirements, while dawdling can be prevented, and while 'overtime' can be avoided, the cost of labor to the employer increases no faster than the rates of money wages. Freight charges constitute another important item in prime costs that probably lags behind wholesale prices on the rise.

Consequently, the rise in the profits made by different business enterprises must vary widely. Obviously, those enterprises are favored which get an early share of increasing business and in the subsequent rise in selling prices. In contrast, enterprises that are late in being reached by the growing demand for goods, and early in being reached by the rise in the prices of raw materials and so forth, may find the revival of prosperity a doubtful blessing for some time. Again, it is an advantage at such seasons to have relatively heavy supplementary and relatively light prime costs. Similarly, it is an advantage to have prime costs consisting largely of wages and freight charges. Now, since these several factors—promptness in being reached by the increase in business and by the rise in prices, the proportion of supplementary to prime costs, and the proportion of prime costs that is made up of labor and transportation costs—are found in all their possible combinations, the diversity in the fluctuations of profits is amply accounted for.

Meager as are the statistics concerning profits, they suffice to confirm the above conclusions. That, within large groups of enterprises or industries, the rate rises promptly with the tide of prosperity there is no doubt. Indeed it is certain in particular cases and probable on the average that profits begin to pick up before the depression is over. Wagon's statistics of the ratio borne by net profits to the share capital of joint-stock companies in 37 German industries even indicate that some years of deepest depression were the most lucrative of the whole business cycle 1891–1900. But these years are decided exceptions, and the years that brought maximum profits to the largest number of industries were the two following the revival of activity in 1895, the year when prosperity culminated (1899), and the year of the crisis (1900). Dermietzel's figures, which reflect the general drift of affairs more clearly than Wagon's, indicate that profits were lowest in the third year of the depression, that they rose a trifle in the last year, and then continued their rise without interruption through the revival of activity and the period of prosperity to a climax in 1899.[27]

2. THE RISE IN STOCK PRICES

Since the market price of a business enterprise rests primarily upon the capitalized value of its current and prospective profits, the prices of stocks vary roughly with the rate of profits. The degree of this correspondence can be determined for the one group of enterprises for which we possess data relating to both profits and stock prices—the American railways. On the whole, the prices of stocks do follow changes in net income, but at some distance, sometimes rising less than profits in periods of revival, for example in 1898, sometimes rising more, for example in 1905 and 1909.[28] The explanation of the discrepancies that mar the parallelism is to be found in the facts that railway dividends have been kept more stable than net income, that the stock market looks forward to future profits in coming years as well as back to net earnings for recent months, that the interest rate at which expected future profits are capitalized is itself subject to variations, and that considerations other than those of an investor intent upon income and safety—such as speculation, manipulation, and contests for control—are frequently potent factors in the market.[29]

But even when stock prices lag furthest behind the gains in net income, they both precede and exceed the rise in wholesale prices.[30] Two factors contribute toward this result. First, as just shown, profits recover some of their earlier losses before the revival sets in, and, as shown in sections ii, 4, and iii, 1, A, commodity prices often do not rise until the movement toward recuperation has continued for several months or even a year. Second, the stock market does not wait for an increase in profits, but discounts it as soon as its occurrence is expected.

The advance in prices is even less uniform among stocks than among commodities.[31] In part these differences arise from dissimilar changes undergone by the profits and financial prospects of the various companies. But there are other differences that recur regularly among the prices of different types of stocks. Low-priced stocks rise more rapidly than high-priced, common stocks rise more rapidly than preferred, and stocks that pay dividends irregularly rise more rapidly than stocks that are firmly established upon an income-yielding basis. The chief reasons for these differences are the greater attractiveness of low-priced stocks to speculators, the greater relative weight of investment demand for dividend-paying stocks, and the superiority of preferred to common stocks in steadiness of yield.[32]

V. Investments

All the processes of a business revival heretofore described might run their course within the circle of business enterprises existing at the close of depressions. But it is characteristic of the money economy that the prospect of good profits leads not only to greater activity among the old enterprises, but also to extensions of their size and to the creation of new enterprises. This expansion of business undertakings is the more important because for a time at least it imparts new energy to the very causes that produced it.

While the investment of fresh capital in business enterprises never ceases altogether, it sinks during depression to a relatively lower ebb than does the rate of current production of such staples as agricultural produce, coal, or even iron. Recovery usually begins before depression has passed away; but not until business has distinctly entered upon the phase of revival do new investments of this character become large again. Sometimes the first year of recuperation brings the maximum investments of the cycle, more often the second or third year. This maximum is likely to be several times as great as the preceding minimum. The growth of industrial equipment is thus very uneven.

These statements, based upon the tables in Part II, Chapter VIII, concerning the applications for business loans, the capital of new joint-stock companies, the increase in railway mileage, the cost of buildings erected, the amount of income reinvested in their own business by banks and railways, etc., accord well with the preceding analysis. Not until work has been provided for the existing industrial equipment by the slow expansion in business during depressions, supplemented by its more rapid strides after revival begins, and not until the profits of existing business enterprises have been raised to a satisfactory level, are there many tempting opportunities for fresh investments. But as these conditions occur often at an early stage of business expansion, so with corresponding frequency the first year or two of revival brings a large aggregate of corporate borrowings on long time.[83]

While our information with respect to savings from year to year is scanty, we have no reason to suppose that their growth is as uneven as that of investments. Hence after a year or two of heavy business borrowings the current supply of investment funds available for the purchase of corporate securities should show signs of being unequal to the demand. At least one such sign has already been found—the rise in interest rates upon long-time loans, which usually begins somewhat later than the rise in discount rates or even in commodity prices. While the return of confidence among investors helps materially to keep this rate from rising promptly with the demand for such loans, it presently has a contrary effect. Let confidence reach the point at which investors become ready to assume considerable risks and the demand for bonds at a fixed rate of interest will begin to shift into a demand for stocks promising a higher, but less certain, rate of dividend. Then corporations seeking to "place" bonds will be obliged to offer greater inducements by raising the nominal rate of interest or selling securities bearing the old rate at a lower price. Combined with the difference of pace at which the demand for long loans and the supply of current savings expand, this movement accounts for the rise in long-time interest rates that usually occurs when prosperity has fairly begun (see iii, 3).

So soon as investments have attained large proportions, another stimulus is imparted to the activity of business. For the establishment of new and the enlargement of old enterprises involve a heavy demand for new industrial equipment—buildings, machinery, furnishings, etc. Then the industries concerned with the supply of the many kinds of goods included in these broad categories come in for their share of prosperity, and add their quota to the increasing demand for materials, equipment, labor, discounts, and long loans. The whole set of processes characteristic of business expansion is thereby rendered still more intense.

VI. The Business Equilibrium

The preceding sections show how the endlessly complicated processes started by an increase in the physical volume of trade convert depression into prosperity. The salient feature of the whole development is that each successive effect reacts to strengthen the causes that produced it, so that the movement toward prosperity gathers momentum as it proceeds.

Every industry wakened to activity stimulates other industries, and when the latter are roused their activity creates a larger demand for the products of the industries from which the stimulus came. The swelling volume of trade presently sends up the prices of certain commodities; every such advance becomes a reason for raising other prices; the latter advances presently cause the first prices to be raised anew, thus starting the whole process over again on a higher level; and the rising of the price level promotes the expansion in business out of which it grew. In combination, the expansions in trade and further advances in prices make those who profit by them optimists; every convert to optimism makes new converts; the latter confirm the faith of the first; and the resulting prevalence of business confidence favors further expansions in the volume of trade and further advances of prices. These developments make workingmen insistent to demand, and employers able to concede higher wages; the resulting increase of family incomes widens the market for the increasing output of consumers' goods and sustains the advances in their prices; meanwhile the higher cost of labor occasions further advances in the prices of commodities at wholesale and retail. Interest rates and rents rise for similar reasons, and their advances have similar effects upon the demand for consumers' commodities, the costs of production, and the level of prices. Finally, every increase in profits resulting from expanding business and the rising level of prices encourages new investments in business enterprises; these new investments swell business still more, drive prices still higher, favor new advances in wages, interest, and rents, and augment afresh the profits of numerous trades.

The more vividly this cumulative growth of prosperity is appreciated, the more difficult becomes the problem why prosperity does not continue indefinitely instead of being but one passing phase of business cycles.

Of course prosperity confers no immunity against disasters that interfere with the course of business; but over many rocks the accumulated momentum of good times may run without serious mishap. The great shortage of the American corn crop in 1901 did not stop the 'boom' then in progress, though it came soon after a spectacular corner in the stock market; the failure of Mr. Walsh's banks in Chicago, the San Francisco fire, and the great coal strike did not stop the 'boom' of 1905–06, though they followed hard one on the other. For such misfortunes affecting a few sections of the business community the superabounding prosperity of the other sections is more than a match. On the other hand, many periods of intense prosperity have ended in years of peace, plenty, and good fortune. The waning, like the waxing of prosperity, therefore, must be due, not to the influence of 'disturbing causes' from outside, but to processes that run regularly within the world of business itself.

The world of business is a system comprising numberless independent enterprises, bound together by industrial, commercial, and financial ties. For the continuance of prosperity it is indispensable that a certain balance be maintained among the fundamental processes that constitute the activity of this system. The demand for goods of every kind must keep pace with the increasing supply, despite the steadily rising prices; the cost of raw materials must not increase too much in comparison with the selling prices of manufactured goods; mercantile collections must grow with mercantile credits; bank reserves must expand with demand liabilities; the cost of living must not rise much faster than money incomes; banks and investors must continue able to provide the ever-increasing loan funds required by business enterprises; and the like. If serious maladjustment occurs in the rate at which any of these factors are growing in relation to the others, some enterprises will lose profits. Then the bonds that unite different enterprises will become channels through which the injury will spread to other enterprises, just as they were recently channels for the spread of prosperity. Unless the original injury is promptly healed, there is grave danger that the cumulation of prosperity will be converted into a cumulation of depression.

It is some such maladjustment among the various factors in the system of business that brings all seasons of expansion to a close and turns prosperity into crisis. The regularity with which this happens suggests that prosperity itself has other effects than those which tend to sustain and intensify business activity. During the earlier stages of a business revival these effects pass unnoticed; but, though slow in developing, their later growth must be cumulative at a higher rate than the growth of the prosperity-producing factors. The next task is to investigate the sources and character of these stresses which accumulate within the system of business until they finally disrupt its equilibrium.

CHAPTER 2

HOW PROSPERITY BREEDS CRISIS

I. Increasing Costs of Doing Business

AMONG THE threatening stresses that gradually accumulate within the system of business during seasons of high prosperity is the slow but sure increase in the costs of doing business.

1. SUPPLEMENTARY COSTS

During the early stages of a business revival, the portion of the total cost of carrying on an enterprise that consists of supplementary charges declines, because their sum remains nearly constant while the number of sales over which they are distributed increases (see Ch. 1, iv, 1). This decline in supplementary costs per unit gradually ceases as the revival blossoms into prosperity. For when current business grows to a point that taxes the full capacity of existing mines and factories, railways and stores, it becomes necessary to enlarge the old or to found new enterprises to care for additional orders. Of course such extensions of the existing industrial equipment involve the enterprises that undertake them in new supplementary charges—interest on the funds invested, rent for the use of new premises, depreciation on buildings, machinery, etc., insurance, salaries for general officials, and the like.

Often these charges are less per unit of product turned out by the new equipment, because improved processes or machinery have been adopted. On the other hand, the initial cost of construction in the midst of prosperity is high, which saddles the new plants from the start with heavy interest charges. Further, when a new plant is founded by a new company, the latter must usually invest considerable sums in building up a trade connection. In this process it is frequently compelled for a time to take customers who have made trouble in their dealings with the old established firms and whose business is likely to prove equally unsatisfactory to the new. These high interest charges, costs of getting established, and losses upon bad debts often overbalance the advantages from improved technical equipment.

Another factor of some moment is the gradual increase in the supplementary costs of the old enterprises themselves—an increase quite apart from that involved in extending plants. When leases expire or bonds fall due while business is expanding, the enterprises concerned must expect ordinarily to pay higher rents and higher interest for renewals. Permanent officers, also, are more likely to claim and to receive an increase in the scale of their salaries when business is good and the cost of living is advancing.

Often more important than this cessation of the decline in supplementary costs per unit is the positive increase that prosperity brings in prime costs.

2. PRIME COSTS OF WEAK ENTERPRISES

When a revival of activity begins, the business enterprises that have been running with few intermissions during the depression are surrounded by a fringe of other enterprises that have closed. Disadvantageous location, antiquated equipment, poor trade connections, weak financial backing, timid or unskillful management—any of these circumstances may have been responsible for their inability to keep prime costs down to the low selling prices that depression brings. Rather than make goods that do not repay even the cost of labor and materials, they have shut their doors.

When prosperity returns and prices rise, these enterprises begin to start up again, one by one. They waste more material, or more labor, or more capital, or more transportation in putting a given output upon the market than do their more fortunate rivals, and at given prices their profits are narrower. But their resumption of business affects all the well-equipped, well-located, and well-managed enterprises in the field: it bids up the prices of materials, labor, etc., and it adds to the supply of goods sent to market, thus increasing the difficulty of advancing selling prices sufficiently to offset the encroachments of costs upon profits.

Many of the strongest enterprises have among their machines or plants some that fall below the current standard of efficiency. Like the weak enterprises, these sections of the industrial equipment are allowed to stand idle when business is dull, but are started again when business becomes brisk. Of course, the average of the prime costs per unit of the goods produced by such an enterprise mounts with every old machine and every ill-located plant it sets at work.

3. THE COST OF LABOR

During the first year or two of a trade revival the average rise in the rate of wages is slow, becoming more rapid in the later stages when employers find it hard to get a sufficient number of hands to fill their orders. Encroachments would seldom be made upon profits, however, did fluctuations in the rate of wages represent the sole changes in labor costs; for wholesale prices usually keep rising faster than wages to the very climax of prosperity.[1] A more serious difficulty is that labor is a highly changeable commodity—its quality deteriorates as its price mounts.

If humanitarian motives are not allowed to interfere with business policy, the less efficient employees are the first to be discharged after a crisis. Hence the relatively small working forces of depression are the picked troops of the industrial army. When revival has ripened into full prosperity, on the contrary, employers are constrained to accept any help to be had. They must take on men who are too old, and boys who are too young, men of irregular habits, men prone to malinger, even the chronic 'trouble makers.' Raw recruits of all sorts must be enlisted and trained in a hurry at the employer's expense. The average efficiency of the working forces is inevitably impaired.

The fact of this deterioration admits of no doubt; but its weight in increasing costs is difficult to determine. Foreign statistics of unemployment show differences of not more than 5 or 6 per cent of the membership of reporting trade-unions between the best and the worst years of a business cycle.[2] Among the masses of unskilled laborers belonging to no trade-union the variations in employment may be greater; but that is a matter of conjecture.[3] In New York State the reported fluctuations are much wider than in France or England. For example, there is a difference exceeding 20 per cent of the membership of the reporting unions between the number out of work in the exceedingly dull year 1908 and the exceedingly busy year 1906.[4] Such differences leave a wide margin for the improvement of working forces during depression, and for a corresponding deterioration during prosperity.

While the relatively inefficient reserve army of labor is thus called into active service, both the standing force and the reserves are kept at work long hours. Now overtime labor is especially expensive to employers, not only because it often commands extra rates of wages, but also because it is tired labor. Few manual laborers possess sufficient strength and vitality to stretch out their working day from 8 or 9 to 10, 11, or 12 hours for weeks or even months at a time without loss of efficiency. At first, the closing hours of the long day, after a time, all the hours of every day find the men less alert and less energetic—unable to accomplish as much work per hour as in less busy seasons. Moreover, the quality of the output declines as nerves become fatigued. 'Spoiled work' increases often at an alarming pace, and the resulting loss of materials and time threatens serious encroachments upon profits.[5]

Quite apart from this difficulty of overtime, men cannot be induced to work at so fast a pace when employment is abundant as when it is scarce. Employers complain that in good times their men 'slow down'; employees complain that in dull times they are 'speeded up.' Whatever may be the merits of this chronic dispute about the fairness of the day's work given for a day's pay in either phase of the business cycle, there is abundant testimony from both sides as to the existence of a considerable difference in the energy exerted. Theoretical writers have strangely neglected this point, but the trade journals make much of it. The most trustworthy body of evidence on the subject, however, is contained in the special report by the federal Commissioner of Labor in 1904 upon *Regulation and Restriction of Output*. This evidence is the more convincing because the influence of business conditions upon the efficiency of labor was not a subject of inquiry. Nevertheless, manufacturers and foremen, trade-union officials, and manual workers both within and without the ranks of organized labor called attention time after time to the fact that the pace of work was slower in the flush times of 1900–02 than it had been in the dull times of 1894–96. In different phrases they all gave the same explanation—men are less afraid of discharge when business is good. A sample bit of testimony may be quoted. The superintendent of a company manufacturing electrical machinery said:

"The absorption of 'driftwood'—that is, the taking on of men who would not be given a job in ordinary times, the temporary employment of tramps, to make it perfectly plain—is the cause of but a small percentage of the decreased output in machine shops. Five years ago men did not restrict their output, union or non-union men, because they wanted to hold their jobs, and a man would do anything and all he was told to do. Now a man knows that all he has to do is to walk across the street and get another job at the same rate of pay. During the hard times we took contracts at any price we could get, and in some places and cases men were driven at high speed to get this work out, so as to lose as little money on it as possible. Men will not keep up that speed rate in these days. We are not restricted in our right to hire and 'fire,' but we are mighty careful nowadays not to discharge a man unless we have the very best of cause, and would not discharge unless we had a case that would preclude a visit from a union committee. We are not looking for visits, nor trouble of any kind."[6]

Among these various factors that coöperate to increase the cost of labor during prosperity—the rise in wages, the employment of undesirables, the payment of extra rates for the tired labor of overtime, and the lessening energy put into their work by old hands and new—we can approximate a quantitative estimate of the first alone. Unless employers grievously exaggerate, however, the last is the most important, and neither of the other two factors is negligible. That this combination of advancing prices for labor and declining efficiency produces a serious increase in the cost of getting work done is beyond question.

Of course, the most serious inroads are made upon profits in those industries where wages constitute a large proportion of the total outlay. A rough index of the variations in this proportion from one industry to another is afforded by table 1, which reproduces the census classification of expenses in thirty-odd branches of manufacturing in 1900. Depreciation charges, insurance against mercantile and trade risks, and cost of selling products are not included by the census, so that the total expenses are somewhat understated and the proportion of wages correspondingly exaggerated. But since on the average wages make over a fifth of the recorded expenses of manufacturing goods, an increase of 5 or 10 per cent in labor cost must cut deeply into profits unless some way of offsetting it can be found.

For other than manufacturing branches we have few data concerning the relations of wages to total expenses. On the interstate railways the proportion mounts nearly to 40 per cent.[7] Among mines, quarries, and lumber companies the average proportion of labor cost must be nearer that of the railways than that of manufacturing companies. Among mercantile establishments, both retail and wholesale, however, it is probably below the proportion in most branches of manufacturing. But the increasing price and declining efficiency of labor during prosperity must become matters of grave concern to employers in most lines of business.

4. THE COST OF MATERIALS

According to table 1 the cost of materials exceeds wages in every one of the leading branches of manufacture, and in a majority is over twice as large. Indeed, on the average it makes practically two-thirds of the total outlay. If wares for resale are substituted for materials, this proportion must run far higher in wholesale stores, while in retail shops it cannot be much lower than in factories on the average and may well be considerably higher. Even the transportation companies and enterprises in the extractive industries have to buy vast quantities of current supplies. Hence an increase in the cost of materials, wares, or supplies is often an increase in the largest single item of expense, and always an increase in an important item. The relative fluctuations in the prices of those commodities that are bought and of those sold are therefore of great, often of decisive, importance in determining profits.

Concerning these relative fluctuations, our definite information consists of index numbers for raw materials, partly manufactured products, and finished goods; also for the same commodities at wholesale and at retail.[8] Now this statistical evidence points to the conclusion that what must be taken as buying prices creep up on selling prices during prosperity.[9] Of course this movement, like the others just traced, threatens a reduction in profits.

TABLE 1

Classification of Expenses in Manufacturing Industries Having Products Valued at More than $100,000,000 in 1900

Industries	Actual amounts in millions of dollars					Proportions of the total in percentages			
	Salaries	Wages	Misc. expenses	Cost of materials	Total	Salaries	Wages	Misc. expenses	Cost of materials
All industries..........	404	2,322	1,028	7,345	11,099	3.6	20.9	9.3	66.2
Agricultural implements..........	8	22	11	44	85	9.4	25.9	12.9	51.8
Boots and shoes......	8	59	11	170	248	3.2	23.8	4.4	68.6
Bakeries.............	6	28	10	95	139	4.3	20.1	7.2	68.4
Carpentering.........	2	71	49	142	264	.8	26.9	18.5	53.8
Carriages and wagons.	4	30	6	57	97	4.1	30.9	6.2	58.8
Railway shops........	6	96	6	110	218	2.8	44.0	2.8	50.4
Car building.........	2	23	3	70	98	2.0	23.5	3.1	71.4
Cheese, butter, etc....	1	6	2	109	118	.8	5.1	1.7	92.4
Clothing, men's......	14	79	52	198	343	4.1	23.0	15.2	57.7
Clothing, women's....	7	33	12	85	137	5.1	24.1	8.8	62.0
Copper smelting......	1	9	2	122	134	.7	6.7	1.5	91.1
Cotton goods.........	7	87	22	177	293	2.4	29.7	7.5	60.4
Flour mills...........	5	18	10	476	509	1.0	3.5	2.0	93.5
Foundries............	32	182	41	286	541	5.9	33.6	7.6	52.9
Furniture............	7	43	11	65	126	5.6	34.1	8.7	51.6
Iron and steel........	12	121	32	522	687	1.7	17.6	4.7	76.0
Lead smelting........	1	5	1	144	151	.7	3.3	.7	95.3
Leather..............	3	23	7	155	188	1.6	12.2	3.7	82.5

Liquors, malt	13	26	109	52	200	6.5	13.0	54.5	26.0
Lumber	11	105	18	318	452	2.4	23.2	4.0	70.4
Planing mills	5	33	7	100	145	3.4	22.8	4.8	69.0
Masonry	2	53	31	87	173	1.2	30.6	17.9	50.3
Paper	5	21	10	71	107	4.7	19.6	9.3	66.4
Petroleum refining	2	7	3	103	115	1.7	6.1	2.6	89.6
Plumbing	3	32	5	65	105	2.8	30.5	4.8	61.9
Printing	36	84	56	87	263	13.7	31.9	21.3	33.1
Silk	3	21	10	62	96	3.1	21.9	10.4	64.6
Slaughtering, etc.	10	34	24	687	755	1.3	4.5	3.2	91.0
Sugar refining	2	7	7	223	239	.9	2.9	2.9	93.3
Tin smithing	3	22	5	50	80	3.7	27.5	6.3	62.5
Tobacco—chewing, etc.	4	7	48	35	94	4.8	8.3	57.2	41.7
Tobacco—cigars	5	41	31	58	135	3.7	30.4	23.0	42.9
Woolen goods	3	25	7	71	106	2.8	23.6	6.6	67.0
Worsted goods	2	20	7	77	106	1.9	18.9	6.6	72.6

SOURCE: *Twelfth Census of the U.S., Manufactures*, Vol. 1, table 1.

While a difficulty of this character seems to be encountered in most branches of business it is likely to become peculiarly acute in those manufacturing industries which use animal and farm products as their leading raw materials. For, following up a suggestion of Sombart's, we have found that these classes of products are more erratic in their price fluctuations than the products of mines and forests.[10] Hence an uncommonly large speculative risk must be borne, or insured against, in such branches of trade as meat packing, flour milling, cotton spinning, woolen weaving, and tanning. Of course this risk exists during all phases of the business cycle, but it is augmented in prosperity by the necessity of carrying larger stocks of raw materials. The census indicates that more than three-fourths of all the "materials purchased in the raw state" by American factories in 1900 belonged to this class which is peculiarly unstable in price.[11]

5. THE COST OF BANK LOANS

Interest upon short-time loans is a minor element of expense in manufacturing operations, according to the American census;[12] but it must be a much more important matter to the mercantile classes. Certainly it is among the costs of doing business that trench upon profits in the later stages of prosperity; for the relative rates of discount rise much more rapidly than the index numbers of wholesale prices—to say nothing of retail prices.[13] But this is a topic of many aspects, which will receive more adequate treatment in section iii.

6. DECLINING ECONOMY OF BUSINESS MANAGEMENT

One final matter may be mentioned: prosperity is unfavorable to economy in business management. When mills are running overtime, when salesmen are sought out by importunate buyers, when premiums are being offered for quick deliveries, when the railways are congested with traffic, then neither the overrushed managers nor their subordinates have the time and the patience to keep waste down to the possible minimum.

The pressure that depression applies to attain the fullest utilization of all material and labor is relaxed, and in a hundred little ways the cost of doing business creeps upward. Still less can attention be given to the adoption of improved methods of organization; for changes in habitual routine are always the source of some confusion and delay when they are being introduced, and when an enterprise has all the business it can handle delay is the one thing to be avoided. Even when the feasibility of making an important improvement is demonstrated to the managers of an enterprise, they often defer its introduction to a less busy season. Progress in industrial technique and in business methods would be slower if business communities were always prosperous.

II. Industrial Equipment and the Investment Market

1. CONSEQUENCES OF INCREASING INDUSTRIAL EQUIPMENT

While the increasing costs of doing business are threatening to encroach upon profits in almost every branch of trade, the rapid extension of industrial equipment is breeding other stresses.

As shown in Chapter 1, v and tables 105–120 of Part II, the repairing of old and the building of new equipment for the handling of business is greatly accelerated by the return of prosperity after a depression. This movement gains momentum as prosperity becomes more intense. Now the laying of new railways, the erection of new office buildings, factories, and power plants, the opening of new mines, quarries, lumber camps, and the like, stimulates all the branches of business concerned with construction work. Not only contracting firms, but also cement mills, brickyards, structural steel works, machine-building companies, lumberyards, etc., etc., become busy. Direct statistical evidence is meager; but there is little doubt that the business done by such enterprises regularly shows a higher ratio of increase in prosperity than is common among establishments that deal either in staple consumers' goods or in the current supplies used by business enterprises.[14] Of course, the continual necessity for repairs and renewals provides a good deal of work for these construction trades at all times, and there is never a year when considerable extensions of old and construction of new plants are not undertaken. But when to this regular work of maintaining the efficiency of the existing equipment and to these odd contracts for new construction is added the rush of orders from the many enterprises that see their own trade outrunning their facilities and from the numerous new projects launched on the rising tide of prosperity, then the construction trades have a season of activity that few of the industries for which they are working can match.

Consequently these trades add a sharply increasing demand to the market forces that are swelling business and lifting the level of prices. For a while their demand for commodities is not accompanied by a corresponding increase in the market supply. What they are making in the way of equipment has been sold in advance to business enterprises and does not come on the market as a factor opposing the advance of prices. While this condition lasts, the demand of construction trades has an especially stimulating effect upon the price level. But, at the same time, the bidding of these trades for labor and materials aids in driving up the costs of doing business in all the various ways described in the preceding section.

A second consequence of the situation is that the movement toward providing new industrial equipment is likely to become especially rapid in the very trades whose business it is to furnish such equipment. The productive capacity of the existing enterprises that at the time of business revival is not used at all or not used to the full is especially large in these lines. But when orders for construction work do begin to come in, they come so fast and are so large and require such quick execution that this wide margin of reserve power is often exhausted in a year or less. Then the foundries, machine shops, cement mills, brickyards, and all the rest become the most eager of all enterprises to install new equipment in the shortest possible time; for they cannot obtain contracts unless they can guarantee prompt deliveries, and the season when contracts are to be had may be brief. Indeed, the *Produktivmittelindustrien* may well show a more rapid expansion of equipment than any of the trades to which they cater.[15]

Further consequences appear as soon as sections of the new industrial equipment are finished and put into active service. Then the enterprises that own the new equipment begin on the one hand to hire operatives, buy raw materials, etc., etc., and on the other hand to pour their products upon the market. This activity serves both to strengthen the forces that are already raising the costs of doing business and to obstruct the advance of selling prices. But, since new construction is not undertaken on a grand scale until a business revival has made considerable headway, and since the work of building and installing the elaborate equipment of today lasts months if not years, prosperity has neared its high tide before the new equipment begins to aggravate seriously the encroachments of costs upon profits.

2. DEVELOPMENT OF STRINGENCY IN INVESTMENT MARKETS

The extension of industrial equipment is financed in part by funds taken out of the current income of business enterprises and reinvested.[16] But most of the necessary funds are obtained by borrowing, by inducing those already interested in enterprises to advance additional capital, or by bringing in new stockholders. As indices of how much money is raised for such purposes, we have the statistics of applications for loans, sales of bonds and stocks, and fluctuations in the interest rate upon long-term loans.[17]

After a year or two of the heavy borrowings of prosperity, this interest rate usually rises to what is regarded by the business community as a high level,[18] and complaint begins to be heard of a 'scarcity of capital.' This is one of the most regularly recurring phenomena of the months that precede the outbreak of a crisis.

The popular explanation of this alleged scarcity is that too much capital has recently been locked up in fixed investments, and that the remaining free capital is insufficient to meet the current needs of business. But all that the available data establish is that the supply of funds forthcoming for long loans is no longer equal to the demand *at the old rate of interest*. It does not necessarily follow that saving has declined, or that the heavy investments of the preceding year or two were made out of past accumulations which are now approaching exhaustion. The stringency may quite as well be due to the diversion of an increasing proportion of the funds seeking investment into other channels than those provided by the loan market. Active businessmen are likely to cease looking elsewhere for investments for their savings when their own special enterprises have in sight more business than can readily be carried with the available working funds. Others may be deterred from lending at the old rate because the advancing price level is reducing the purchasing power of fixed money incomes, or because they think it may reduce the purchasing power of the principal when it comes to be repaid. Still others who do not think their interests out so clearly may be impressed by the patent fact that bonds have been falling in price. The statistics and market reports show that the purchases of stocks increase while the purchases of bonds are falling off.[19]

But, whatever the cause—which cannot be determined until more definite knowledge is obtained concerning the fluctuations of savings and the promptness with which savings are invested—the effect is certain. The terms exacted for long loans become onerous.

3. DECLINE IN INVESTMENT BORROWING

When the market rate of interest for long-term loans has risen one-quarter, one-half, or, on some classes of business, 1 per cent above the level that had prevailed during the preceding depression, the financial managers of large business corporations begin to restrict their borrowings to the narrowest possible limits. Two shifts, indeed, are open to them: they may endeavor to follow the change in the appetite of investors by raising more capital on stocks and less on bonds, and they may take up money on one-, two-, or three-year notes at a high rate of discount instead of selling long-term bonds. That they adopt both these courses freely is proved by the evidence.[20] But it is also clear from the tables of Part II, Chapter VIII, that public applications for capital usually decline heavily in the year preceding a crisis.

Of course this decline means, not that the desire on the part of business enterprises to secure funds has shrunk, but that the men in control are unwilling to saddle their companies for a long series of years with the heavy fixed charges that would result from borrowing under the prevailing conditions. They prefer to defer the execution of their plans until funds can be procured on better terms.

4. CHECK UPON ORDERS FOR NEW CONSTRUCTION

High rates of interest, however, are not the sole, in many cases they are not even the most important, cause for deferring the execution of plans calling for new construction. The high prices demanded by contractors as the climax of prosperity approaches frequently count for more.

Evidence is given in Chapter 1, v, that many contracts for permanent improvements are let in the early days of revival, or even in the late days of depression. Much of the work then undertaken requires a year, two years, three years, or even more to execute. To safeguard themselves against an advance in prices, the firms that are contracting to construct houses, office buildings, factories, machinery, roadways, sewers, canals, docks, bridges, and the like enter into subcontracts with enterprises that provide the necessary iron, steel, copper, lumber, cement, brick, tile, stone, etc. When feasible, the latter enterprises in their turn often enter into contracts with still other houses from which they buy materials or supplies. Now most of these enterprises bind themselves without definitely knowing how much business other enterprises in the same branch of trade are booking. It often happens, therefore, that contractors and their subcontractors sell to investors more construction than can readily be executed within the contract time. This condition of trade is discovered when the contractors look about for labor and materials to perform the work they have undertaken. Then prices rise rapidly and large bonuses are often offered for quick deliveries. One result is that many building contractors and manufacturers find that what promised to be lucrative bargains turn out to be losing bargains. More important is the further result. When bids are invited for additional construction, contractors are forced to ask much higher prices than those they would have asked a year or so earlier.[21]

Of the projects for permanent improvements some are so pressing that the contracts are let despite the onerous terms demanded. But other projects, many and large, can be and are postponed to a season when the initial outlay will be less. Thus the high costs of construction that characterize prosperity combine with the high interest charges upon long loans to reduce the number and the size of fresh contracts let.

Activity does not slacken at once in the trades that do contract work and furnish materials. For the finishing of the contracts already in hand may keep everyone as busy as ever for several months to come. Indeed, the mills making structural steel, etc., may be under high pressure to get out work on which bonuses for quick delivery are expected at the very time their order books for the coming quarters are scantily filled, and while their selling agents are having great difficulty in drumming up custom.[22]

This change in the situation promises to relieve one of the stresses that are becoming acute. The provision of new equipment will decline, and therewith the increase both in competition for an already scant supply of labor and materials and in the new products seeking sale. But at best only the pace at which the stress is accumulating is relieved. Moreover, the relief lies in the future, and as a rule it is not felt until after the crisis has occurred. And worst of all, this problematical relief to the enterprises that would have to meet the competition of the new equipment is offset by the sudden apparition of acute strain approaching in the industries that provide equipment. Particularly when they have extended their own plants to handle the recent flood of contracts do they suffer when this tide recedes. How serious is the danger their threatened embarrassment entails for the whole community of business enterprises will appear in the sequel (sec. iv, 2, B, and sec. v).

III. Tension in the Money Market

1. DEMAND FOR SHORT-TERM LOANS

The advance in interest rates during a period of high prosperity is relatively much greater in the money than in the investment market.[23] For, while certain of the factors that drive up interest rates operate in both markets, others are peculiar to the market for discounts.

As pointed out in Chapter 1, iii, 3, the bank accommodation needed by the business community grows not only with the increase in the physical volume of business but also with the rise in prices. Were no other factor to be considered, it would therefore cumulate rapidly. But there are other factors.

Expectation of large profits, combined with the prevalence

of an optimistic bias in judging business chances, disposes men
of affairs to undertake as much business as possible upon their
working capitals. Indeed, not a few venture beyond the line
of safety, and failures ascribed to inadequacy of capital become
numerous (cf. Ch. 3, ii, 4). Of course, this effort to make one's
own capital support as much business as possible involves borrowing a larger proportion of the funds required than is common during depressions or revivals. That is to say, the demand
for bank loans increases even more rapidly than the pecuniary
volume of business.

Among the factors that differentiate the demand for short-
term loans from the demand for long-term loans is a smaller
degree of elasticity. When interest rates rise, short loans asked
for do not contract so much as investment borrowings. Many
investment projects require that everything to be used shall
be bought new. Then the whole annual cost of the undertak-
ing, apart from operating charges, may be treated from the
accountant's viewpoint as the interest on the sums invested.
But in the majority of short-term loans the practical business
problem relates to the additional service that may be got by
the use of additional funds from equipment already on hand
and for which the cost has already been allowed. Then the interest on the projected loan cannot be treated as the entire expense. On the contrary, it may be a minor item, and an advance
in the rate of 1 or 2 per cent may make so small a fraction of the
whole cost as not to deter men from borrowing.

Again, in borrowing for long periods, the businessman must
consider probable selling prices in the years to come. Experience teaches him that it is folly to expect an indefinite continuance of the active demand for his goods and the high prices that
prevailed during the 'boom.' Hence his enterprise, which for
the present might support heavy fixed charges without disaster,
will face more serious difficulties in the next depression. But
in borrowing for 60 to 90 days, or even for a year, the businessman is prone to count upon being able to turn over his goods

promptly at prices equal to or higher than those prevailing at the moment. Hence he has less reason to hesitate because of an increased cost of loans.

Finally, the temporary shifting of a part of the investment demand for loans to the money market by the substitution of short-term notes for bonds increases the demand for bank accommodation (see sec. ii, 3). For these notes are 'peddled' not only among individual investors, savings banks, insurance companies, and others who might have bought bonds, but they are offered also to commercial banks and there added to the applications for discounts coming from the regular classes of local customers.

2. SUPPLY OF SHORT-TERM LOANS

Directly or indirectly the supply of short-term loans comes chiefly from banks.[24] Since the commodity loaned by a bank is usually some form of bank credit, an expansion of loans causes a corresponding expansion in demand liabilities.[25] And since these liabilities to pay on demand must be protected by an adequate stock of cash, the amount the banks of any country can lend is ultimately limited by the money they hold.[26] How, then, does prosperity affect the amount of money held by the banks?

For the United States alone do we have regular statistics concerning the stock of money in the country and its distribution between the banks and the public. The influence of prosperity upon the total stock of money available for use will be discussed presently. For immediate purposes the pertinent fact is that even when the total stock is growing most rapidly, American banks are unable to prevent their quota from being diminished by the activity of business. Of the money withdrawn from the banks day by day and week by week for paying wages and the like, the greater part flows back in a few days through the deposits of shopkeepers, streetcar companies, restaurants, places of amusement, etc. But the entire amount does not flow back. For when employment is full and wages are rising, millions of men carry each a little more money than when times are dull. And when trade is active thousands of retail shops carry each a little more 'change' than when daily sales were smaller. Hence, as table 77 and charts 48 and 49 (Part II) show, the banks' proportion of the total declines gradually from the time depression begins to relax to the time prosperity reaches its zenith.

This loss of money by the banks to the public is sometimes more than offset by an increase in the stock divided between these two claimants. For example, the actual amount of lawful money in the clearinghouse banks of New York and in the national banks as a whole increased during the prosperous years 1897–99. At other times the decline in the quota exceeds the gain from the total to be divided; for example, in 1905–06, when both groups of banks lost cash.[27] But, whatever the net change in the actual amount of money in banks, prosperity checks the possible expansion of short-time loans so far as it increases the proportion of money suspended in active circulation at the expense of the proportion held by the banks as reserves.

3. DEVELOPMENT OF STRINGENCY

Since the demand for short-term loans expands at a peculiarly rapid rate, since their supply is limited by the amount of cash in banks, and since the banks lose cash to the public, prosperity ultimately produces a tense money market.

The coming of this result is deferred by the elasticity of the limit set by cash reserves upon the expansion of bank loans. During depressions bank reserves become larger in proportion to demand liabilities than bank managers think needful, so that periods of prosperity open with a considerable excess of lending power above current demands.[28] But, owing to the processes just traced, the excess is gradually used up, and after a time bank managers are facing the difficult problem of precisely how much farther it is prudent to go in lending additional credit on the basis of their available cash. In America hard and fast rules concerning the minimum ratios of reserve to be held are imposed by law upon all national and many state banks. But, on the one hand, these rules are administered with much circumspection, and, on the other hand, business judgment affirms that the circumstances of the time, the character of a bank's clientele, its relations with other banks, and the liquidness of its assets other than cash ought always to be taken into account in determining whether it is really overstepping the limits of prudence. Hence there is in practice considerable leeway within which the responsible officials exercise their own judgment.

The net resultant of this situation as shown by bank reports is that during prosperity the expansion of loans regularly proceeds at such a pace as to reduce the ratio of reserves to demand liabilities by a considerable though variable margin. The national banks of America, for example, have allowed their reserve ratios to fall from 3 to 6 per cent below the high records of the years preceding the revival of activity. The clearing-house banks of New York have let their ratios drop below 26 per cent, and frequently a trifle below the accepted minimum of 25 per cent.[20] Just where bankers will draw their line against further expansion of loans it is therefore impossible to say. But it is certain that they will draw such a line firmly somewhere within fairly definite limits. As these limits are approached the bankers put up their discount rates and become more exacting in their acceptance of new applications for loans. Business men then find that short-term loans are both more expensive and more difficult to obtain.

That this development of stringency in the money market imposes a severe strain upon business prosperity cannot be doubted; but its precise bearings must be considered in connection with the other strains arising from the increasing costs of doing business, the tension of the market for bonds, and the difficulties faced by the enterprises producing industrial equipment. Before attacking this central problem it is necessary to dispose of a point recently mentioned only to be set aside—the interrelations between prosperity and the quantity of money in circulation.

4. INTERRELATIONS BETWEEN PROSPERITY AND THE QUANTITY OF MONEY IN CIRCULATION

With the quantity of gold that passes into monetary use prosperity and its consequent developments have a highly complex set of interrelations: (1) The advance in the cost of supplies, the decline in the efficiency of labor, etc., cause costs to encroach upon profits in gold mining more seriously than in most other lines of business. For the gold-mining company cannot increase the selling price of its product one jot. Hence the increase in the gold output is somewhat checked. Certain of the poorer mines may be closed, and in the better mines low-grade bodies of ore are temporarily passed over.[30] (2) Of the gold extracted, a decidedly larger quota is diverted from coinage to industrial uses by the growing demand that prosperity begets for jewelry, etc.[31] (3) Of the gold used as money in any country, a larger part is likely to be exported if prices have risen more rapidly there than in other commercial nations, because such a state of the markets stimulates imports of merchandise and checks exports.[32] All these influences act in the direction of reducing an increase or augmenting a decrease in the quantity of gold money. On the other hand, (4) prosperity stimulates the production of gold by spreading a taste among investors for speculative securities promising a high rate of return, thereby making it easier to raise capital for developing new mines. (5) Further, the adverse influence of prosperity upon the balance of payments on merchandise account may be more than offset by its favorable influence upon the balance on investment and banking account. For prosperity encourages the sale of securities to foreign capitalists, and by establishing high discount rates in the local money market encourages the international banking houses to keep large balances in the financial centers. Thus the net effect of prosperity upon the quantity of gold coin depends upon two opposing sets of factors of which the relative strength varies from time to time. But, whatever this net effect, in recent times it has certainly been overshadowed by the influence of other factors not directly dependent upon the condition of business—the progress of mining and metallurgical technique, the discovery of new gold deposits, and the maintenance of order in the chief producing districts.

The supply of paper money issued by the government is usually controlled by imperious necessities of public finance or by major public policies, with neither of which the changing phases of business cycles have more than an indirect connection. As for the quantity of paper money issued by banks, the influence of prosperity depends largely upon the provisions of law concerning issue, security, and redemption. These provisions are too elaborate to be rehearsed here. The present purpose may be met, however, by recalling the conclusion established by the statistics of bank-note circulation in table 76, Part II. Only a slight degree of correspondence appears between the average quantity of bank notes outstanding in each year and the fluctuations in business activity—a conclusion that holds for the elastic systems of France and Germany as well as for the inelastic systems of America and Great Britain.[33]

Not until we come to deposit currency do we find the influence of prosperity upon the quantity of the circulating medium to be both clear in its bearing and decisive in its weight. By making businessmen more eager to borrow and banks more willing to lend, good times produce a rapid expansion of credit currency. In the United States, the one country where the quantities can be measured, this expansion has regularly shown a higher ratio than the concomitant expansion of bank reserves or even of the total monetary stock.[34] Prosperity also causes the credit currency, and in less measure money, to circulate more rapidly.[35] In these two ways business activity automatically provides means by which the vastly increased payments required by the expanding pecuniary volume of trade are readily effected.

So much concerning the effect of prosperity upon the quantity of the currency. What of the counter effects of changes in the quantity of the currency upon prosperity?

Here the one important factor to deal with is changes in the supply of gold money, since gold is nowadays the vital element in bank reserves, and since the supply of gold is dominated by factors not intimately related to business cycles.

An abundant supply of gold favors a revival of business activity by giving the banks liberal reserves and thereby increasing their ability to lend credit at moderate rates of interest. This feature of the situation grows more important as the revival ripens into full prosperity. For the banks usually have a considerable reserve of lending power in the earlier stages of revival, even though the gold supply has been contracting; while, as the climax of prosperity approaches, the banks are usually straining every resource to meet the heavy demand for loans, even though the gold supply has been expanding. That is, an increasing supply of gold favors the continuance of prosperity by retarding the accumulation of one of the stresses characteristic of its later stages—namely, tension in the money market.

IV. Decline in Prospective Profits

1. DEFENDING PROFITS AGAINST ENCROACHMENTS OF COSTS

The gist of the first part of this chapter is that prosperity leads to an increase in the cost of doing business—an increase that threatens to diminish profits. The decline in supplementary costs per unit ceases; equipment of less than standard efficiency is brought back into use; the price of labor rises while its efficiency falls; the cost of materials, supplies, and wares for resale advances faster than selling prices; discount rates go up at an especially rapid pace, and all the little wastes incidental to the conduct of business enterprises grow steadily larger.

So far all is clear. But it has not been shown that this rise of money costs necessarily entails a fall of money profits. For do not the higher cost prices paid by any person mean higher selling prices for someone else? In that case, does not an increase in costs promise to augment the net incomes of sellers just as much as it threatens to reduce the net incomes of buyers? Is there, then, any real danger that the *average* rate of profits, taking all business enterprises together, will be encroached upon?

(1) With reference to those items among the increasing costs which consist of higher prices paid by one set of business enterprises for goods bought from other enterprises it is indeed true that the increase in expenditures is just balanced by the increase in receipts. But, though from the accountant's viewpoint the gains and losses are equal, this offsetting does not make them negligible. For the additions to cost and the additions to income are most unevenly distributed—a condition that threatens to disturb confidence by bringing serious loss upon certain enterprises.

(2) Part of the additional costs consists of higher prices paid to persons not belonging to the business community proper, such as wage earners and farmers, and it is by no means certain that other enterprises will get back what any given enterprise pays out. For the additions to money income scattered among millions of men are not all spent promptly in ways that add to the profits of business.

(3) Against the other items of increasing cost—the use of old-fashioned equipment, the diminishing efficiency of labor, and the declining economy of business management—no compensating gains can be set. They represent a serious addition to the expense of accomplishing given results in most if not in all establishments—an addition that constitutes an immediate encroachment upon profits whenever it occurs and benefits no other enterprise in anything like equivalent measure. Thus

there is no escaping the conclusion that the increase in costs makes grave difficulties for the whole community of business as well as for particular enterprises.

But, granted so much, a problem still remains: Why cannot businessmen defend their profit margins against the threatened encroachments of costs by marking up their selling prices? That simple expedient would remove the difficulty at a stroke.

Once squarely put, this question is not easy to answer squarely. It sounds well to say that the advance of selling prices cannot be continued indefinitely. But this plausible statement challenges the abrupt question: Why not? The only rejoinder that lies upon the surface is that the advance in the price level would ultimately be checked by the inadequacy of the quantity of money. Indefinitely high prices necessitate indefinitely large credits for merchants, manufacturers, etc., and these credits must be sustained by indefinitely large bank reserves. Except under an irredeemable paper standard, the quantity of money does not increase rapidly. Hence the time must come, soon or late, when bank reserves seem scanty in comparison with the demand liabilities reposing upon them. Then confidence in the solvency of the banks would become impaired, and the whole movement of expansion and advancing prices would end in a grand panic. As a sketch of what might happen, this analysis has a certain academic interest. But other causes check the rise of prices before the banks have allowed themselves to be jeopardized in this fashion. And, what is more to the point, this analysis does not really bear upon the problem in hand. For the problem is not, What prevents the general level of prices from rising indefinitely? but, What prevents business enterprises from maintaining a profitable adjustment between the advance in two sets of prices, those which constitute costs and those which constitute returns? To show why a rise in the general level of all prices must come to an end is not to explain the accumulation of stresses between these two parts of the system of prices.

Thus we come back to our problem. During the earlier stages of prosperity no insuperable obstacle is encountered in defending profits by raising selling prices. What processes create such obstacles in the later stages?

2. HINDRANCES TO THE CONTINUED ADVANCE IN SELLING PRICES

A. Public Regulation, Contracts, and Custom

In certain important and many unimportant lines of business the encroachments of costs upon profits cannot be prevented because governmental regulation, established custom, business policy, or long-term contracts impede the advance of prices.

American street railways, for example, are usually prohibited by the conditions of their charters from charging more than a five-cent fare, and even when legally free to do as they like they seldom find it good policy to depart from the customary price. Such enterprises as gas, electric-lighting, and water companies usually have their basic rates fixed by agreements with the public authorities, and cannot raise their tariffs except by negotiation at considerable intervals. Enterprises in this position find their share in prosperity limited to the advantage derived from an increase in the physical volume of their business. Often their fixed charges make so large a proportion of their total expenses that increasing sales suffice to keep their profits rising for some time after prime costs have begun to advance. But there is a limit upon the number of patrons they can serve with their existing plants, and as this limit is approached a further advance in the cost of materials, labor, etc., is bound to reduce their profits.

State and federal legislation has recently brought most American railways into the class of enterprises whose charges are subject to public supervision. And experience has shown that public commissions are much less ready to permit than railway managers are to propose advances in freight and passenger rates. For a public commission is prone to consider, not whether costs are encroaching upon profits, but whether current profits constitute a fair return upon the capital invested. This attitude may be wholly justifiable upon broad grounds of public policy; but the continuation of business prosperity may be imperiled by allowing costs to encroach upon profits, even though the rate that remains to the companies would have seemed amply remunerative in the earlier days of revival.[36]

As examples of enterprises that hesitate to raise prices because they sell to a wide circle of individual consumers at prices stereotyped by business policy or by custom, we may cite the newspapers, the weekly and monthly periodicals, and the manufacturers of trade-marked goods which are advertised widely at fixed prices. The first group, however, may raise its advertising rates, and perhaps the second may reduce the quality of its wares.

Early in every period of prosperity many other enterprises sign contracts that bind them to deliver at fixed prices goods that conform to strict specifications. When these contracts make up the bulk of their business, and require many months to execute, the selling firms are nearly helpless if their profits are threatened by rising costs.

All enterprises that have difficulty in protecting profits by raising prices have peculiarly strong motives for resisting the advance in the cost of materials, labor, etc. But, so far as they are buying staples or supplies made from staples that are used by many other industries, they must get their shares in competition with enterprises that are free to raise selling prices. The gas company must bid for coal against the neighboring foundry, the newspaper must pay enough for paper to keep lumbermen cutting logs for it instead of for the planing mill, etc. And neither the gas company nor the newspaper can prevent its employees from slackening the intensity of their effort. Inability to raise selling prices certainly does not confer immunity against the rise in buying prices.

B. Increase in Capacity for Producing Goods

The obvious point has already been made that when new industrial equipment is placed in active service both the demand for labor, materials, etc., and the current supply of products are enlarged. Hence the encroachments of costs and the difficulty of advancing selling prices are both aggravated (sec. ii, 1). The resulting strain grows progressively more severe so long as prosperity continues to stimulate investment in new equipment. Must not the day come when, in all the industries affected, selling prices can no longer be raised?

It is conceivable that under a supremely systematic and far-sighted direction of economic activity the rate at which new industrial equipment was provided in every branch of industry might be adjusted to the rate at which the demand for its products increased with such nicety as to prevent the overstocking of any market. Needless to say, such system and such foresight are not attained by the present business community. The provision of new equipment for business use is left to the initiative of any individual who will risk his own funds or who can persuade investors to risk theirs in the venture. Caution is enforced by the penalty of pecuniary loss if the enterprise does not find a profitable market for its wares. But a year or more is usually required to carry such a project from the stage of inception to the stage when an elaborate plant stands ready to begin operations. With the crude criteria available at present, no one can forecast accurately so far in advance the prices at which given quantities of a commodity can be sold. As a result, many of the forecasts that are made go wrong. The provision of industrial equipment proves inadequate to meet the demand that exists at profitable prices in some branches of trade, and more than adequate in other branches. The whole tenor of prosperity, however, is in the direction of augmenting errors of the latter kind. The optimistic temper that prevails disposes most men to underrate the risks and to overrate the probable gains. Even active and experienced men of affairs do not escape this infection of overconfidence, and the mass of investors are especially subject to it. Indeed, the credulity of the latter class offers a tempting opportunity to enterprising promoters, who launch plausible schemes, sell them out to the general public, and abandon them to their fate.[37]

The twist given by overconfidence to forecasts of future demand, always difficult to make with accuracy, thus leads in every period of prosperity to an overstocking of certain markets. To check the prosperity out of which the movement grows it is not necessary that investments should return no profits or involve heavy losses. Difficulty arises whenever the increase in the capacity of certain kinds of mines or factories, or of the sawmills, railways, etc., in certain districts, proceeds fast enough to keep selling prices from rising as rapidly as costs. For a decline in orders from the industries first affected spreads trouble among other branches of business by a process analogous to that by which activity is propagated (see Ch. 1, ii, 1–2). And, what is more serious still, an actual or even a prospective decline of profits in a few important industries suffices to create financial difficulties of grave concern to all industries (see sec. v, 3).

C. Advance in Interest Rates

Rising rates of interest of course count among the increasing costs of doing business that threaten to reduce profits. But they have other effects that must be counted among the obstacles that prevent selling prices from being raised sufficiently to cancel increasing costs.

As shown in section ii, 4, the discouragement of long-term borrowing, caused by the rise of interest rates, makes it difficult for the trades engaged in construction work of all kinds to obtain new contracts. Investors will not pay these high rates. Nor will they let contracts freely at the high prices that contracting firms are forced to charge in order to meet their own high costs. And when contractors of various kinds begin to restrict their orders for materials and supplies, the decline of demand threatens to stop the rise of prices in other industries, if not to cause a fall.

In the money market there is little evidence that the demand for short-time loans falls off when interest rates mount high; but it is clear that banks restrict their loans when the ratio of reserves falls dangerously low (see sec. iii, 3). Of course, inability to borrow means inability to buy—a check upon the expansion in the demand for a vast variety of goods and hence an added obstacle in the way of further price advances.

High discount rates also impede the efforts, often made toward the end of a prosperous period, to maintain selling prices by keeping goods off the market and allowing the current output to pile up in huge stocks, which are held for sale at a more opportune moment. This policy interrupts the inflow of cash from sales, and makes it necessary to borrow money to pay running expenses. A temporary relief from a threatened fall of prices may be obtained in this way, but the potential danger becomes more grave. The heavy interest cost of 'carrying' the unsold stocks saps the financial strength of even the largest enterprises and makes long persistence in this course hazardous. If buyers get wind of the situation, they hold off for the drop in prices they expect will come when the stocks are finally 'sacrificed.' In short, there can be but one end to such a policy when initiated under the business conditions of waning prosperity, and that disastrous end is hastened by high discount rates.

D. Underconsumption

If certain of the theories reviewed in the first chapter of Part I are sound, the greatest obstacle in the way of defending profits by advancing selling prices is the lagging of consumers' demand behind the supply of consumers' goods. May goes so far as to say that a glutting of the markets can be prevented only by combining an increase in wages with a decrease in prices—

only by such double stimulation can demand be kept up to supply. Aftalion holds simply that the increasing supplies of consumers' goods cause marginal utilities to fall, and thus bring on a decline in the price level.[38]

Such theories are speculative solutions of a quantitative problem, which is commonly formulated in the question, Does the increase in consumers' demand keep pace with the increase in consumers' supply? but which is more accurately stated by asking, Does consumers' demand grow fast enough to absorb the forthcoming supplies at the continually rising prices that must be charged to prevent costs from encroaching upon profits?

To answer this question categorically would require more refined and more extensive statistics of demand, supply, and prices than are to be had.[39] One significant fact, however, is established in Part II, Chapter IV. According to the monthly figures in table 4 of that chapter, producers' goods reached their highest point and began their decline earlier in 1907 than did consumers' goods. Likewise, according to the monthly figures of tables 5 and 6 (Part II), raw materials began to fall in price before the products manufactured from them. Now, if the chief stress arose from the lagging of consumers' demand behind the supply of consumers' goods, one would expect the opposite result to be registered by the index numbers. Consumers' goods would be the first to fall in price, and this decline would extend to the prices of producers' goods and of raw materials. This extension might take place promptly; but certainly these other classes of commodities would not be the first to fall. What is known about the behavior of prices, then, favors the view that the impossibility of defending profits against the encroachments of costs is experienced earlier by enterprises that handle raw materials and producers' goods. This conclusion is confirmed by current reports concerning retail trade, jobbing, and manufacturing when crises are approaching. The technical journals usually report that the factories and wholesale houses are restricting their orders some weeks, if not months, before they report that retail sales are flagging.

Until the underconsumption theories have been shored up by more convincing evidence than has yet been adduced in their favor, therefore, the view must prevail that the difficulty of warding off encroachments upon profits by advancing costs comes to a head earlier in other lines of business than in those concerned with consumers' goods. The latter industries may well have troubles of their own, troubles that would presently become acute if left to themselves. These gradually accumulating difficulties, however, usually cut but a small figure, because before they have reached a critical stage they are overshadowed by graver troubles arising in other quarters.

3. THE CRITICAL POINT

To sum up: The very conditions that make business profitable gradually evolve conditions that threaten a reduction of profits. When the increase in business, at first a cause and later both a cause and a consequence of rising profits, taxes the productive capacity of the existing industrial equipment, the early decline of supplementary costs per unit of output comes gradually to a standstill. Meanwhile, the expectation of making satisfactory profits induces active bidding among business enterprises for materials, labor, and loan funds, and sends up their prices. At the same time, the poorer parts of the industrial equipment are brought back into use, the efficiency of labor declines, and the incidental wastes of management rise. Thus the prime costs of doing business become heavier. After these processes have been running cumulatively for a while, it becomes difficult to advance selling prices fast enough to avoid a reduction of profits by the encroachment of costs. In many industries the increase in industrial equipment has been so rapid that the full output can scarcely be marketed at the high prices that must be asked. In the trades engaged in construction work new contracts decline when the rise in long-term interest discourages borrowing, and when the cost of construction becomes excessive in the eyes of investors. The decline in bank reserves ultimately makes the banks disinclined to expand loans further—which diminishes the ability of many enterprises to buy as freely as they had planned. The high discount rates also clog the effort to forestall a decline of prices by holding stocks of commodities off the market. In other trades prices are more or less stereotyped by public regulation, custom, contract, or business policy. It may also be that the purveyors of consumers' goods in general find difficulty in sell-. ing their supplies at sufficiently high rates to maintain profits unimpaired, though index numbers and market reports indicate that these difficulties come to a head earlier in other branches of trade.

Since these various stresses become more severe the longer prosperity lasts and the more intense it becomes, and since a setback suffered by any industry necessarily aggravates the stress among others by reducing the market for their products, a reduction in the rate of profits must inevitably occur. But both the analysis and the statistics of profits in Part II, Chapter IX, show that this reduction comes much later in some branches of business than in others, and varies widely in its severity. Even in the same industry different enterprises have exceedingly dissimilar fortunes, partly because of unlike advantages of location and business connection, partly because each enterprise encounters its own peculiar set of unforeseen business conjunctures, partly because of unequal energy and skill among the managers. Indeed, what quantitative information we possess indicates that in the very last year preceding a crisis a large number, perhaps a majority, of enterprises are still making profits as high as or higher than in any preceding year. That is, if an average rate of profits could be computed for a whole country, it would not be surprising to find it reaching its climax just before the crisis breaks out. But this result would not mean that there had been no serious encroachment upon profits. On the contrary, it would mean that the critical point is reached and a crisis precipitated as soon as a decline of present or prospective profits has occurred in a few leading branches of business and *before that decline has become general*. To understand why, it is necessary to examine the bearings of the rate of prospective profits upon outstanding credits.

V. Undermining Business Credit

1. RELATIONS BETWEEN CREDIT AND PROFITS

Toward the end of an expansion virtually all business enterprises have become enmeshed in the network of credit. Customers prefer to buy 'on time,' and in their turn sellers insist upon receiving similar terms from those from whom they buy. Numberless contracts are outstanding that require work to be done by one enterprise for another in advance of payment. And nearly all enterprises above the smallest size borrow from the banks. This seeking for credit, indeed, is not purely voluntary. Where the increase in business made possible by the use of borrowed funds adds more to profits than the interest adds to costs, borrowing becomes compulsory in sharply competitive trades. For a man who uses borrowed funds in addition to his own capital can make higher profits than a rival who refuses to 'run into debt,' if both sell at the same price. Then the borrowing competitor, if he is aggressive, can undersell his less daring rival and still make a fair rate of profit while driving the latter out of business. Thus even the reluctant among businessmen are constrained to ask as well as to grant credit.[40]

To bring out the relation between these credits and profits it will now be necessary to recite a few familiar facts of business practice. The credit an enterprise can command depends primarily upon the estimate set by lenders upon its value as a going concern. Several elements are commonly considered in framing such estimates: the amount, nature, and condition of the physical property owned by the enterprise, including stocks of materials and finished goods as well as real estate and equipment; the number and character of the contracts, patent rights, franchises, securities, etc., that it holds; its pecuniary obligations already outstanding; the balance between its bills due and bills receivable; the good will it enjoys; the business prospects of the branch of trade in which it is engaged, etc. Now all the property owned by a business enterprise, both tangible and intangible, is valued primarily upon the basis of the money that can be made by its use. Good will, also, is valued according to its estimated contribution toward profits. Pecuniary obligations of all sorts have to be considered because they represent deductions that must be made from gross receipts before net profits can be computed. And business prospects mean precisely the prospects of making money. That is, profits, present and prospective, are by far the most important single element in deciding how much a business enterprise is worth and how large a line of credit can safely be granted it. Indeed, if the available data concerning present and prospective profits were sufficiently full and sufficiently trustworthy to be accepted without being checked by any other methods of estimate, a business enterprise might be rated simply by capitalizing these profits at the current rate of interest.[a]

Whatever form credit assumes, in fine, whether it is a bank loan, mercantile credit, or a contract requiring the performance of services for future payment, whether it is supported by collateral security or not, the present and prospective profits of the applicant constitute an element, usually the crucial element, in determining how much may be granted.

2. EFFECT OF PROSPERITY ON CREDIT

In its earlier stages, by broadening the basis upon which credit is granted, prosperity increases the amount prudent judges are willing to extend. All who deal in staple commodities by methods that enable them to pledge their stocks to lenders can obtain increasing advances as the prices of their goods rise.

The concomitant advance of stock-exchange securities per-
forms a like service for those with shares and bonds to offer as
collateral. And the increasing profits of business enterprises,
together with their brighter prospects in the immediate future, justify them, not only in their own opinion but also in
the opinion of lenders, in requesting more liberal lines of
credit. The effect of these definite changes in the business situation is heightened by the prevailing spirit of confidence.
On the same facts submitted by an applicant for discounts
bankers will pass a more favorable verdict; the credit men of
wholesale houses have less critical eyes for the orders sent in
by retail dealers; and manufacturers are more easily induced
to make up goods to be paid for after delivery.

As prosperity grows more intense, a pyramiding of credits
begins. The larger advances obtained in one form or another
by most business houses help to swell their profits. In turn, the
higher profits, present and prospective, give these enterprises
both a business motive and a business justification for demanding larger credits. If their applications are granted and followed by further increases of profit, the enterprises make still
larger demands, and so on. At the same time, the high rate of
profits disposes businessmen to use their own funds to control as many enterprises as possible; that is, to finance their
ventures with borrowed money to the extreme limit permitted
by lenders (cf. sec. iii, 1). Similarly with the other bases of
credit. Prosperity leads to a rapid advance in the prices of commodities; then higher prices force the dealers to borrow more
funds to finance their purchases, and, on the other hand, enable them to borrow more money on their warehouse receipts,
etc. So, too, with stock-exchange securities, when used as collateral for loans. Every rise in the quotations entitles holders
to request larger advances, and if these advances are invested
in further purchases on the exchange they aid in screwing up
quotations, and the higher quotations increase the borrowing
power of the owners once more.

This process does not run long without encountering-obstacles. The advance in interest rates is one, because it cuts down the capitalized value of given prospective profits. The fall of bond prices, which usually comes after a year or two of prosperity, is another, because it reduces the borrowing power of men having this class of collateral. Stock prices are subject to frequent relapses, even in the best of times. The like is true of commodity prices, particularly for the great agricultural staples. And the credit based on the business rating of enterprises has its ups and downs; for the prospective profits of different enterprises vary endlessly, bankruptcies occur in every year to inculcate caution among lenders, and every year has its seasons of relative dullness and doubt. But, despite these minor checks, the grand total of credits rises year by year until the climax of prosperity is reached.[42]

Accordingly, that climax finds business enterprises trusting one another liberally for the payment of goods sold upon time, contracting freely to produce goods for future delivery, and also borrowing on the grand scale made possible by high profits and easy optimism. At this stage of the cycle the typical business enterprise has outstanding heavy financial obligations to creditors, but relies confidently on the still larger sums that will fall due from its debtors, plus the sums represented by its unsold goods and unfilled contracts, to bring in the necessary funds in good season.

3. EFFECT UPON OUTSTANDING CREDITS OF A DECLINE IN PROSPECTIVE PROFITS

Upon such a structure of interlocking credits, the encroachments of costs upon profits combine with the tension in the money and investment markets to impose an ever-increasing strain.

The course can be followed most clearly with reference to credits granted upon stock-exchange collateral in New York while the 1907 panic was brewing. Table 2 gives the lowest and highest points touched between January 1904 and September 1907 by interest rates, and commodity and security prices, together with the level at which all these factors stood in the last-named month—just before the panic began.[13]

TABLE 2

EXTREME FLUCTUATIONS IN INTEREST RATES AND IN INDEXES OF COMMODITY AND SECURITY PRICES, NEW YORK, JANUARY 1904 TO SEPTEMBER 1907

Item affected	Lowest point	Highest point	Standing just before the panic, Sept. 1907
	Interest rates (percentages)		
Average yields on investments in 10 railway bonds	3.80, Aug. 1905	4.27, Sept. 1907	4.27
Discount on 60–90-day commercial paper............	3.75, June 1905	6.79, Sept. 1907	6.79
	Indexes of commodity prices		
Raw materials..............	117.3, Oct. 1904	136.9, June 1907	132.8
Manufactured goods........	110.3, Sept. 1904	130.3, Sept. 1907	130.3
	Indexes of security prices		
Ten railway bonds..........	113.1, Mar. 1904	118.6, Aug. 1905	105.6
Ten preferred stocks........	143.5, June 1904	188.5, Aug. 1905	123.0
Ten common stocks.........	183.5, June 1904	311.5, Jan. 1906	205.0
Forty common stocks.......	165.5, May 1904	279.5, Jan. 1906	197.0

Bond prices began to rise before the depression of 1903–04 was over. Two or three months later stock prices moved upward, and, after another two or three months, commodity prices. Discount rates did not advance until eight or nine months after commodities, and two months more passed before investment rates of interest turned the corner. The early advance of securities, the slightly later advance of commodities, and the continued decline of interest rates, all helped to broaden the basis of credit.

Substantially the reverse order was observed on the fall. Bonds and preferred stocks touched their highest points in August 1905, common stocks in January 1906, and raw materials in June 1907, while manufactured goods and interest rates on both long and short loans continued to advance until the panic broke out. Of course, the fall in security prices was partly a consequence of the rise in interest rates; for a bond or stock expected to bring in interest or dividends at a specified rate is worth less on an investment basis when 'money' brings 6 per cent than when it can be had for 4 per cent." But, whatever the cause, the fall in the prices of securities began to undermine the credit of borrowers who depended upon this type of collateral considerably more than a year before the panic occurred. The strain was felt earlier in bonds, but it became much more severe in stocks—especially in common stocks. Borrowers whose credit depended upon the prices of raw materials they could use directly or indirectly as collateral did not suffer in the same way until the summer before the panic, and then the decline in the prices of their wares was much more moderate than the decline in stock prices. Finally, those who could make a similar use of manufactured goods had a nominally increasing security to offer until the panic actually began.

Now, the money value of an enterprise as a going concern and the price of shares in business enterprises are matters of the same sort. No doubt, the listing of shares on a stock exchange gives opportunity for the occurrence of many fluctuations in prices that find no parallel in a banker's rating of the business enterprises that apply for loans." But, if the enterprise has difficulty in financing its plans for permanent improvements, the banker is less disposed to take its paper. A mere rise in interest rates will tend to depress its capitalized value in the banker's eyes, in the same way that a tight money market tends to depress the prices of stocks. Most of all, the moment that prospective profits decline, even though present profits continue large, the banker revises his estimate of how much credit the enterprise may reasonably be granted. In short, the business factors that cause stocks to fall in the later stages of prosperity have a similar effect upon the credit ratings of business enterprises. The latter fact is less clear solely because these ratings are not made upon an open market, and are not quoted in the newspapers.

Accepting the prices of shares in business enterprises, then, as the best available index of the current valuations set by men of affairs upon going concerns, we may inquire how general and how severe was the decline in market ratings before the panic of 1907. The *Financial Review* gives stock quotations for 63 manufacturing, mining, gas, electric, street railway, and miscellaneous companies in January 1906, January 1907, and September 1907. Adding our 40 transportation companies, we have a list of over one hundred business enterprises for which the changes in current valuation during the period preceding the crisis are recorded. Between January 1906 and 1907—the culminating year of prosperity—shares in 21 of these companies rose in price, while in 82 companies shares fell. That is, the market value of four out of five of these enterprises had fallen nine months before the panic. But the average decline was rather moderate as stock-market fluctuations go—9 per cent of the prices in January 1906. As the stresses gathering during prosperity became more intense, this decline grew greater in degree and became all but universal. The shares of only one enterprise—the American Cotton Oil Company—rose between January and September 1907; those of 102 fell. The average drop in these eight months was 28 per cent.[46]

While we cannot prove by direct evidence that this decline in the values set by the stock market on shares in large corporations fairly represented the change in the values set by credit men upon smaller business enterprises, still we can scarcely doubt that lenders of all classes were growing more and more conservative in their ratings of applicants for loans. Of course this change in mental attitude was no mere whim or emotional aberration, but the mature conclusion of much thinking about the changes in business prospects that prosperity itself was bringing. When this growing conservatism in judging what a business enterprise was worth had reached a certain point it became an independent force reacting powerfully upon the situation within which it had arisen.

Let the estimated money values set upon business enterprises decline seriously, then creditors become apprehensive that their margins of security will shrink to nothing. Certainly the overwhelming majority of enterprises are still solvent; probably a very large proportion are still making high profits; perhaps more than half are doing better than at any previous stage of the business cycle. But the creditors of those enterprises which have suffered most severely from the encroachments of costs, from the decline in new orders, or from some unfortunate conjuncture; or maybe the creditors who happen to be most nervous—certainly numerous creditors of some sort become sufficiently alarmed to refuse to renew maturing loans. Then their debtors must pay up.

When prosperity has evolved such a condition of business, the process of liquidation, once begun, spreads rapidly and promptly brings into its sweep even the creditors who are least nervous and the debtors who are most prosperous. For the efforts of the men called upon for settlement to raise money presently increase the uneasiness of other creditors and create new difficulties for the enterprises whose prospects of profits have not been dimmed hitherto. The analysis of the process by which liquidation spreads over the whole field of business, however, belongs in the next chapter; for when the demand for reduction of outstanding credits becomes general the cycle passes from the phase of prosperity into the phase of crisis.

CHAPTER 3

CRISES

I. The Beginning of Liquidation

WE HAVE seen that the very conditions of business prosperity ultimately beget a downward revision of credits. For prosperity produces a vast expansion of credits based primarily upon the capitalization of large expected profits. When profit margins are threatened by the encroachments of costs, when these encroachments cannot be offset by further advances in selling prices, and when the rate at which profits are capitalized is reduced by the rise in interest, then creditors press their claims.

The beginning of this process of liquidation is sometimes prematurely brought on by the collapse of some conspicuous enterprise that has lost heavily in speculative ventures. Such failures, however, are more often signs that liquidation has already started than causes of its beginning. At other times crop failures, political disorders, uncertainties about the monetary standard, the outbreak of war or a drop in prices following upon peace, crises in foreign countries, or other events that do not arise from the domestic business situation give the impetus to liquidation before prosperity has run its full course. But the preceding description of the processes going forward in a period of business activity shows that, even in the absence of any disquieting event from the outside, prosperity itself gradually accumulates stresses that impel creditors to demand repayment of a part of their advances.

There is no general rule concerning the spot in the business system at which this process of forcing debtors to pay up begins. If violent fluctuations in the prices of certain important materials threaten losses to manufacturers or merchants, the trades concerned may be the first to lose credit. Contractors or others engaged in providing industrial equipment are especially likely to be early victims, because their orders fall off as soon as the bond market becomes stringent and the cost of construction becomes heavy. Or there may be some district of the country, rather than some line of business, where the great lenders of the financial centers think that the expansion of credits has proceeded faster than the expansion of security for repayment. Or it may be merely that certain individual creditors take the conservative tack before others, and put the screws on whatever enterprises happen to have borrowed from them. The spot where liquidation begins, however, is less important than the manner in which it spreads from enterprise to enterprise, from trade to trade, and from town to town.

Say, then, that some creditor more cautious than his fellows, or the creditor of some enterprise more heavily involved than most, gives notice that a maturing debt will not be renewed or extended. The debtor has various ways of raising funds. He may apply to some other lender, he may put pressure upon those who owe him money, he may offer liberal inducements to settle accounts not yet due, he may persuade other creditors to allow more time on sums due them, he may force cash sales of wares on hand, he may 'sacrifice' his securities or other property. If any of these shifts prove successful in getting the necessary funds, the debtor escapes bankruptcy himself. But his efforts increase the business difficulties of others. If he borrows from some bank, that institution is brought nearer the point where it must restrict its loans to other would-be borrowers. If he applies pressure to his own debtors he lands them in the same predicament he is facing. If he persuades other debtors to pay before their time or other creditors to defer their claims, he at least diminishes the means at their disposal. Finally, if he sells commodities, securities, or other property at a sacrifice for cash he injures the market for others. Thus, though the earlier attempts to force a liquidation of outstanding credits may cause no failures, they increase the likelihood that further attempts will have more serious results.

They also increase the likelihood that similar attempts will be made by other creditors. Both creditor and debtor have an interest in concealing such matters as the refusal to extend a loan; but the steps the debtor takes to raise money give an inkling of his plight to the businessmen he approaches on the subject. A suspicion that some creditor is becoming apprehensive and that some debtor is having trouble in meeting his obligations is all that is needed to decide other hesitating creditors to put on the screws. And each new effort to reduce outstanding credits spreads wider the knowledge of what is going on, and strengthens the movement toward liquidation.

The more general such a movement becomes, the more difficult it is to carry through without disaster. For the money and investment markets promptly become more tense than ever. The demand for loans that falls upon any bank is swelled not only by the men who are being pushed to settle by other banks and by mercantile or manufacturing concerns, but also by the men who seek to fortify their position by having funds in readiness to meet demands that may be made upon them. For, when a serious crisis is thought to be impending, it seems wiser to pay interest on money that may not be needed for some time than to risk inability to obtain it later. In addition, enterprises that have bonds maturing or that must raise money to pay for contract work nearing completion fall back upon the banks because investors will not take their long-time obligations. This sudden increase in the demand for loans to meet outstanding obligations much more than makes up for the decrease in the demand for loans to finance fresh business ventures. On the other hand, banks are particularly loath to increase loans at such seasons if they can help it. Their reserves were reduced to a low point by the preceding prosperity, and experience teaches that if the situation goes from bad to worse they may be subjected to heavy demands from depositors and require very large reserves to maintain their own prestige. Further, the risk of loss on bad debts increases with the demand for loans. Heavy failures are likely to occur, and no one can tell what enterprises will be crippled by them. The one certainty is that the banks holding the paper of bankrupt firms will suffer delay and perhaps a serious loss on collection. Hence each bank is disposed to limit its efforts to 'taking care of its own customers.'[1]

Such a restriction of loans, however prudent it may seem from the viewpoint of a single bank, aggravates the stress. On the one hand, it increases the likelihood that some of the enterprises already trying to raise money will fail and be pushed to the wall; on the other hand, it increases the general uneasiness and makes the pressure for liquidation more general and more intense. Thus matters run along for some days or weeks, the strain becoming more severe until the bankruptcy of one or more conspicuous enterprises publishes abroad the gravity of the situation.

What happens then depends primarily upon the leading banks. The crisis may degenerate into a panic, or its severity may be greatly mitigated by effective measures of relief. The best way of presenting these alternatives is to describe two instances in detail—a typical panic and a typical crisis.

II. A Typical Panic—The United States, 1907

Since 1890 the United States has had two great panics, while Great Britain, France, and Germany have had none. We are therefore confined to the study of American experience in 1893 and 1907. The phenomena of these two panics are sufficiently alike to make a review of one suffice for present purposes. The later is preferable, not only because it is closer to contemporary interests, but also because more material is available concerning it, and because it is not complicated by a monetary problem.[2]

1. BEGINNING OF THE 1907 PANIC

It was a series of bank failures in New York that turned the crisis of 1907 into a panic.

Months before the panic broke out, tension in the investment market had caused a slackening of new construction. Copper was among the commodities for which demand dropped. Its price fell from 26 cents a pound early in the year to 20 cents in July, 15½ cents in September, and 12 cents in October. Of course, the prices of stocks in copper mining companies also fell heavily. In turn this fall embarrassed the capitalists who were large owners of copper stocks and who presumably depended on these securities to serve as collateral for heavy loans. Among these capitalists, one, F. A. Heinze, organized a pool to bolster up the prices of shares in the United Copper Company. On October 14 the pool succeeded in running up the prices of this stock on the 'curb' from 37¼ to 60. But this success was brief. Next day the price declined again, and on the 16th it tumbled to 10. Gross & Kleeberg failed, alleging that the brokerage firm of Heinze's brother would not take stock, bought for their account. The next day the latter firm—Otto Heinze & Company—suspended.

This episode in copper stocks made trouble because F. A. Heinze was president of the Mercantile National Bank. It was believed that he 'owned the control' of this institution, and it was suspected that he had taken advantage of that fact to obtain large loans upon the security of the stocks that had fallen so heavily in price. Naturally, the bank's depositors became alarmed and began to withdraw their accounts. The suspicion spread quickly to seven other banks controlled by Messrs. C. W. Morse, E. R. and O. P. Thomas—men believed to have close business affiliations with the Heinzes. The names and

deposits of these banks, some of which were members of the
Clearing House, were published (see tabulation on this page).

Distrusting their ability to meet the demands of depositors,
these institutions appealed to the Clearing House for help.
After examination to determine their condition, the Clearing
House pledged its aid on condition that the Heinze, Morse,
and Thomas interests withdraw from control. These arrange-

Bank	Capital and surplus	Deposits on Oct. 12
Mercantile National Bank*........	$ 8,043,600	$11,569,400
Consolidated National Bank.......	2,114,700	3,913,300
National Bank of North America*..	4,407,600	13,320,000
Mechanics and Traders Bank*.....	2,943,300	19,001,000
New Amsterdam National Bank...	1,266,600	5,132,900
Fourteenth Street Bank*..........	1,416,200	7,392,300
Hamilton Bank...................	488,700	7,210,000
Hudson Trust Company...........	1,106,000	3,828,000
	$21,786,700	$71,366,900

* Member of the Clearing House.
SOURCE: *Bradstreet's*, October 26, 1907.

ments were completed by Sunday, October 20, when it was generally believed that danger of a panic had been averted.

But next day confidence received a yet more serious shock.
The president of the Knickerbocker Trust Company was cred-
ited with being interested in certain of the Morse enterprises.
Distrust resulted in a succession of unfavorable clearing-house
balances, and on Monday the National Bank of Commerce announced that it would no longer act as clearing agent for the
trust company. Tuesday, October 22, the Knickerbocker
opened its doors to a run, and suspended after three hours,
during which it claimed to have paid out some $8,000,000.[3]

The Knickerbocker Trust Company, with deposits of about
$62,000,000, was the third largest institution of its kind in New
York. Its failure caused widespread alarm, and precipitated
runs on the Trust Company of America (deposits $64,000,000)
and the Lincoln Trust Company (deposits $22,400,000). To
add to the distrust, several of the Westinghouse companies

went into the hands of a receiver on October 23, and the Pittsburgh Stock Exchange was closed. Next day several runs began on banks and trust companies in New York, and the Hamilton and Twelfth Ward banks suspended payments as a safety measure. The day following several other suspensions were announced by banks and trust companies—one in Manhattan, four in Brooklyn, and one in Providence.

2. THE SCRAMBLE FOR MONEY

The salient feature of the panic precipitated by this epidemic of bank troubles was a desperate scramble for money. To the New York banks actually subjected to runs, and to the banks that feared they might be, large supplies of currency were a matter of self-preservation. Out-of-town banks, knowing that panic in New York would spread to the rest of the country, and remembering that remittances had been scaled down or refused in 1893, ordered the return of their balances with reserve agents and 'called' the loans they had outstanding with stockbrokers. Timid depositors sought to get their money into their own hands, and many large businessmen locked up such sums as they could get hold of in order to be fortified against emergencies and prepared to take advantage of favorable opportunities—such as stock sales at bargain prices or a premium on currency.

The first relief measures were directed toward enabling the Trust Company of America and the Lincoln Trust Company to meet the run by their depositors. On October 23 a committee of trust-company presidents was formed to aid them by advancing cash and securities to be used as the basis of loans. The Secretary of the Treasury deposited $35,000,000 in the national banks within four days, and much of the large share allotted to New York was transferred to the threatened trust companies. Meanwhile, to prevent the further collapse of prices on the Stock Exchange, a pool was formed to lend $25,000,000 on call on October 24, and $10,000,000 on the

25th. But not until the 26th, four days after the suspension of the Knickerbocker Trust Company, did the New York Clearing House begin to issue clearing-house loan certificates.[4]

While this measure improved the situation by enabling the banks to lend more freely, it was combined with another measure that intensified the scramble for money. Although the New York bank reserves had not declined seriously by October 26—for most of the millions absorbed by the trust-company runs and shipped to out-of-town banks had been provided by the government deposits—the banks began to restrict their payments of cash as soon as the issue of clearing-house loan certificates was authorized. Then out-of-town banks, thinking themselves in desperate need of lawful money for reserves, and employers who could not get from their banks enough money to pay wages, were compelled to buy currency at a premium from brokers. A premium on currency was first reported by the press on October 30. Early in November it rose as high as 4 per cent, remained above 1 per cent until the second half of December, and did not disappear until the last two or three days of the year.[5]

Of course the existence of the premium gave depositors an additional incentive for drawing money out of the banks, and gave those who received money an additional incentive for refusing to deposit it. Moreover, mutual distrust among banks and distrust of banks by the general public was augmented by the refusal to honor in full checks and demands for remittances. On the other hand, the premium may have induced some men who had locked up money in safety deposit boxes to sell their hoards. But the scramble for money was certainly rendered more rather than less intense by the restriction of payments on the part of the New York banks.

The $35,000,000 transferred from the federal subtreasuries to the national banks was the first addition to the supply of money in circulation. But much more was needed, and the banks resorted to an increase of their notes and an importation of gold. Neither measure, however, gave prompt relief. Not until after the first of November did bank notes begin to increase rapidly, and not until the week ending November 9 were the first shipments of gold received.[6]

Meanwhile the panic had spread rapidly from New York to the interior. In two-thirds of the cities having more than 25,000 inhabitants the banks followed the example of the metropolis in suspending cash payments to a greater or less degree.[7] Since lawful money could not be provided quickly enough to meet the insistent demand, a variety of substitutes for cash came into use. An attempt by A. P. Andrew to ascertain the amount of this illegal and inconvertible paper money yielded an estimate of $334,000,000.

	Millions of dollars
Clearing-house loan certificates (large)	238
Clearing-house loan certificates (small)	23
Clearing-house checks	12
Cashiers' checks	14
Manufacturers' pay checks	47
Total	334

But this record was far from complete, and Dr. Andrew thought it safe to "place an estimate of the total substitutes for cash above 500 millions."[8]

Developments in New York can best be followed by aid of table 3. Before the panic began, money was being shipped westward from New York for crop-moving purposes at about the usual rate; but the time was close at hand for this movement to decline.[9] The panic quadrupled the outflow in the last week in October and caused it to increase still further throughout the first half of November. Thereafter the shipments declined; but the current did not set in favor of New York until the first of the new year—three weeks later than usual. Of course these figures mean that the restriction of payments by the New York banks was far from total; on the contrary, they supplied the interior banks with nearly $125,000,000 between the outbreak of the panic and the end of the year. Only a small part of these funds, however, came out of the reserves of the banks. At first the bulk was provided by the Treasury, and

TABLE 3

RECORDED MOVEMENTS OF MONEY INTO AND OUT OF THE CLEARING-HOUSE BANKS OF NEW YORK CITY DURING THE 1907 PANIC

(In millions of dollars)

| Week ending | Bank reserves | Net gain (+) or loss (−) by | | | | Net gain (+) or loss (−) in bank reserves |
		Shipments to and from interior	Sub-treasury operations	Imports and exports of gold	Totals of the three preceding columns	
October 5........	261.8	− 3.9	− 1.0	+ .1	− 4.8	− 7.6
12........	261.2	− 4.9	+ 1.0	+ .2	− 3.7	− .6
19........	267.6	− 4.4	+ 4.0	....	− .4	+ 6.4
26........	254.7	−16.3	+21.0	− 1.3	+ 3.4	−12.9
November 2........	224.1	−17.0	+ 9.5	− .5	− 8.0	−30.6
9........	219.8	−17.4	+15.0	+ 7.3	+ 4.9	− 4.3
16........	218.7	−22.6	− 6.1	+21.1	− 7.6	− 1.1
23........	215.9	−17.3	+ .6	+12.4	− 4.3	− 2.8
30........	217.8	−10.6	− .6	+16.5	+ 5.3	+ 1.9
December 7........	222.5	− 9.0	+ 3.5	+13.8	+ 8.3	+ 4.7
14........	226.6	− 6.8	− 2.8	+ 9.5	− .1	+ 4.1
21........	233.1	− 5.2	+ 1.4	+ 5.7	+ 1.9	+ 6.5
28........	242.6	− 2.2	+ 2.4	+ 4.1	+ 4.3	+ 9.5
January 4........	250.6	+ 5.5	− 4.3	+ 5.3	+ 6.5	+ 8.0
11........	269.0	+13.4	− 4.6	+ 3.6	+12.4	+18.4
18........	295.2	+12.3	+ 3.5	+ .5	+16.3	+26.2
25........	318.9	+20.6	+ 1.5	+ .4	+22.5	+23.7

Compiled from the *Commercial and Financial Chronicle.* The interior movements and subtreasury operations are for weeks ending one day earlier than indicated by the table. For the weeks ending November 15 to January 10, the *Chronicle* gives the net result of subtreasury operations and gold imports together; but as it also gives the gold imports separately it is easy to segregate the two movements.

when that source began to fail the gold that had been ordered from Europe began to arrive. Indeed, these receipts of money from the government and from abroad exceeded the western shipments during the first seven weeks of the panic.

ven by table 6. In ordinary times domestic rates
uctuate within limits set by the cost of shipping
luding insurance and the loss of interest during
between San Francisco and New York 40 cents
d dollars is the usual shipping point, so long as

TABLE 5

ES AND NET DEPOSITS WITH RESERVE AGENTS HELD BY THE
NATIONAL BANKS OF DIFFERENT CLASSES ON AUGUST
22 AND DECEMBER 3, 1907

(In millions of dollars)

sses of anks	August 22		December 3		Gain (+) or loss (−)	
	Millions of dollars	Percentage of reserves	Millions of dollars	Percentage of reserves	Millions of dollars	Percentage of reserves
Cash reserves						
reserve cities:						
York.........	218.8	26.5	177.1	20.5	−41.7	− 6.0
cago...........	66.1	25.2	54.0	23.1	−12.1	− 2.1
Louis..........	26.8	23.0	21.0	19.6	− 5.8	− 3.4
rve cities........	190.3	13.4	162.6	12.9	−27.7	− .5
ntry banks.......	199.6	7.6	246.0	9.9	+46.4	+ 2.3
Net deposits with reserve agents						
eserve cities........	166.5	....	139.7	....	−26.8	....
ountry banks.......	410.0	....	356.0	....	−54.0	....

From O. M. W. Sprague, *Crises under the National Banking System* (Publications of the National Monetary Commission), pp. 305, 308, 309, 310. A slight mistake in Sprague's figures for the gain in cash by the country banks has been corrected by reference to the *Report of the Comptroller of the Currency*, 1908, p. 195.

paper money is available for remittance.[12] But in November
1907 rates as high as $2 prevailed in places as close to New York
as Boston and Philadelphia. In some towns the extraordinary
rates were premiums and in other towns discounts. The whole
machinery for making payments was thrown out of gear for a
month or two, and the resulting embarrassment to business
houses and banks must have been severe.[13]

If the data are trustworthy, then, the decline in New York
bank reserves was caused mainly by a local drain—the runs on
the trust companies for which the clearing-house banks found
money, and hoarding.[10] The heavy loss of cash, however, was
confined to the first two weeks of the panic, and after the fifth
week the reserves began to rise steadily. At the lowest ebb the
bank statement showed not less than $215,851,100 of specie
and legal tenders on hand, equal to 19.98 per cent of the deposits. It was therefore not actual lack of money, but timidity
in using bank reserves that explains the restriction of payments and the resulting premium on currency.[11]

Table 4 shows how the money in circulation was increased.
Between the last days of September and of October only 14
millions were added to the monetary stock; but the Treasury
transferred 57 millions from its vaults to the banks, so that the
amount in circulation increased about 70 millions. Thereafter
the increase came chiefly from the importation of gold and the
issue of new bank notes. Between the end of October and the
end of December the circulation of gold coin and certificates
rose 105 millions, bank notes 84, silver dollars and silver certificates 6, subsidiary silver 8, and greenbacks 2 millions. In
the hurry of the panic, banks did not stop to take out gold certificates, but used gold coin with unaccustomed freedom. The
very unpopularity of the latter medium rendered it more acceptable to banks that were endeavoring to restrict withdrawals
of deposits. In all $273,000,000 were added to the money in
circulation between September 30 and the end of the year.
But even this huge sum was far from adequate; for, if Andrew's
estimate is not exaggerated, twice as much unlawful currency
was provided in the form of substitutes for cash. The monetary
demands created by a panic seem to be insatiable, for a relatively small decrease in the use of credit instruments makes a
large increase in the need for money.

Still more striking results would appear had we for these
months data concerning the distribution of the money in cir-

culation between the banks and the public. But Secretary Cortelyou has prepared an interesting substitute in the shape of an estimate of the money absorbed by the public during the panic. According to his figures, the national banks of the whole

TABLE 4

MONEY IN THE TREASURY AS ASSETS AND THE ESTIMATED AMOUNT IN CIRCULATION DURING THE 1907 PANIC

Description	September 30, 1907	October 31, 1907	November 30, 1907	December 31, 1907	January 31, 1908
	Money in the Treasury as assets (in millions of dollars)				
Gold coin and bullion....	200	167	174	189	177
Gold certificates........	81	71	72	60	41
Silver dollars............	4	2	...	...	9
Silver certificates.......	13	7	3	4	11
Subsidiary silver........	8	7	3	5	11
U.S. notes..............	4	3	2	1	8
Treasury notes..........	...	...	...	...	...
National-bank notes.....	20	15	7	11	30
Total..............	329	272	261	270	286
	Estimated amount in circulation (in millions of dollars)				
Gold coin..............	562	574	640	649	641
Gold certificates........	640	677	676	707	770
Silver dollars............	85	89	91	91	90
Silver certificates........	461	464	469	468	453
Subsidiary silver........	125	127	133	135	131
U.S. notes..............	343	343	345	345	339
Treasury notes..........	6	6	6	5	5
National-bank notes.....	584	595	649	679	665
Total..............	2806	2876	3008	3079	3094
Estimated stock of money	3135	3149	3269	3349	3380
Percentage in the Treasury as assets.........	10.5	8.6	8.0	8.1	8.5
Percentage in circulation.................	89.5	91.4	92.0	91.9	91.5

Compiled from the *Reports of the Treasurer of the United States.*

country lost less cash tha...
tion on this page). In ...
metropolis participated in ...
up what they laid hands o...
clearly by table 5 (see p. 84)...

Reduction in cash held by the na...
banks, August 22 to December 3...
Net importations of gold, Novembe...
December 31......................
Increase in government deposits in the ...
tional banks, August 22 to December ...
Increase in bank-note circulation, Augu...
22 to December 3.....................
Reduction in cash held by the state banks...
and trust companies of New York City,...
August 22 to December 19............

Total............................ 2...

Compiled from the *Response of the Secretary of the Treasury to Sen...
cember 12, 1907 (60th Cong., 1st Sess., Sen. Doc. 208),* pp. 14, 15.

reserve cities the banks used their reserves, th...
meet the demands for money; but in the smaller ...
banks that were forcing substitutes for cash up...
increased their own holdings of lawful money.

3. DEMORALIZATION OF THE MARKETS FOR LOAN...
INVESTMENTS

This desperate scramble for cash threw the money mar...
confusion.

Business journals testify that collections were serious...
terfered with, so that many enterprises were temporarily ...
prived of the regular remittances of funds on which they h...
been counting to meet their current expenses and their fina...
cial obligations.

More precise information concerning the confusion that ...
reigned in all matters pertaining to payments between differ-

TABLE 6

EXCHANGE RATES ON NEW YORK IN EIGHT CITIES DURING THE 1907 PANIC

Week ending	Boston	Philadelphia	Cincinnati	Kansas City
October 26	$0.25 discount	Par	$0.25 discount	$0.25 premium
November 2	0.25 discount	....	0.50 discount	0.25 premium
9	0.30 premium	$2.50 premium	Par–0.25 discount	1.00 premium
16	1.50 premium	5.00 premium	Par–0.60 discount	1.00 premium
23	2.00 premium	2.50–4.00 premium	Par–0.60 discount	1.00 premium
30	Par	2.00–3.00 premium	1.00 premium	1.00 premium
December 7	0.25 discount	1.50–2.50 premium	0.30–0.50 discount	1.00 premium
14	0.30 discount	2.50 premium	0.50 discount	1.00 premium

Successive weeks of:	Chicago	St. Louis	New Orleans	San Francisco
October 1	$0.25 discount	$0.75 discount	$0.75 discount	$0.20 premium
2	0.20 discount	0.45 discount	0.35 discount	0.60 discount
3	0.20 discount	0.60 discount	0.35 discount	0.70 discount
4	0.25 discount	2.00 discount	0.75 discount	10.00 discount
November 1	0.25 discount	0.30 discount	1.50 discount	7.50 discount
2	Par	2.50 premium	2.00 discount	Unsalable
3	0.25 premium	4.00 premium	1.50 discount	Unsalable
4	1.00 premium	6.00 premium	1.00 discount	Unsalable
December 1	1.00 premium	2.00 premium	0.80 discount	5.00 discount
2	Par	2.00 premium	0.40 discount	3.50 discount
3	Par	4.00 premium	0.40 discount	4.00 discount
4	0.50 discount	3.00 premium	0.75 discount	4.00 discount
5	0.50 discount	2.00 premium	0.85 discount	

Data for the first four cities from Sprague, *History of Crises under the National Banking System*, pp. 291, 292; for the second four cities from Kemmerer, *Seasonal Variations in the Relative Demand for Money and Capital in the United States*, p. 372. All the quotations are for $1000 of New York exchange.

Other anomalies were observed in the market for foreign exchange. It was fortunate for the country that few finance bills were outstanding when the panic broke out. In October

1906 the Bank of England had been forced to advance its rate of discount to 6 per cent in order to check an outflow of gold to America. It took advantage of the occasion to warn the other London banks that the accepting of more finance bills for New York account would menace the stability of the local market. The monetary stringency of the following months in America was partly caused by this step. New York financiers were forced to settle for their old bills as they matured and could get no further advances of moment. Moreover, an unusually small amount of anticipatory bills had been drawn in the summer of 1907 against shipments of produce. Hence, when the export movement of wheat and cotton began in the autumn, the proceeds of the bills of exchange were not required to settle old debts, but supplied credits against which gold could be demanded.[14] The panic also caused a rapid decline in imports of commodities, so that the favorable balance of payments on merchandise account reached unprecedented proportions.[15]

All this was highly favorable to the banks, and, as we have seen, enormous amounts of gold were imported—63 millions in November, 43 in December, and 10 in January. The curious feature of the situation was that these importations were made in the face of quotations for sterling bills high above the import point. Under ordinary circumstances the import point for sight exchange, with discount at 6 per cent, is about $4.84¼, and the export point about $4.88.[16] Just before the panic, the actual rates for bankers' sight bills were approximately $4.86. In the first turmoil they dropped as low as $4.82¼ on October 26—considerably below the import point. But a quick rally brought them up to $4.86¾–$4.88 on November 2. During this whole month the lowest quotation was $4.85–$4.85¼, while the highest quotation was $4.88½–$4.88¾.[17] That is, tens of millions of gold were engaged for import at prices for bills always well above the import point and sometimes exceeding the export point. Of course, the explanation is that the importing banks could sell the gold 'to arrive' at a premium of perhaps 1 to 3 per cent. It does not follow that the premium on currency facilitated imports; but simply that this premium affected the nominal prices of bills of exchange, when the bills were paid for in checks upon banks that were restricting withdrawals of cash.

TABLE 7

PRICES AND VOLUME OF BUSINESS ON THE NEW YORK STOCK EXCHANGE
DURING THE 1907 PANIC

	September	October	November	December	January
	Relative prices of bonds and stocks (Average actual prices 1890-99 = 100)				
West Shore R. R. bonds..	95.4	94.5	90.9	92.9	95.9
Ten railway bonds.......	105.6	103.3	99.5	101.6	105.8
Ten preferred stocks.....	123.0	126.0	117.5	123.5	124.5
Ten common stocks......	205.0	169.5	152.5	161.5	166.5
Forty common stocks:					
Grand averages........	197.0	171.5	159.0	167.0	174.5
Averages of highest relative prices.......	204.0	192.0	169.0	176.0	186.0
Averages of lowest relative prices.......	190.0	151.0	149.0	158.0	163.0
	Volume of business transacted				
Par value[a] of:					
bonds sold............	25.0	50.0	63.0	60.0	86.0
stocks sold...........	1088.0	1551.0	849.0	1072.0	1396.0
Actual value of shares sold...................	902.0	1127.0	617.0	779.0	1016.0
Millions of shares sold....	12.2	17.3	9.7	12.6	16.6

[a] In millions of dollars.

Data concerning prices of securities from the tables in Chap. 4 (secs. iii and iv). Data concerning volume of business from the "Quotation Supplement" of the *Commercial and Financial Chronicle*, and the *Financial Review*.

On the Stock Exchange the panic wrought havoc with prices. Common stocks were most seriously depressed, but preferred stocks also fell heavily (table 7). Even high-grade railway bonds sold off several points. The lowest prices in all classes of securities were touched in November. December brought a distinct rally, and in January, the first month after the panic, prices for bonds and preferred stocks were higher than in September, the last month before the panic. Common stocks, however, were slower in recovering.

The one encouraging feature of the market was that sales at these low prices were not large. During the severe liquidation of March 1907 over 32 million shares of stock had changed hands in a single month. In October the sales were not much over half and in November less than a third of this volume. Doubtless the drastic decline of the spring and summer months had already forced most of the weaker holders to dispose of their stocks. In addition, the banks made considerable effort to sustain the market, first by contributing to the money pools of October 24 and 25, and, after clearing-house loan certificates had been issued, by refraining from forcing repayment of call loans, and by taking over loans called by the trust companies and out-of-town banks. Indeed, this policy of forbearance was compulsory. Brokers and their customers could not have found the money to settle had all the banks stopped lending on the one hand, and on the other called in their outstanding loans. And had the banks endeavored to get back their money by selling the stocks pledged with them as collateral, the resulting fall of prices in a market where no one could borrow would have wiped out their margins of security and left them with heavy losses.

Judging from the comments of the press on the sudden increase in 'odd-lot' sales, the purchasers at this season were largely small investors. The low prices offered tempting bargains to all who had funds available for payment. Bond sales were much heavier relatively than stock sales, both because purchasers faced smaller risks in taking bonds under panic conditions and because the slighter decline in price made the man who was forced to raise money by parting with his securities prefer to let bonds go rather than stocks.

The most violent manifestations of the panic appeared in the market for short-time loans. Unfortunately, we have statis-

tics of discount rates for New York City alone.[18] The best compilation of these figures, published in the *Financial Review*,
is partly reproduced in table 8 for the weeks preceding, during,
and following the panic. The exceedingly high rates for call
loans are the most spectacular feature of this exhibit.[19] But we
have seen that these rates did not force such a ruinous liquidation as might have been expected. In any case, the eccentricities
of the call-loan rate possess less significance for general business than the demoralization of the market for time loans and
commercial paper.

Rates of 12 per cent and over are bad enough, but far worse
are the entries 'no business' and the footnotes explaining that
the quotations in the table are purely nominal, because no
loans were being made.[20] At a pinch, the merchant and the manufacturer may be able to pay 10–15 per cent for loans during a
month or two. Not to be able to get loans at all is a far worse
plight. And many enterprises must have found themselves in
this predicament for six or eight weeks. No doubt most of the
strong banks 'took care of' such regular customers as seemed
to be really solvent. But the enterprises that relied largely for
loans upon selling their commercial paper through note brokers had no such protection.

Further light is thrown on the extreme stringency of the
money market during the panic by table 9. The New York
banks increased their loans more than 10 per cent in the very
height of the panic; in Boston and Philadelphia the changes
were slight; but in the other cities the banks contracted loans,
slightly in St. Louis, heavily in Chicago, New Orleans, and
San Francisco. The exceptional action of the New York banks
is accounted for by the need of the trust companies to liquidate
loans, whenever possible, and by similar action on the part of
outside banks. "These two groups of lenders more than exhausted the possibilities of contraction in New York, and a
part of their loans had to be taken over by the clearing-house
banks to prevent a general disaster."[21] Of course, the extreme

TABLE 8

INTEREST RATES IN NEW YORK CITY DURING THE 1907 PANIC

Week ending		Premium on currency	Call loans			Time loans				Commercial paper		
			At stock exchange		At banks and trust companies	Sixty days	Ninety days	Four mos.	Six mos.	Double name	Single name	
										Choice	Prime	Good
		Range	Range	Average	Min.					Sixty–ninety days	Four–six mos.	Four–six mos.
Oct.	4	....	3 – 10	5	3	5¾– 6	6 – 6½	6 – 6½	6 –6½	7	7	....
	11	....	2½– 6	5	3	6 – 6½	6½– 7	6½	6	7 [e]	7 [e]	7 –7½ [e]
	18	....	2¼– 10	5	3	6	6½	6	6	7 [e]	7 –7½ [e]	7½ [e]+
	25	....	5 –125	40	6	6½– 7 [d]	6½– 7 [d]	6½–7 [d]	6 [d]	7 –7½ [e]	7 –7½ [e]	....
Nov.	1	1 –3	3 – 75	50	[c]	12 –16	12 –16	No business		No business		
	8	1 –4	4 – 25	22	[c]	....	12 –15	No business		7 –7½ [e]	7 –7½ [e]	....
	15	2¼–4	5 – 15	10	[c]	12 –15	12 –15	No business		7 –7½ [e]	7 –7½ [e]	....
	22	1½–3½	3½– 15	10	[c]	12 –15	12 –15	No business		No business		
	29	¾–1¾	3 – 12	7	[c]	....	12 –15	No business		8	8	....
Dec.	6	½–2	3 – 13	6	[c]	No regular rates: All business by special agreement						
	13	½–1½	2 – 25	18	[c]	8 –10	8 –10	8	7 –8	8 [e]	8 [e]	....
	20	½–1¼	6 – 17	12	[c]	12	10	8	6 –7	8 [e]	8 [e]	....
	27	¼–1¼	6 – 25	20	[c]	12	10 –12	....	7½–8	8 [e]	8 [e]	....
	31 [a]	⅛– ⅜	5 – 20	17	[c]	10	10	6	....	8	8	....
1908												
Jan.	3 [b]	....	5 – 20	10		10	10	7	6	8	8	....
	10	....	2 – 9	6	4	6½	6	6	6	6¾–7½	6¾–7½	....
	17	....	2½– 6	4	3	5¼– 5½	5¼– 5½	5¼–5½	5½–6	6½–7	6½–7	7½
	24	....	1½– 3	2	1½	4	4½	4½	5	5½	6 –6½	6½–7
	31	....	1½– 2	1¾	1½	3 – 3½	3 –3½	4½	4½	5½–6	5½–6	6 –6½

SOURCE: *Financial Review*, 1909, pp. 40, 41.
[a] Covers business for last two days of year.
[b] Covers business for first three days of year.
[c] Banks and trust companies out of the market.
[d] Nominal rates; no offerings.
[e] Quotations entirely nominal; no business.

TABLE 9

LOANS, DEPOSITS, AND RESERVES OF THE CLEARING-HOUSE BANKS
OF SEVEN CITIES DURING THE 1907 PANIC

Week ending	Loans (millions of dollars)	Deposits (millions of dollars)	Reserves	
			Amount (millions of dollars)	Ratio (per cent)
	New York City			
October 5.............	1089	1037	262	25.3
12.............	1083	1026	261	25.5
19.............	1077	1026	268	26.1
26.............	1088	1024	255	24.9
November 2.............	1148	1052	224	21.3
9.............	1187	1087	220	20.2
16.............	1192	1089	219	20.1
23.............	1188	1080	216	20.0
30.............	1198	1083	218	20.1
December 6.............	1186	1075	223	20.7
13.............	1175	1067	227	21.2
20.............	1165	1059	233	22.0
27.............	1148	1051	243	23.1
January 4.............	1133	1048	251	23.9
11.............	1117	1052	269	25.6
18.............	1127	1090	295	27.1
25.............	1136	1127	319	28.3
	Chicago			
October 5.............	279.7	405.2	62.7	15.5
12.............	276.7	402.8	62.8	15.6
19.............	277.1	398.9	59.0	14.8
26.............	279.3	391.6	54.5	13.9
November 2.............	276.0	384.3	53.9	14.0
9.............	271.2	376.8	55.7	14.8
16.............	270.8	372.4	55.8	15.0
23.............	265.1	370.5	58.1	15.7
30.............	261.1	371.1	63.8	17.2

TABLE 9—(*Continued*)

Week ending	Loans (millions of dollars)	Deposits (millions of dollars)	Reserves	
			Amount (millions of dollars)	Ratio (per cent)
Chicago—(*Continued*)				
December 6	258.0	369.8	65.3	17.7
13	255.0	363.4	65.6	18.1
20	252.5	363.2	66.5	18.3
27	250.2	358.9	69.0	19.2
January 4	247.3	363.3	71.5	19.7
11	244.0	371.8	74.8	20.1
18	243.5	381.2	76.0	19.9
25	246.3	389.5	77.4	19.9
Boston				
October 5	190.3	214.8	21.6	10.1
12	190.8	213.3	21.6	10.1
19	191.7	224.2	22.4	10.0
26	191.2	222.1	22.8	10.3
November 2	192.5	222.2	20.8	9.4
9	191.5	214.7	19.9	9.3
16	190.9	217.7	19.2	8.8
23	190.4	213.7	18.6	8.7
30	190.7	212.1	17.1	8.1
December 6	191.9	214.7	17.4	8.1
13	190.6	211.3	18.2	8.6
20	189.5	209.4	19.3	9.2
27	190.1	210.0	20.5	9.8
January 4	191.1	218.9	21.9	10.0
11	188.9	216.3	23.8	11.0
18	188.6	216.0	25.1	11.6
25	188.1	210.3	25.8	12.3
Philadelphia				
October 5	224.3	252.9	54.7	21.6
12	223.0	251.3	53.6	21.3
19	222.0	254.8	55.6	21.8
26	219.8	246.3	52.7	21.4

TABLE 9—(*Continued*)

Week ending	Loans (millions of dollars)	Deposits (millions of dollars)	Reserves	
			Amount (millions of dollars)	Ratio (per cent)
	Philadelphia—(*Continued*)			
November 2................	219.6	236.2	47.4	20.1
9................	221.2	233.8	45.9	19.6
16................	222.2	233.3	44.8	19.2
23................	223.0	230.7	44.8	19.4
30................	224.2	231.2	44.5	19.2
December 6................	224.4	230.2	44.8	19.5
13................	224.8	230.5	43.0	18.7
20................	224.8	229.5	43.1	18.8
27................	225.1	231.1	43.3	18.7
January 4................	224.6	235.3	45.7	19.4
11................	223.1	233.9	46.5	19.9
18................	222.9	235.5	48.1	20.4
25................	221.4	234.1	50.0	21.4
	St. Louis			
October 5................	171.7	203.4	24.9	12.1
12................	168.2	200.6	23.9	11.9
19................	168.4	198.4	22.0	11.0
26................	167.8	194.5	22.4	15.2
November 2................	167.3	189.0	21.3	11.3
9................	167.4	188.8	21.7	11.5
16................	168.1	188.6	23.9	11.5
23................	167.1	186.9	24.8	13.2
30................	166.4	187.0	25.6	13.6
December 6................	166.7	186.7	25.7	13.8
13................	166.1	186.5	26.0	13.9
20................	165.3	185.1	26.2	14.2
27................	163.1	184.3	26.8	14.5
January 4................	162.4	182.6	26.0	14.3
11................	160.3	181.0	26.4	14.4
18................	157.5	180.4	26.7	14.2
25................	154.1	176.6	27.2	15.3

TABLE 9—(*Continued*)

Week ending	Loans (millions of dollars)	Deposits (millions of dollars)	Reserves	
			Amount (millions of dollars)	Ratio (per cent)
New Orleans				
October 5...............	65.9	54.8	5.4	9.9
12...............	66.2	54.3	4.8	8.8
19...............	66.5	52.7	4.4	8.3
26...............	66.0	53.3	5.1	9.6
November 2...............	65.8	52.8	4.6	8.7
9...............	64.9	52.9	5.0	9.5
16...............	64.8	52.9	5.5	10.4
23...............	62.5	53.1	5.6	10.5
30...............	62.3	52.9	5.9	11.2
December 6...............	62.0	52.1	5.8	11.0
13...............	61.3	52.0	5.6	10.8
20...............	60.3	51.5	6.1	11.8
27...............	59.1	51.9	6.2	11.9
January 4...............	60.3	51.5	6.1	11.8
11...............	59.1	51.9	6.2	11.9
18...............	58.2	51.6	6.3	12.2
25...............	57.3	51.5	6.0	11.7
San Francisco				
October 5...............	93.0	108.2	13.8	12.8
12...............	93.3	108.3	13.1	12.1
19...............	94.6	111.0	13.7	12.3
26...............	93.4	108.3	12.0	11.1
November 2...............	90.1	99.5	12.0	12.1
9...............	88.8	96.1	11.3	11.8
16...............	89.1	94.3	12.5	13.2
23...............	88.0	92.7	14.0	15.1
30...............	87.1	91.4	15.3	16.7
December 6...............	86.3	90.3	15.7	17.4
13...............	85.5	90.5	16.7	18.5
20...............	85.0	90.1	17.9	19.9
27...............	84.1	89.7	17.8	19.8

TABLE 9—(Concluded)

Week ending	Loans (millions of dollars)	Deposits (millions of dollars)	Reserves	
			Amount (millions of dollars)	Ratio (per cent)
	San Francisco—(Continued)			
January 4...............	83.5	91.7	17.7	17.7
11...............	82.6	92.0	18.6	20.2
18...............	82.2	92.5	19.5	21.1
25...............	81.1	92.7	19.5	21.0

Compiled from E. W. Kemmerer, *Seasonal Variations in the Relative Demand for Money and Capital in the United States* (Publications of the National Monetary Commission), pp. 258, 264, 269, 274, 275. The data for Boston and Philadelphia are compiled from the *Commercial and Financial Chronicle*.

reluctance of the banks to make new or even to extend old loans aggravated the panic among businessmen who needed to borrow.

Deposits fell off faster than loans were contracted in Chicago, St. Louis, and San Francisco. One might expect the difference to be explained by a reduction in reserves, but it is not. Even where reserves declined, the loss of cash is not sufficient to sustain the theory that the banks were paying off depositors in cash taken from their vaults. If such withdrawals were permitted on a considerable scale, despite the restriction of payments, they were more than offset by funds imported from Europe, obtained from New York, or raised by selling bonds. In New Orleans the decline in deposits was very slight, and in New York deposits increased some $63,000,000 in the first four weeks of the panic, because of the $115,000,000 expansion in loans. The difference between these two sums—$52,000,000— is nearly equaled by the concomitant drop of $49,000,000 in the reserve.

Finally, table 9 shows again how tenaciously the banks held to their cash in the face of the most urgent demands from their customers. Though the New York banks displayed great nervousness in restricting payments, their course was bolder than that pursued by the banks in these other cities, except Boston and Philadelphia. After losing a relatively small sum in the first or second week of the panic, the banks of Chicago, St. Louis,

TABLE 10

Business Failures, Weekly, United States, during the 1907 Panic, Compared with the Number in the Corresponding Weeks of the Four Preceding Years

Week ending	Corresponding weeks in				
	1907	1906	1905	1904	1903
October 3	177	136	189	195	197
10	192	192	183	196	203
17	194	170	178	227	216
24	220	184	178	180	217
31	223	163	160	200	216
November 7	226	146	166	184	250
14	259	222	198	190	234
21	265	212	224	193	167
28	258	174	188	184	239
December 5	272	216	203	231	241
12	284	220	226	239	239
19	300	227	235	249	243
26	248	161	212	218	209
	1908	1907	1906	1905	1904
January 2	345	185	220	278	262
9	435	283	286	295	315
16	431	234	279	304	266
23	408	252	276	228	242
30	359	211	228	239	216

Compiled from *Bradstreet's*.

New Orleans, and San Francisco all began to gain once more. By the end of November their percentages of reserve were higher than in the weeks preceding the panic. Had the New York banks set the example of attempting to quiet the panic by meeting all demands in full, it is probable that the scramble for cash would never have assumed great dimensions and that the banks in other towns would have been able to maintain the same policy. But with restriction begun in New York, a timid policy may have been compulsory upon the banks in smaller places.

Concerning the policy pursued by banks in other towns, our information is slight. The last report of the national banks before the panic was made August 22, and the next report not until December 3. The changes between these two dates cannot with confidence be ascribed to the effect of the panic. The drift of this evidence, however, indicates that a moderate contraction of loans was practiced throughout the country, while deposits everywhere fell much more rapidly than loans. As already shown, reserves decreased a little in most of the reserve cities and increased in the country districts.[22]

4. REACTION OF MONETARY STRINGENCY UPON GENERAL BUSINESS

On the one side, the panic intensified the process of liquidation—that is, the process of forcing the settlement of outstanding accounts. On the other side, it made the raising of money extremely difficult. The restriction of payments by the banks, the slowness of collections, the confusion of domestic exchanges, the fall in the prices of securities, the demoralization of the discount market, and the contraction of bank loans, one and all added to the troubles of debtors who were being pressed for payment.

Business failures increased, but as table 10 indicates, the increase was not very great during the weeks when the panic was at its worst. On the other hand, the number increased as the panic relaxed after the first of the year. The explanation is partly that banks and other lenders made special efforts to allay distrust so long as the danger was most threatening, and partly that January 1 settlements brought affairs to a head with many weakened firms.

As brought out in Part II (Ch. IX, ii, 1), just before and during a crisis the increase in the liabilities of firms that fail is more rapid than the increase in their number. The difference during the 1907 panic is clear in Dun's figures by quarters (table 11). It would be still more striking were bank suspensions included with these commercial and manufacturing bankruptcies. The reason for the greater average size of enterprises dragged down by a panic than of those that fail during

TABLE 11

BUSINESS FAILURES, NUMBER AND AVERAGE LIABILITIES, UNITED STATES,
BY QUARTERS, 1907–1908

Quarter	Number of failures	Average liabilities
1907		
1st quarter............................	3,136	$10,228
2nd quarter...........................	2,471	15,173
3rd quarter...........................	2,483	18,714
4th quarter...........................	3,635	22,379
1908		
1st quarter............................	4,909	15,422
2nd quarter...........................	3,800	12,805
3rd quarter...........................	3,457	15,997
4th quarter...........................	3,524	12,099

Dun's Review, January 8, 1910, p. 11.

prosperity or after the panic has yielded to depression lies in the changes in the relative importance of the causes that bring about failure. For years Bradstreet's has endeavored to ascertain the leading cause for every failure it records. Lack of capital and incompetence usually account for more than half the failures, while fraud, inexperience, etc., bring up the proportion 'due to the faults of those failing' to about four-fifths. In a panic, however, failures that are 'not due to the faults of those failing,' but to the failure of others, competition, or what Bradstreet's calls "specific conditions" become, if not more numerous relatively, more important financially. Thus in the prosperous years 1905 and 1906 about a quarter of the defaulted

CRISES

liabilities were ascribed to causes beyond the control of the failing firms, while in 1907 this proportion increased to more than one-half, and in 1908 remained above one-third.[23] During a panic a considerable number of large concerns, furnished with adequate capital and well managed, are among the victims of these unfortunate conjunctures, and it is primarily their fall that swells the average liabilities.

On commodity prices panic has a sharply depressing influence. As stated in the closing section of Chapter 2, several groups of commodities had passed their maximum prices several months before the panic of 1907 began. Raw mineral products began to decline after February, raw forest products after April, twenty miscellaneous raw materials after May, and goods manufactured from them after June. June also marked the turning point for all the producers' goods for which we have data. On the other hand, raw animal and farm products, especially subject to seasonal influences, rose after midsummer to maxima in October.[24] Consumers' goods also rose until October and did not begin to decline until December, while the retail prices of foods rose slightly during the panic itself. These maxima are indicated by italics in table 12.

Thus, upon most classes of wholesale prices the influence of the panic was limited to accelerating a fall already in progress, or to diminishing the effect of seasonal conditions that tended toward an advance. However, the recorded quotations from which the index numbers are computed probably fail to reflect the full severity of the reaction in commodity markets. For there are broad hints in the contemporary issues of the financial periodicals that heavy reductions from list prices were quietly made in private negotiations by overstocked houses, as one means of raising money.[25]

Business as a whole continued to increase slowly for some time after wholesale prices began to decline. Such at least is the conclusion suggested by the statistics of bank clearings in tables 13-15. Owing to the influence of seasonal factors upon

TABLE 12

RELATIVE PRICES OF COMMODITIES, BY MONTHS, 1907–1908, PRICES AT WHOLESALE IN THE UNITED STATES

Month	Retail prices of foods (1)	Consumers' goods (2)	Producers' goods (3)	Raw materials (4)	Manufactured articles (5)	Raw materials			145 farm products (9)	All commodities (10)	Bradstreet's index no. (11)	England (Sauerbeck) (12)
						Mineral (6)	Forest (7)	Animal (8)				
1907												
January	120	116	140	144	130	146	170	145	124	127	8.9	80
February	120	117	142	147	131	*148*	171	*145*	127	129	9.0	81
March	119	117	143	147	133	146	174	136	131	129	9.1	80
April	119	115	143	146	134	143	*177*	133	127	129	9.0	81
May	119	116	144	*149*	135	144	174	131	134	130	8.9	*82*
June	119	116	*144*	148	*136*	143	171	130	138	130	9.0	82
July	120	117	141	146	135	141	170	131	134	130	9.0	81
August	120	120	141	144	132	137	170	135	131	130	8.9	79
September	122	122	138	148	134	134	168	137	135	131	8.8	79
October	123	125	134	148	134	131	164	142	*141*	*132*	8.9	79
November	123	*125*	134	139	133	128	162	136	135	129	8.7	77
December	*124*	123	130	135	129	122	153	130	135	126	8.5	76
1908												
January	. . .	120	128	136	129	120	151	125	136	124	8.3	76
February	. . .	118	128	131	128	119	153	120	134	123	8.1	75
March	. . .	118	127	134	127	120	151	120	136	122	8.0	74
April	. . .	117	127	133	127	119	154	122	134	122	8.1	74
May	. . .	115	123	132	125	118	153	119	136	121	8.0	74
June	. . .	114	123	129	123	116	148	121	136	119	7.7	73
July	. . .	115	124	131	122	116	148	128	137	120	7.8	73
August	. . .	114	124	135	121	118	146	131	135	120	7.9	72
September	. . .	113	123	135	122	117	146	136	129	119	7.9	73
October	. . .	113	124	133	121	118	151	140	130	120	8.0	72
November	. . .	113	125	134	121	120	153	144	128	120	8.1	72
December	. . .	115	126	136	123	121	157	147	129	121	8.2	72

Column (1) is from the *Bulletin of the Bureau of Labor*, July 1908, p. 187.—"simple average"; columns (2) and (3) are from Part II, table 4; columns (4) and (5) are from Part II, table 5; columns (6), (7), (8), and (9) from Part II, table 7; column (10) from the materials used in making Part II, table 7—"grand totals" of all commodities raw and manufactured; column (11) from *Bradstreet's*, and column (12) from the *Journal of the Royal Statistical Society*. Italic figures indicate maxima.

the clearings, comparisons between corresponding periods in
1907 and 1906 possess more significance than comparisons between successive months or weeks of 1907.

So far as New York is concerned, clearings in 1907 ran steadily behind the records of 1906 except in March and July. But

TABLE 13

BANK CLEARINGS IN AND OUTSIDE NEW YORK CITY, 1906–1907,
AND GAIN OR LOSS

(In millions of dollars)

Month	New York		Outside New York		1907 compared with 1906 Gain (+) or loss (−)	
	1906	1907	1906	1907	New York	Outside New York
January	11,239	9,638	5,095	5,383	−1,601	+ 288
February	8,324	7,332	4,153	4,461	− 992	+ 308
March	8,377	9,562	4,630	5,063	+1,185	+ 433
April	8,543	7,668	4,359	4,969	− 875	+ 610
May	8,793	7,335	4,444	5,047	−1,458	+ 603
June	7,816	6,369	4,433	4,767	−1,447	+ 334
July	7,256	7,312	4,392	5,037	+ 56	+ 645
August	8,834	6,891	4,310	4,637	−1,943	+ 327
September	8,314	6,030	4,199	4,522	−2,284	+ 323
October	9,344	8,196	5,206	5,584	−1,148	+ 378
November	8,608	5,500	5,048	4,159	−3,108	− 889
December	9,227	5,350	5,058	4,057	−3,877	−1,001

Compiled from the *Financial Review*.

most of, if not the entire decline was due to dullness upon the
Stock Exchange.[26] It is impossible, however, to segregate the
clearings that originate in the sales of stocks and bonds from
those which originate in other transactions, so that we cannot
be certain that general business in New York was less before
the 1907 panic than during the preceding year of high prosperity.[27] Outside New York, it was certainly greater in every
month of the year until November, if clearings may be trusted
as an index. But after midsummer the gains were considerably
smaller than they had been from April to July, and probably

TABLE 14

BANK CLEARINGS IN AND OUTSIDE NEW YORK CITY AND IN SIXTEEN OTHER CITIES DURING THE 1907 PANIC

(In millions of dollars)

Week ending	New York	Outside New York	Chicago	Boston	Phila-delphia	St. Louis	Pittsburgh	San Francisco	Baltimore
October 3	1724	1176	259	159	149	64.5	55.6	45.0	31.2
10	1580	1141	249	144	130	67.7	50.0	44.3	32.8
17	1778	1257	271	172	152	76.2	52.3	47.3	29.6
24	1948	1247	265	171	151	73.2	55.3	43.7	32.8
31	1846	1176	244	178	152	61.5	52.7	40.6	31.7
November 7	1357	1029	208	138	122	55.9	46.9	....	26.4
14	1373	994	200	138	125	55.5	51.9	30.9	29.0
21	1316	970	198	137	118	57.8	49.6	28.0	28.0
28	981	749	153	94	95	45.1	44.8	20.6	20.5
December 5	1455	1017	205	131	139	60.5	55.2	30.3	27.3
12	1320	952	191	125	110	58.8	47.6	29.2	26.3
19	1243	951	191	124	117	58.0	45.3	31.2	26.0
26	1031	792	166	100	95	50.2	42.0	24.5	20.0
January 2	1062	844	168	131	103	53.1	43.5	26.0	19.7
9	1545	1071	213	152	131	65.5	48.4	32.6	28.3
16	1674	1055	216	168	122	61.7	42.8	34.4	26.2
23	1664	1054	229	161	123	62.8	44.9	35.1	25.5
30	1345	942	214	132	104	57.1	44.8	33.3	24.3

TABLE 14—(Continued)

Week ending	Kansas City	Cincinnati	New Orleans	Minneapolis	Cleveland	Detroit	Louisville	Los Angeles	Omaha
October 3	37.7	26.4	17.7	29.9	19.8	14.5	14.1	10.4	11.6
10	39.9	25.8	17.7	32.4	17.2	13.0	13.1	11.2	12.9
17	39.6	27.5	19.0	36.9	20.3	14.9	13.9	12.9	13.5
24	40.9	27.5	20.4	36.0	17.7	14.8	13.4	11.2	12.7
31	39.5	24.6	19.6	29.2	17.4	14.3	14.4	9.0	13.7
November 7	34.5	23.5	18.4	24.8	15.9	14.0	11.5	9.7	10.2
14	31.1	21.3	18.7	22.5	16.7	13.2	10.2	9.2	10.4
21	29.2	21.7	19.5	23.2	15.9	14.2	9.1	8.7	10.5
28	23.6	16.8	15.5	19.4	12.2	10.7	7.1	6.1	8.3
December 5	26.7	22.6	22.9	26.5	15.4	12.7	10.7	7.3	10.3
12	29.2	20.7	21.6	25.3	15.0	13.9	8.9	9.9	10.7
19	31.1	21.9	23.2	24.2	15.3	13.6	9.0	7.2	10.5
26	25.7	17.9	19.8	19.6	13.0	10.7	7.6	5.8	9.4
January 2	25.5	19.9	20.7	19.5	12.7	11.1	8.1	6.4	8.5
9	33.1	29.8	20.9	23.4	18.6	14.1	11.6	8.9	11.3
16	34.9	27.0	22.2	22.9	16.1	13.2	11.8	9.6	12.9
23	34.9	25.2	22.7	20.9	17.4	13.9	11.7	9.4	11.7
30	32.7	24.1	18.1	18.6	14.7	11.3	11.0	7.6	11.0

Compiled from *Bradstreet's*.

TABLE 15

BANK CLEARINGS IN AND OUTSIDE NEW YORK CITY AND IN SIXTEEN OTHER CITIES, PERCENTAGE OF INCREASE OR DECREASE DURING THE 1907 PANIC FROM CORRESPONDING WEEKS OF PRECEDING YEAR

Week ending	New York	Outside New York	Chicago	Boston	Philadelphia	St. Louis	Pittsburgh	San Francisco	Baltimore
October 3	-24.8	+ 4.2	+16.2	- 6.5	-12.2	+14.3	+ 1.3	- 8.4	+ 8.2
10	-21.3	+ 3.6	+14.7	-17.4	- 4.5	+14.2	+ 6.6	+ 1.4	+13.5
17	-17.8	+ 5.6	+20.2	-11.0	- 8.6	+21.9	+ 8.8	+ 3.3	- 2.5
24	- 7.7	+12.6	+20.1	- 3.0	+ 1.9	+22.3	+ 7.9	+ 2.2	+21.2
31	+ .7	+ 8.5	+13.8	+ 9.7	+ 1.0	+ 6.0	+ 2.2	-14.8	+ 8.2
November 7	-24.9	- 6.1	- 3.0	-13.3	-14.7	+ .1	+ 1.7	....	....
14	-35.1	-19.0	-15.3	-21.2	-22.0	-18.0	- 1.8	-82.4	- 8.3
21	-42.3	-19.9	-18.6	-26.9	-25.8	-13.4	- 5.8	-48.1	-10.2
28	-39.7	-20.6	-18.9	-30.6	-27.7	-16.6	- .8	-48.7	-15.7
December 5	-37.5	-21.3	-22.7	-29.5	-23.2	-10.6	- 4.6	-46.6	-19.0
12	-38.9	-18.1	-14.4	-26.0	-27.7	-11.3	-12.0	-36.6	-14.7
19	-48.2	-20.0	-20.3	-30.9	-26.0	- 9.6	-11.2	-30.8	-19.8
26	-43.5	-20.2	-17.9	-28.3	-29.1	- 8.5	-14.7	-35.4	-24.8
January 2	-48.1	-25.0	-25.8	....	-33.2	-13.2	-16.9	-41.7	-34.6
9	-31.1	-13.4	-10.7	-23.7	-17.0	- 3.9	-12.7	-28.0	-10.6
16	-23.7	-15.6	- 9.2	-29.7	-17.7	-10.9	-19.0	-26.4	-15.8
23	-25.2	- 8.3	+ .7	-17.7	-14.4	- 3.1	-18.1	-25.3	-11.4
30	-28.0	-13.1	- 6.2	-18.6	-28.5	- 1.3	-18.8	-26.4	-17.1

TABLE 15—(Continued)

Week ending	Kansas City	Cincinnati	New Orleans	Minneapolis	Cleveland	Detroit	Louisville	Los Angeles	Omaha
October 3	+36.8	+ 1.7	−13.7	+12.4	+ 9.6	+10.1	+ 9.2	−12.0	+10.9
10	+37.9	+ 5.7	−28.5	+19.5	+ 1.1	+ 5.6	+ 7.3	− 2.1	+13.0
17	+26.4	− 4.5	−17.6	+24.4	+ 2.9	+ 6.6	+ 7.1	+10.1	+18.3
24	+36.7	+10.8	−16.6	+45.1	+14.6	+26.4	+ 8.6	+ 1.0	+25.9
31	+36.8	− 2.1	− 6.0	+29.9	− 7.2	+20.9	+11.2	− 9.6	+39.5
November 7	+20.7	−15.9	−32.1	− 8.0	− 4.6	+15.6	− 9.7	−17.1	+ 3.2
14	− 1.0	−16.7	−30.9	−19.9	−13.9	−34.1	−23.8	−35.6	+ 3.8
21	+ .6	−22.1	−29.8	+ .6	− 9.2	−40.5	−25.3	−30.9	+ .1
28	+ 2.0	−18.8	−31.4	− 2.0	− 7.5	−10.5	−25.0	−44.9	+ 1.5
December 5	−14.8	−19.8	−24.0	− 4.8	−14.3	−14.9	−22.2	−45.8	− 6.0
12	− 5.7	−19.5	−22.1	+ 2.9	−11.5	− 5.8	−33.9	−22.2	− 2.9
19	+ .4	−17.7	−16.8	+ 7.5	−20.5	− 9.2	−34.0	−47.9	−12.0
26	− 5.1	−19.3	−10.7	− 4.6	−15.2	−11.5	−31.3	−40.0	+ .8
January 2	− 5.4	−20.2	−11.9	+ 1.4	−32.9	−15.9	−36.5	−42.2	−10.0
9	− 1.1	− 6.9	−20.4	+11.9	− 7.2	− 4.9	−25.9	−32.9	+ 6.1
16	+ 4.4	−21.0	−16.6	+27.4	−14.2	−10.2	−22.3	−35.1	+18.4
23	+10.8	− 7.8	− 4.0	+24.4	+10.4	+ 2.6	− 8.5	−25.1	+17.1
30	+15.0	−10.5	−20.6	+21.5	−10.7	− 5.3	− 7.2	−36.7	+10.9

Compiled from *Bradstreet's*.

would have turned presently into moderate losses, even had the crisis not become a panic.

From the detailed figures by weeks (table 15) it is evident that, just before the panic, Boston, Philadelphia, and New Orleans were running steadily behind their records of the preceding year, and that San Francisco and Los Angeles were barely keeping even. But the middle-western towns were still gaining sufficiently to keep the totals for the country outside New York above the totals of 1906.

The first effect of the panic in the great business centers of the East was to increase financial transactions, such as the sale of securities by embarrassed banks and individuals, and the shifting of loans. These transactions availed to put the clearings even of New York, Boston, and Philadelphia temporarily above the records of 1906. But business of more ordinary kinds was restricted so promptly that the special panic operations cut little figure in the totals after the end of October. The eastern cities, which had been running behind before the panic, now showed losses of a quarter, a third, or even a half in comparison with the corresponding weeks of the preceding year. Still more notable is the speed with which the trouble spread from New York to the Gulf and to the Pacific. During the very first week of the panic a majority of the towns had smaller gains over 1906 or actual losses. From the third week of the panic to the end of the year the restriction of business, measured from the level of 1906, averaged about 20 per cent outside New York and about 40 per cent in New York. Among the leading towns, Kansas City, Minneapolis, and Omaha fared least badly—perhaps because their industries are so largely concerned with footstuffs. In general, the industrial sections of the East lost more heavily than the agricultural sections of the Middle West; for the harvests were on the whole profitable to American farmers.

From notes in the business periodicals we can gather how this contraction of business came about. At the first hint of trouble from the banks, merchants began to limit their purchases. 'Hand-to-mouth' buying became the order of the day. Wholesale dealers and manufacturers received telegrams canceling orders already placed or requesting deferred deliveries. Other concerns found they could not obtain the specifications necessary for making up goods ordered on contracts. On the other hand, sellers often hesitated to ship goods, fearing that the consignees would be unable to pay. Not a few houses withdrew commercial travelers already in the field, and stopped soliciting orders for a time. Here and there inability to get money for pay rolls caused a temporary stoppage of work.

Such interruptions to the usual course of wholesale trade and manufacturing, with their reactions upon transportation, mining, and the like, became epidemic in the first fortnight of the panic. But retail trade continued to be reported 'fair' for several weeks, especially in the Middle West. No doubt the approach of the Christmas shopping season and of cold weather was largely responsible for sustaining the business of shopkeepers in 1907. But the same phenomenon was remarked upon in 1893, when the panic occurred in summer. Retail trade, in fact, seems not to be curtailed seriously outside the largest cities until a panic has closed many industrial enterprises, put others on short time, and led to the widespread discharge of wage earners. Then, of course, the shopkeeper's sales fall off, as had those of the wholesale merchant and manufacturer several weeks earlier.

III. A Typical Crisis—Great Britain, 1907

Since our example of a panic is taken from American experience in 1907, our example of a crisis had best be taken from the simultaneous experience of Great Britain.

1. BEGINNINGS OF REACTION

Definite signs that the business 'boom' had passed its zenith appeared in Great Britain as early as midsummer 1907, that is, several months before the American panic.

Among the symptoms of reaction that called forth contemporary comment were the following. British railway stocks fell in the first half of 1907 without any apparent reason save that investors were holding aloof.[28] A series of high-grade loans failed to find subscribers. The Bristol Corporation, the Middlesex County Council, the East Indian Railway, and finally the Manchurian Railways, supported by an unconditional guarantee from the Japanese government, tried one after another to raise money and were "more or less cold-shouldered by the public."[29] While the shipbuilding yards were kept busy most of the year executing orders received in 1906 or even in 1905, their outlook for the future was dismal, since few new contracts were in sight.[30] The iron and steel trades were in a similar position. Though the mills were working at high pitch for the moment, and though stocks of pig iron were very low, the price of 'Cleveland warrants' began falling in July, since both domestic and foreign demand for future delivery was declining.[31] Indeed, manufacturers were not eager to take new business at the ruling quotations, because of high production costs. The *Economist* explained that the price of coal was "a crushing tax on present and prospective industry,"[32] and that producers of iron were trading practically at a loss in executing orders booked at a time when materials and fuel were much cheaper.[33] The building trades also were dull in almost all sections of the country.[34] Among the railways, gross receipts grew steadily, but operating expenses grew faster, so that the ratio of net to gross receipts declined.[35] Sauerbeck's index number of prices at wholesale reached its summit in May, and fell in every subsequent month. After July town clearings in London ran in most weeks below the records of 1906. Imports began to gain less after April. Perhaps most significant of all signs of reaction was the rise in the percentage of unemployment, which since March 1906 had been less than in the corresponding month of the preceding year. In July 1907 it began to run steadily higher than in 1906 (tables 16–22).

By midsummer 1907, then, the tide of British business began to recede, because of the cumulation of stresses described in Chapter 2. But only in the markets and industries most sensitive to coming events was the change noticed. Current business outside the financial markets did not slacken: railway receipts continued to rise, country clearings in London and clearings in most of the provincial towns continued to exceed the high records of 1906, and the rate of gain in exports was not retarded.[36] Nevertheless, the difficulties already present on the stock exchange and in the bond market, and definitely foreshadowed in shipbuilding, the iron trade, and the labor market were certain to extend in a short time over the whole field of business. The more acute difficulties experienced in foreign countries, then, did not cause the British crisis of 1907—they did no more than hasten its development and make it more severe.

2. EFFECT OF FOREIGN CRISES

London's position as the world's free market for gold exposes British business in an exceptional degree to disturbance from financial troubles in other countries; and the exceptionally high ratio of foreign commerce to domestic trade in Britain makes her business exceptionally sensitive to depression among her customers. The year 1907 brought severe stresses from the first source, the year 1908 from the second.

Egypt had a serious crisis in spring 1907, South Africa in late summer and early autumn, Holland in the first half of October, the United States and Hamburg in the second half, Portugal in November, and Chile in December.[37] Each disaster affected in some way the delicate mechanism of the London money market and later the demand for British products. Incomparably greatest, however, was the effect of the panic in New York.

The first consequence of the crash in America was the fall of 'Yankee rails' on the London stock market. No large failures followed; indeed, dealers were said to be pleased by what they described as the emancipation of the home and foreign markets from 'American bondage.'[38] The second consequence, withdrawals of gold from the Bank of England for export to New York, had more serious results.

On October 16 the Bank of England had a reserve of $116,000,000, equal to 49 per cent of its deposit liabilities to the banks and the public. Meanwhile its loans made 63.6 per cent of deposits (table 16). In both respects the Bank was stronger than usual; for the averages of these ratios in 1900–09 were 46.8 and 70.0 per cent respectively.[39] Since the middle of August the Bank rate had stood at the moderately high level of 4½ per cent, and the market rate for 60-day bills was 4.13 per cent (table 17). In all respects the Bank had the situation well in hand.

The first heavy withdrawals of gold were made in the week ending November 2—$13,436,000.[40] During the next two months $97,700,000 in gold was exported (table 18). Meanwhile, since the holiday shopping season was approaching, the domestic withdrawals of currency from the Bank exceeded the deposits in most weeks.[41] To meet this enormous drain, the Bank of England advanced its discount rate from 4½ to 5½ per cent on October 31, to 6 per cent on November 4, and to 7 per cent on the 7th. It also received some $15,000,000 in American eagles from the Bank of France early in November,[42] and induced the India Council to release into its general fund about $7,500,000 of gold that had been 'earmarked.'[43] These measures proved amply sufficient. Between October 23 and November 6 the reserve fell $31,000,000; the next week the gold from France was largely instrumental in raising it $17,000,000; another decline of $6,000,000 followed; but thereafter gold

TABLE 16

BANK OF ENGLAND, BANKING DEPARTMENT, WEEKLY RETURNS,
AUGUST 7 1907 TO JANUARY 29 1908

Week ending	Capital and rest (1)	Public deposits (2)	Other deposits and seven-day bills (3)	Government securities (4)	Other securities in banking department (5)	Reserve notes and specie (6)	Ratio of	
							Reserve to deposits (7)	Loans to "other deposits" (8)
	Millions of dollars						Percentage	
1907								
August 7	88	31	214	78	140	115	47	65.4
14	88	32	208	71	136	121	50	65.4
21	88	37	226	71	153	127	48	67.7
28	88	37	228	71	151	131	49	66.2
September 4	89	31	233	70	151	132	50	64.8
11	89	37	229	70	148	136	51	64.6
18	89	42	229	70	150	140	52	65.5
25	89	45	221	70	149	136	51	67.4
October 2	89	42	213	70	150	125	49	70.4
9	86	32	220	77	144	117	47	65.5
16	86	26	209	72	133	116	49	63.6
23	86	34	213	72	145	117	47	68.1
30	87	35	219	70	170	101	40	77.6
November 6	87	33	212	70	176	86	35	83.0
13	87	34	220	70	168	103	40	76.4
20	87	38	212	70	170	97	39	80.2
27	87	38	210	70	159	106	43	75.7
December 4	87	27	216	70	153	107	44	70.8
11	87	26	219	70	147	115	47	67.1
18	87	25	212	70	145	109	46	68.4
25	87	27	212	70	161	96	40	75.9
1908								
January 1	87	37	256	77	199	104	36	77.7
8	87	26	220	79	135	118	48	61.4
15	88	22	217	70	131	126	53	60.4
22	88	33	211	70	128	134	55	60.7
29	88	43	205	70	126	141	57	61.5

Compiled from *Statistics for Great Britain, Germany, and France, 1867–1909* (Publications of the National Monetary Commission), pp. 120, 121.

TABLE 17

London Discount Rates, by Weeks, August 1907 to January 1908

Week ending	Discount rates				Deposit allowances	
	Bank rate	Sixty-day bills	Six-month bills	Call money	Banks	Discount houses
1907						
August 2........	4.00	3.56	4.19	2.75	2.50	2.75
9........	4.00	3.94	4.44	2.00	2.50	2.75
16........	4.50	4.50	5.00	3.00	3.00	3.25
23........	4.50	4.63	5.19	2.50	3.00	3.25
30........	4.50	4.19	4.88	2.50	3.00	3.25
September 6........	4.50	3.94	4.69	2.13	3.00	3.25
13........	4.50	3.81	4.38	2.25	3.00	3.25
20........	4.50	3.69	4.13	1.75	3.00	3.25
27........	4.50	3.69	4.25	3.63	3.00	3.25
October 4........	4.50	3.88	4.25	3.63	3.00	3.25
11........	4.50	3.94	4.44	2.25	3.00	3.25
18........	4.50	4.13	4.44	2.88	3.00	3.25
25........	4.50	4.50	4.75	3.38	3.00	3.25
November 1........	5.50	5.69	5.56	4.50	4.00	4.25
8........	7.00	6.75	6.44	5.00	4.00	5.25
15........	7.00	7.00	6.13	5.00	4.00	5.25
22........	7.00	6.94	6.13	6.50	4.00	5.25
29........	7.00	6.38	5.13	5.25	4.00	5.25
December 6........	7.00	5.88	4.75	3.50	4.00	5.25
13........	7.00	6.06	5.13	4.00	4.00	4.75
20........	7.00	6.06	4.94	4.50	4.00	4.75
27........	7.00	6.38	5.13	6.50	4.00	4.75
1908						
January 3........	6.00	5.00	4.63	4.88	4.00	4.25
10........	6.00	4.63	4.31	4.13	4.00	4.25
17........	5.00	4.31	4.06	3.63	3.50	3.75
24........	4.00	3.75	3.50	3.25	2.50	3.00
31........	4.00	3.63	3.31	3.75	2.50	3.00

Compiled from *Statistics for Great Britain, Germany, and France, 1867–1909* (Publications of the National Monetary Commission), pp. 61, 62.

TABLE 18

Net Gold Imports and Exports, Great Britain, by Months, 1906-1908

(In millions of dollars)

Month	1906 Imports	1906 Exports	1907 Imports	1907 Exports	1908 Imports	1908 Exports	Net imports (+) or exports (−) 1906	Net imports (+) or exports (−) 1907	Net imports (+) or exports (−) 1908
January	11.6	16.1	22.3	18.2	15.7	14.3	− 4.5	+ 4.1	+ 1.4
February	27.2	7.7	18.1	14.5	20.2	17.7	+19.5	+ 3.6	+ 2.5
March	25.9	10.1	21.4	11.3	18.5	7.0	+15.8	+10.1	+11.5
April	13.6	28.1	17.8	8.7	27.5	16.7	−14.5	+ 9.1	+10.8
May	22.2	20.4	23.9	14.1	15.8	21.6	+ 1.8	+ 9.8	− 5.8
June	11.6	3.1	10.6	18.6	15.5	23.6	+ 8.5	− 8.0	− 8.1
July	13.4	7.5	18.1	10.7	22.1	24.7	+ 5.9	+ 7.4	− 2.6
August	21.4	4.4	19.4	8.5	14.0	18.9	+17.0	+10.9	− 4.9
September	14.3	40.6	12.7	17.0	24.1	24.7	−26.3	− 4.3	− 0.6
October	15.7	43.1	20.6	28.2	14.9	24.7	−27.4	− 7.6	− 9.8
November	26.7	10.8	55.1	74.0	13.8	25.9	+15.9	−18.9	−12.1
December	20.4	15.5	37.9	23.7	22.4	23.2	+ 4.9	+14.2	− 0.8
Year	224.0	207.4	277.8	247.5	224.5	243.1	+16.6	+30.3	−18.6

Compiled from *Statistics for Great Britain, Germany, and France, 1867-1909* (Publications of the National Monetary Commission), p. 65.

began to flow into England freely and by December 11 the reserve was again at $115,000,000, equal to 47 per cent of the deposits. The usual end-of-the-year settlements caused a new drop in the reserve after the middle of December, so that the ratio was 36 per cent on January 1; but the managers knew that the strain was over and reduced Bank rate to 6 per cent on the 2nd, and to 5 per cent on the 16th. Meanwhile the reserve had mounted to sums larger both absolutely and in proportion to deposits than before the American panic began.

This increase in the reserve after the first fortnight of the heavy withdrawals, while due partly to the $22,500,000 of gold obtained from the Bank of France and the India Council, and partly to the inflow of funds from the interior after the holidays, was also due in large measure to imports from other countries. In fact, imports of gold in November and December amounted to $93,000,000—only $4,700,000 less than exports." Never was the efficacy of an advance in Bank rate as a means of attracting gold more strikingly demonstrated.

3. THE CRISIS IN INDUSTRY AND COMMERCE

Though the Bank of England succeeded in meeting the double strain imposed by the approach of crisis at home and the call for help from New York, it was obliged to maintain the extraordinarily high discount rate of 7 per cent for nearly two months. During this time the market rate for 60-day bills averaged nearly 6½ per cent and for 6-months bills nearly 5½ per cent (table 17). While these rates were much lower than those reported in New York (table 8), they were much higher than English business was accustomed to paying. The tense condition of the money market, therefore, had a powerful effect in hastening and aggravating the crisis that had been developing slowly since midsummer.

This crisis, however, proved mild and tame in comparison with the American panic. There was no hint of suspension or even of limitation of payments by the banks, and therefore no scramble for money. There was no fear that solvent borrowers with acceptable security would be refused bank accommodation, and therefore no needless failures and no wholesale destruction of credit. In the very fortnight when the Bank of England lost $31,000,000 in cash it increased its loans by the same amount. If the loans declined after November 6, it was not because the Bank was refusing to lend, but because businessmen were refusing to borrow at 7 per cent.

On the Stock Exchange the crisis had less effect than might have been expected, largely because of a fortunate coincidence. In September the Executive Council of the Amalgamated Society of Railway Servants had decided to take a ballot upon the advisability of calling a general strike. But Mr. Lloyd George intervened, and news that the dispute would be adjusted without a conflict was published on the day the Bank of England raised its rate to 7 per cent.[45] While this good news did much to buoy up the market, stock prices sank to the year's lowest point in November. Recovery was prompt, however, and, if the 'index number of stock-exchange values' compiled by the *London Bankers' Magazine* may be trusted, the general level of prices was higher in January than it had been in September.[46]

Another fortunate circumstance helped to mitigate the effects of the crisis upon industry and commerce. The British farmers reaped exceptionally large harvests in 1907 and sold them for exceptionally high prices.[47] While agriculture employs a much smaller proportion of the population in the United Kingdom than in the United States, still the ability of the farming classes to buy freely was an important factor in counteracting the shrinkage in the demand for commodities from other sources. Nevertheless, the recession of activity, already started, became more marked in the last three months of the year.

In November, the *Economist* sought the opinions of representative firms in many branches of trade concerning the effect

TABLE 19

MERCHANDISE IMPORTS AND EXPORTS, GREAT BRITAIN, BY MONTHS, JANUARY 1907 TO MARCH 1908, AND PERCENTAGE OF GAIN (+) OR LOSS (−) FROM CORRESPONDING MONTHS OF PRECEDING YEAR

Month	Food, drink, and tobacco		Raw materials and articles mainly unmanufactured		Articles wholly or mainly manufactured		Miscellaneous and unclassified		Grand total	
	Amount in millions of dollars	Gain or loss (per cent)	Amount in millions of dollars	Gain or loss (per cent)	Amount in millions of dollars	Gain or loss (per cent)	Amount in millions of dollars	Gain or loss (per cent)	Amount in millions of dollars	Gain or loss (per cent)
Imports										
1907										
January...	96.1	+ 0.2	130.8	+31.6	66.4	+ 4.2	1.2	− 0.9	294.6	+13.2
February..	79.5	− 1.4	116.9	+32.1	60.1	− 1.7	1.1	+ 5.9	257.6	+11.3
March.....	95.7	+ 0.6	115.8	+ 2.9	68.6	− 0.3	.9	−19.4	281.0	+ 8.4
April......	95.5	+10.2	112.3	+39.8	67.5	+10.7	.9	− 2.3	276.3	+20.5
May.......	99.1	+ 0.1	91.6	+12.1	64.5	− 5.8	.9	−12.3	256.0	+ 2.1
June......	100.3	− 2.7	74.8	+ 9.7	56.6	− 7.1	1.0	+11.6	232.6	− 0.2
July.......	105.0	+ 3.4	82.2	+14.8	65.9	+ 5.5	1.0	− 2.3	254.1	+ 7.4
August....	106.0	+18.4	71.7	+ 3.5	61.3	− 4.8	.9	−18.5	239.9	+ 0.8
September..	98.6	+ 1.7	78.9	+ 0.5	56.8	− 1.3	1.0	+26.3	220.6	+ 0.6
October....	119.0	+12.4	95.8	+ 2.8	64.9	− 1.3	.9	−18.4	280.6	+ 5.5
November..	108.9	+11.1	106.7	− 1.6	61.5	− 3.4	.9	− 4.9	278.1	+ 2.5
December..	101.0	+ 7.9	112.8	+ 1.1	57.9	− 3.6	.9	+ 0.6	272.5	+ 2.4
1908										
January...	97.1	+ 1.0	121.5	− 7.0	54.9	−17.5	.8	−32.0	274.3	− 6.8
February...	91.1	+14.5	102.2	−12.4	60.7	+ 0.7	1.2	+ 9.5	255.1	− 0.9
March......	107.3	+12.0	81.4	−29.5	64.0	− 6.8	.9	− 1.5	253.6	− 9.7

TABLE 19—(Continued)

				Exports					
1907									
January....	7.3	− 1.0	18.9	+18.9	141.8	+13.9	2.7	+35.5	170.6	+13.9
February...	6.8	+ 5.8	19.0	+26.2	128.3	+ 9.7	2.0	+19.2	156.1	+11.5
March......	6.9	− 3.9	20.1	+13.7	139.7	+10.1	2.2	+ 1.6	169.0	+ 9.7
April.......	7.2	+12.1	21.1	+29.8	136.7	+28.2	2.4	+ 9.1	167.5	+27.3
May........	7.8	+ 2.4	22.6	+25.0	146.8	+17.7	2.4	+ 2.1	179.7	+16.4
June.......	8.4	+12.7	21.9	+38.6	128.5	+ 3.7	2.3	+18.6	161.1	+ 8.1
July........	11.2	+22.1	24.8	+30.6	158.3	+19.9	2.6	− 3.7	196.8	+20.9
August.....	11.4	+19.3	23.7	+28.9	143.5	+ 8.9	3.2	+40.9	181.8	+11.5
September..	11.3	+ 8.7	23.6	+33.3	133.9	+13.2	2.3	+ 0.4	171.1	+15.1
October....	11.6	+ 0.3	25.7	+28.8	146.3	+14.3	2.9	+27.5	186.5	+15.3
November..	11.8	+ 4.1	24.4	+35.2	135.3	+ 5.5	3.0	+ 2.6	174.5	+ 8.7
December..	9.1	+ 7.8	21.9	+27.1	125.8	+ 1.0	2.6	− 7.5	159.3	+ 4.2
1908									
January....	7.4	+ 1.1	20.6	+ 9.1	137.0	− 3.4	2.5	− 6.8	167.4	− 1.8
February...	7.1	+ 4.2	20.3	+ 6.8	125.9	− 1.8	2.2	+ 9.2	155.5	− 0.3
March......	7.2	+ 4.4	20.5	+ 1.8	130.4	− 6.6	1.9	−13.5	160.1	− 5.2

Compiled from the monthly trade supplements of the *Economist* (London).

TABLE 20

CLEARINGS IN LONDON, BY WEEKS, 1906–1908, AND PERCENTAGE OF GAIN OR
LOSS FROM CORRESPONDING WEEKS OF PRECEDING YEAR

Week ending		Town clearings			Country clearings		
		Millions of dollars		Gain or loss (per cent)	Millions of dollars		Gain or loss (per cent)
1907	1906	1907	1906		1907	1906	
July 3	July 4	1,460	1,483	− 1.6	105	98	+ 7.1
10	11	1,134	995	+14.0	123	113	+ 8.8
17	18	1,198	1,146	+ 4.5	112	104	+ 7.7
24	25	913	908	+ .6	95	88	+ 8.0
31	Aug. 1	1,151	1,237	− 7.0	95	88	+ 8.0
Aug. 7	8	1,042	864	+20.6	96	86	+11.6
14	15	899	1,126	−20.2	101	98	+ 3.1
21	22	1,111	931	+19.3	102	87	+17.2
28	29	880	907	− 3.0	84	75	+12.0
Sept. 4	Sept. 5	1,102	1,321	−16.6	93	91	+ 2.2
11	12	878	836	+ 5.0	102	86	+18.6
18	19	1,007	1,244	−19.1	96	90	+ 6.7
25	26	905	864	+ 4.7	89	82	+ 8.5
Oct. 2	Oct. 3	1,268	1,340	− 5.4	94	94	0.0
9	10	1,053	916	+15.0	124	112	+10.7
16	17	1,154	1,197	− 3.6	114	106	+ 7.5
23	24	935	965	− 3.1	102	93	+ 9.7
30	31	1,245	1,301	− 4.3	98	92	+ 6.5
Nov. 6	Nov. 7	1,069	1,016	+ 5.2	120	105	+14.3
13	14	975	1,128	−13.6	104	93	+11.8
20	21	1,138	997	+14.1	112	99	+13.1
27	28	940	924	+ 1.7	94	83	+13.2
Dec. 4	Dec. 5	1,151	1,362	−15.5	99	100	− 1.0
11	12	872	956	− 8.8	108	92	+17.4
18	19	1,151	1,252	− 8.1	106	99	+ 7.1
24	26	834	717	+16.3	79	57	+38.6
1908	1907	1908	1907		1908	1907	
Jan. 1	Jan. 2	1,096	1,518	−27.8	79	94	−16.0
8	9	1,114	1,128	− 1.2	123	113	+ 8.8
15	16	1,025	1,347	−23.9	108	102	+ 5.9
22	23	1,105	1,070	+ 3.3	107	97	+10.3
29	30	976	967	+ .9	95	86	+10.5
Feb. 5	Feb. 6	1,287	1,430	−10.0	112	109	+ 2.8
12	13	949	1,002	− 5.3	103	91	+13.2
19	20	1,127	1,265	− 6.4	90	90	0.0
26	27	915	978	−10.9	104	96	+ 8.3

TABLE 21

PROVINCIAL CLEARINGS IN ENGLAND, BY WEEKS, 1907–1908, AND PERCENTAGE OF GAIN OR LOSS FROM CORRESPONDING WEEKS OF PRECEDING YEAR

Week ending	Manchester Amount in millions of dollars	Manchester Gain or loss in comparison with 1906 (per cent)	Liverpool Amount in millions of dollars	Liverpool Gain or loss in comparison with 1906 (per cent)	Birmingham Amount in millions of dollars	Birmingham Gain or loss in comparison with 1906 (per cent)	Newcastle-on-Tyne Amount in millions of dollars	Newcastle-on-Tyne Gain or loss in comparison with 1906 (per cent)	Bristol Amount in millions of dollars	Bristol Gain or loss in comparison with 1906 (per cent)
1907										
July 6	37.1	+ 6.5	24.3	+26.6	9.3	+10.5	6.2	− 3.1	3.9	+ 5.2
13	30.4	+ 5.4	20.7	+19.4	5.5	+ 0.8	5.3	+22.3	2.9	+ 0.4
20	30.9	+17.5	18.7	+41.1	5.1	+11.0	4.6	− 1.7	2.7	+ 6.5
27	27.7	+ 8.0	13.8	+ .2	4.8	− 2.4	5.2	− 6.4	2.8	− 3.7
Aug. 3	34.7	+14.1	19.8	+17.4	8.4	+ 8.0	5.8	−11.6	3.5	+ 3.6
10	28.2	+12.6	13.8	+15.1	3.6	+19.8	4.6	− 2.4	2.1	+ 2.5
17	29.5	+10.8	16.6	+ 2.0	5.0	+ 8.4	6.5	+ 6.7	2.7	− 7.1
24	24.1	+13.8	14.5	+ 3.7	3.8	− 5.0	6.0	+13.8	2.5	0.0
31	28.6	+12.9	16.3	+13.3	4.7	−11.1	5.1	+ 5.2	2.5	− 4.4
Sept. 7	31.4	+12.1	16.9	+ 8.8	7.7	+27.2	5.6	+ 2.6	2.9	+12.0
14	26.6	+ 5.9	16.4	− 0.01	4.4	+ 5.1	5.1	− 4.7	2.6	+ 5.8
21	26.8	+12.1	20.2	+56.6	4.1	− 4.3	5.4	+ 2.9	2.4	− 0.1
28	27.4	− 0.5	17.2	− 5.7	4.2	−10.7	5.2	+ 8.8	2.4	− 8.3
Oct. 5	38.3	+13.1	20.4	− 3.3	8.2	+12.2	6.5	− 3.8	3.6	− 6.2
12	30.4	+ 1.9	17.3	−15.2	4.8	− 1.7	4.8	− 3.6	2.8	+ 0.3
19	30.2	+10.4	17.4	−17.3	5.2	− 6.5	4.5	−12.0	3.1	+ 8.7
26	27.2	+ 1.8	17.4	+ 2.4	4.3	− 8.7	4.7	− 9.8	3.2	+11.6

TABLE 21—(*Continued*)

Week ending	Manchester		Liverpool		Birmingham		Newcastle-on-Tyne		Bristol	
	Amount in millions of dollars	Gain or loss in comparison with 1906 (per cent)	Amount in millions of dollars	Gain or loss in comparison with 1906 (per cent)	Amount in millions of dollars	Gain or loss in comparison with 1906 (per cent)	Amount in millions of dollars	Gain or loss in comparison with 1906 (per cent)	Amount in millions of dollars	Gain or loss in comparison with 1906 (per cent)
1907										
Nov. 2	35.5	+12.1	22.4	+ 8.7	7.7	− 2.8	6.1	+18.9	3.3	+ 6.6
9	32.1	+19.7	16.5	+10.5	6.1	+29.2	4.9	+24.4	2.9	+ 7.9
16	31.6	+ 6.0	19.9	+ 1.8	5.4	− 0.3	6.0	+ 5.5	3.1	− 4.9
23	27.8	+ 8.8	16.8	− 1.5	4.5	− 9.7	6.1	+11.7	2.8	+ 2.7
30	29.9	+ 2.6	20.3	+ 7.1	4.7	−18.6	5.2	+ 2.3	2.7	+ 2.8
Dec. 7	35.8	+34.1	19.3	+13.1	7.9	+ 1.9	5.9	− 6.8	3.2	− 7.6
14	30.1	+ 0.7	19.9	+ 2.0	4.9	+ 7.9	5.7	+ 3.9	2.6	− 0.9
21	29.2	+ 6.7	18.8	+ 5.5	5.3	−18.1	5.8	− 4.0	4.0	+18.5
28	36.6	−14.3	16.2	− 0.6	5.3	− 1.8	6.7	+86.1	2.9	−20.8
1908										
Jan. 4ª	23.0	− 3.6	14.2	−11.0	6.8	− 9.0	3.7	−43.0	2.8	−13.0
11	30.9	+ 2.9	17.8	− 5.1	4.8	− 6.2	5.2	+12.8	3.0	0.0
18	31.9	+ 2.0	21.1	− 4.7	5.1	−10.9	5.1	− 3.6	2.9	− 9.2
25	27.2	+ 1.9	19.2	+12.2	4.4	−13.5	4.8	−15.3	2.8	− 3.8
Feb. 1	31.0	− 5.7	18.8	−14.1	5.8	−26.1	4.4	−14.0	3.0	−13.9
8	35.7	+17.1	19.2	+ 8.2	7.1	+ 9.2	4.5	−21.1	3.5	+ 4.5
15	31.8	+ 6.5	18.5	−11.1	5.3	− 9.6	4.2	−26.7	3.3	+ 7.7
22	26.5	− 3.1	17.8	− 2.5	4.9	−12.2	4.2	−24.8	2.9	− 4.0

ª Entries for January 4 cover only the first four days of 1908.

of 'dear money' upon their business. The replies indicated that there had not as yet been any serious interruption of manufacturing; but the passing of the 'boom' was generally admitted. Not a few manufacturers who had been troubled by the heavy cost of production seemed to welcome the change. In particular, the high prices of raw materials had become a

TABLE 22

TRADE-UNION MEMBERS, PERCENTAGE UNEMPLOYED, UNITED KINGDOM, AT END OF EACH MONTH, 1904–1908

Month	1904	1905	1906	1907	1908
January	6.1	6.3	4.3	9.9	5.8
February	5.6	5.7	4.1	3.5	6.0
March	5.5	5.2	3.4	3.2	6.4
April	5.5	5.2	3.2	2.8	7.1
May	5.8	4.7	3.1	3.0	7.4
June	5.5	4.8	3.2	3.1	7.9
July	5.6	4.7	3.1	3.2	7.9
August	5.9	4.9	3.3	3.6	8.5
September	6.3	4.8	3.3	4.1	9.3
October	6.3	4.6	3.9	4.2	9.5
November	6.5	4.3	4.0	4.5	8.7
December	7.1	4.5	4.4	5.6	9.1
Average	6.0	5.0	3.6	3.7	7.8

From the *Fourteenth Abstract of Labour Statistics of the United Kingdom*, 1908–09, p. 7.

serious burden, and many firms had been "unable to recompense themselves by charging more to their customers." The most pessimistic opinions came from trades like jute and linen that depended largely upon the American market. But no serious disasters were expected, for manufacturers had received such a long warning of the crisis that speculation had been kept within narrow limits.[48]

These views are amply confirmed by the statistical record. The dwindling gains of imports and exports over twelve months before turned after the first of the year into positive losses (table 19). Country clearings in London held out longer, but town clearings and clearings in the provincial centers of trade showed losses or diminished gains (tables 20 and 21). Finally, unemployment, instead of declining after the end of the year as usual, continued to rise until the percentage was more than twice that of the preceding year (table 22).

Thus British business, like American business, passed from a state of high prosperity in the summer of 1907 into a state of marked depression in the summer of 1908; but the transition was accomplished without a serious epidemic of bankruptcies and without violent interruption of the usual processes of producing and distributing goods.

IV. The Close of Crises

No certain dates can be assigned for the beginning or end of crises. For the strains that force liquidation of credits accumulate slowly and the demand for settlement of outstanding credits may become widespread before the public is aware of what is going on and before the pace of activity has sensibly abated. Further, in a large country this process of liquidation may begin at some business center, while the tide of prosperity is still rising elsewhere, and spread rather gradually. On the other hand, the strains relax as gradually as they gather and the crisis merges into depression in the same unobtrusive fashion that it emerges from prosperity.

For example, it is impossible to say precisely when the crisis of 1907 began in the United States. Stringency in the money and investment markets became severe in 1906; the stock market was in difficulties at least as early as January 1907, and a crash occurred in March; the prices of raw mineral products began to decline after February; complaints of the encroachment of operating expenses on profits became common in the spring; bond issues began to find few takers about the same time; several large industrial plants went into the hands of receivers in the summer because they could not obtain loans, and a crisis was brewing toward the end of 1906 and in the early part of 1907. Nonetheless, general business continued to rise month after month. To say precisely when the crisis began is therefore to select some arbitrary criterion and apply it irrespective of other conditions.

Panics, on the other hand, may be dated with more assurance. The suspension of the Knickerbocker Trust Company on October 22 marks the beginning of the panic of 1907, and with less definiteness the crash of industrial stocks and the bank failures of May mark the beginning of the panic of 1893.

The ending of a crisis, whether accompanied by panic or not, is the cessation of intense demand for prompt liquidation. When the banks have been able to satisfy the needs for both currency and deposit credits, solvent debtors gradually meet their obligations as they mature, and insolvent debtors fail and pass from the management of business enterprises. There are losses to be written off, but confidence in the safety of the remaining credits is restored. Meanwhile little is borrowed to finance new business ventures, and that little upon a broad margin of security to the lender and on exceedingly conservative estimates of profit to the borrower. Interest rates relax, and money accumulates in the banks. In short, the crisis ends because the members of the business community have withstood, on the whole successfully, the test of ability to meet their financial obligations.

When a panic has occurred, with a restriction of payments, a scramble for money, contraction of loans, heavy failures, and so forth, the process of recuperation is slower but possesses the same general character. Despite the intense stress of the demand for money, the percentage of firms that fail is very small. According to *Bradstreet's* it was 1.46 in 1893, .70 in 1907, and .94 in 1908. *Dun's Review* gives 1.28 per cent in 1893, .82 per cent in 1907, and 1.08 per cent in 1908. The great majority of enterprises reassure their skeptical creditors by actually paying, or proving their ability presently to pay, what they owe.

Meanwhile the importation of gold, the increase in bank notes, and the issue of substitutes for money gradually relieve the worst of the monetary stringency. Just as soon as banks become able and willing to pay in cash, hoarding ceases, and money locked up in deposit boxes comes back into circulation. Presently the banks find themselves with a superfluity of cash and reduce interest rates. The contraction of business brings with it a meager demand for credit, while borrowing to meet maturing debts declines. Anxiety concerning the collection of old accounts may still be great, failures may remain numerous or even increase, but the inability to borrow on good security is a thing of the past. The acute stage of the liquidation—the crisis—is over, and depression—the dragging stage of the liquidation—begins.

V. Prevention of Panics

Experience supports the current belief that occasional crises are inevitable in a full-blown money economy, the workings of which are still imperfectly understood. Just as definitely, experience supports the belief that panics can be avoided. The difference between crisis and panic is a matter of degree, but in this case matters of degree have grave importance. To save solvent firms from failing for lack of loans they can repay, to save capable managers from being forced to part with the control of properties they are developing effectively, to save employers from having to discharge men because banks will not furnish money for pay rolls—in short, to prevent the more violent manifestations of business confusion from occurring—is a service of great value to a country.

The American panics of 1893 and 1907 were ushered in by a series of heavy failures. But the downfall of the Comptoir d'Escompte in 1889 in France, of Barings in 1890 in England, and of the Bank of Leipzig in 1901 in Germany were no less alarming than the failure of the Knickerbocker Trust Company in 1907 in America. Had the former failures occurred in the United States, panics would have followed; had the latter failure occurred in England, France, or Germany, there would have been no panic. For in any of these European countries the shock to confidence would have been allayed by the prompt intervention of the other banks. A syndicate of the strongest financial institutions in the country would have taken charge of the embarrassed concern and guaranteed payment to its depositors. More important still, the central bank would have taken the lead in a policy of lending freely to all necessitous businessmen who could provide adequate security for repayment. Most important of all, a restriction of payments on the part of the leading banks would not have been made—it would not even have been feared. Failures would not have been avoided, for enterprises that had become insolvent through mismanagement or misfortune would have gone into the hands of receivers; but the bankruptcies would not have been swelled by the inability of solvent concerns to get bank accommodation. Interest rates would have risen, but not to 10 and 12 per cent, and commercial paper would not have become unsalable. The process of liquidation would have proceeded with its concomitant decline in prices and trade; but the transition from prosperity to depression would have been far less violent.

The difference in efficiency for purposes of withstanding strain between the American and the English banking organization and banking practice stands out with startling clearness from the accompanying figures concerning bank reserves.

	Bank of England reserve			Banks of New York reserves		
	Date	Millions of dollars	Per cent	Date	Millions of dollars	Per cent
Before the panic	Oct. 9	117	100	Oct. 12	261	100
Lowest point	Nov. 6	86	74	Nov. 23	216	83
After the panic	Jan. 8	118	101	Jan. 11	269	103

American importations of gold from London actually caused a greater relative fall in the Bank of England reserve than occurred in the combined reserves of the New York clearing-house banks. Yet no one feared for a moment that the great British bank would hesitate to honor in full all legitimate demands made upon it from home or abroad, while the New York banks advertised their weakness by restricting payments almost at the outset of the strain.

The crucial importance of the policy followed by the leading banks in determining whether a crisis shall become a panic arises because the banks are the chief source of short-time loans and the chief organs for increasing the currency on short notice. Since a crisis occasions a liquidation of outstanding credits, the imperative need of the moment is for sufficient bank accommodation to enable solvent debtors to meet the demands made upon them for payment. If the banks can inspire the community with confidence in their ability to satisfy this need, the process of liquidation can be carried through with a minimum of loss and confusion.

Defects of both banking law and practice, therefore, may fairly be held responsible for the recurrence of panics in the United States. Legislation that prohibits any except national banks from issuing notes and requires them to deposit government bonds as security prevents a rapid increase in the currency when it would be most effective in checking an incipient panic.[59] But the need would not be fully met even by the most elastic system of bank-note issue. For the majority of business enterprises require deposit credits rather than money to meet their accruing obligations. Elasticity of lending power is needed more than elasticity of currency. At present American banks in the country districts, and still more in the reserve and central-reserve cities, make a practice in good times of keeping reserves little above the minimum required by law. Indeed, the end of a prosperous period commonly finds the great majority of city banks with reserves barely above or just under the limit.[60] These reserves are not small; indeed, they are larger in proportion to deposits than the reserves carried in other countries that avoid panics.[61] But there is no adequate machinery in the American system of thousands of small, independent banks for putting the available funds where they are most needed. Each institution in country districts must fend for itself, and many banks not threatened keep idle in their vaults money that under a higher type of organization might be used effectively to calm uneasiness and avert disaster in other places. In the towns, the issue of clearing-house loan certificates does something toward enabling the banks to coöperate with one another. In recent panics, however, this measure has been shorn of one of its original elements—the equalization of reserves among the banks by assessments levied upon institutions that have more money than they require and the distribution of the proceeds among the institutions whose reserves are running low.[52] As matters stand now, by means of the clearing-house loan certificate city banks can keep all their cash for the use of their depositors and correspondents, instead of having to use a large proportion for the payment of clearing-house balances. But it does not enable the bank that has heavy demands for currency from country banks or from local customers to obtain funds from its neighbors. Thus, even in the reserve and central-reserve cities, the available money is prevented from flowing to the places where it is most needed. Of course the avoidance of restrictions upon payments is thereby rendered more difficult. The banks most exposed to demands for money—that is, the city banks that make a specialty of soliciting deposits from country institutions—are tempted to restrict their remittances early in any season of strain, because they cannot count definitely upon support from their neighbors.[53]

Granting that much of the difficulty of meeting the strains imposed upon banks by crises arises from the lack of organic interrelations among the institutions, we still have to admit that the American banks have made a fetish of the reserve requirements of the national-bank act. Just at the moments of hesitation when timidity on the part of the banks spreads fear among businessmen and when boldness inspires confi-

dence, the banks have been timid. Instead of using their reserves promptly and liberally, they have sought to keep them
intact or even to increase them by withdrawing money from
other banks in which they have placed deposits. Willingness
to 'go below the legal reserves' on occasions when alarm is
spreading would probably do more to check panics in the
United States than the practice of holding larger reserves in
ordinary times. Certainly, the latter measure would give little
relief unless it were combined with the former policy.

CHAPTER 4

BUSINESS DEPRESSION

I. How Crisis Breeds Depression

1. ABORTIVE REVIVALS OF ACTIVITY

IN BOTH 1893 and 1907 the passing of the panic in America was promptly followed by an increase in business activity. Newspapers and technical journals reported the reopening of mills and factories that had been closed during the panic, the return to the road of commercial travelers who had been recalled, the freer buying of goods, and so forth. Optimists, encouraged by such reports, began to predict a speedy revival of prosperity. The crisis, they argued, had arisen from impaired confidence. If confidence could be restored, no real reason would remain why business should not be resumed on the scale prevailing before the panic. The supply of labor, the stock of raw materials, the equipment for transporting and manufacturing goods had not been reduced in quantity or quality by runs upon the banks or by insolvencies. Everyone was eager to be at work. Let business men 'look on the bright side,' combat skeptics by talking prosperity instead of hard times, prove their faith by their works, and all would be well once more.[1]

After both panics a few weeks sufficed to prove the falsity of such predictions and the futility of such a policy. The little burst of activity that followed the panic subsided and hope gave place to renewed discouragement. The acute strain that had marked the panics did not recur, but a slow liquidation dragged on through many months.

The failure of these 'sunshine movements' lends point to the question, Why are crises followed by depressions? Why do so many mills that reopen their gates after the season of severe stress is over presently close again? Is the reason solely that the majority of businessmen will not or cannot shake off their gloomy forebodings? Or are there elements in the business situation as left by the crises that make a period of depression inevitable—elements beyond the control of sentiment?

While a decline in current new orders and contracts for future performance begins some months before the crisis (cf. Ch. 2, ii, 4), yet the close of the crisis finds many factories, mines, contracting firms, and the like with a considerable amount of work still to be performed. A temporary stoppage of operations during a panic may be caused by inability to obtain money for pay rolls, or by doubts concerning the ability of consignees to pay for goods when delivered. But when the banks have ceased to limit payments, and when indiscriminate distrust of the solvency of business enterprises has disappeared, then work is promptly resumed upon these leftover orders and contracts. Other concerns find themselves caught with stocks of raw materials, already on hand or contracted for, far larger than are required by current consumption when orders are light. Their best way of raising money to meet maturing obligations is often to work up and sell these materials, even though very low prices have to be quoted to force a market. Such conditions account for the reopening of many business enterprises in the weeks immediately following a panic.

But, unless large new orders and contracts are obtained speedily, these business enterprises soon reach the end of their order books or surplus stocks. Then they reduce their working forces, put their plants on part time, or close altogether. As a matter of fact, in neither 1894 nor 1908 did the new business prove sufficient to support the mills that had reopened. Hence the reports of the second, third, and fourth months after the panics told a disappointing tale of new suspensions of industrial operations.[2]

It is the paucity of new orders, then, that blights the hope of a quick restoration of prosperity after a severe crisis. Businessmen may be ready to talk prosperity in the hope that others may be induced to buy; but in their own purchases they practice extreme conservatism. Confidence may be restored in the sense that no one longer doubts the solvency of the banks, or the ability of anyone fairly entitled to credit to borrow. But confidence in the sense of sanguine expectations of profitable prices and a large volume of business is not restored, and cannot be restored by cheerful conversation. Experience enforces the contrary belief that prices will fall and business shrink for some time to come. The processes that work out these results must now be described.

2. THE CUMULATION OF DEPRESSION

A. The Volume of Business

The wholesale discharges of workingmen, which occur during a crisis and again when the leftover contracts and accumulated stocks of materials have been worked off, cause a decline in consumers' demand. Many business and professional men likewise are compelled to retrench their family expenditures. Few people may starve; but tens and hundreds of thousands are forced to put up with a less varied or a less abundant diet. Other lines of expenditure are reduced more sharply than the purchases of food. Clothing and furniture are used longer before being discarded and are replaced at urgent need by cheap articles. Fuel and light are economized to an uncomfortable degree; amusements, travel, and all the dispensable adjuncts to comfort are pared down. Accumulated savings, personal credit at retail shops, and personal property that can be pawned are gradually eaten up by those hardest pressed. As these resources are exhausted, the straits of many families become worse and their purchases of commodities are progressively reduced. Hence the calls upon private and public charity usually increase and consumers' demand usually decreases as the period of hard times drags on.[3]

In general, the current business demand for the raw materials and partly finished products from which consumers' goods are made shrinks with the shrinkage of family expenditure. Indeed, for a time this business demand shrinks even faster than consumers' demand; for either merchants or manufacturers may fill their orders for a while after the crisis from their leftover stocks, which are likely to be larger than they care to carry in a dull market. On the other hand, in order to keep at least a skeleton organization together, manufacturers sometimes make goods for which they have no present sale. But operations of this last kind must necessarily be small.

Information concerning the current demand for such producers' goods as are used in repairs and renewals of existing plants is scanty. Every period of intense activity brings out all the weak points of the active establishments, and leaves many of them in a somewhat run-down condition. The first lull in activity affords a favorable opportunity for overhauling plants and bringing their equipment up to the highest standard of efficiency. But what has been proved to be technically desirable may not be financially expedient. Many alterations are planned as soon as the reduction in orders gives the managing staffs leisure; but their execution is often deferred until a resumption of active demand for products is in sight. On the whole, a leisurely course is probably taken by the majority of enterprises, so that the demand for repairs and renewals is light during at least the first quarter or two of depression.

Concerning the demand for all the variety of goods that enter into new construction work it is possible to speak with more confidence. While many of the existing factories are standing idle, while many buildings lack tenants, while the railways have light traffic, etc., there is little inducement to enter upon

the provision of new equipment. While investors have the recent decline in the price of securities fresh in mind, there is
little use in issuing any but the best accredited grade of bonds.
Finally, while a further fall of prices is in prospect, it is vain
to expect the larger capitalists to take up new projects which
can probably be executed more cheaply after the lapse of a year
or two. Engineers, architects, and the like may be kept busy pre-
paring plans for future use; but in the early stages of depression few contracts for new construction are actually started.
Hence the demand for this kind of work continues the decline
that began in the latter days of prosperity.

The processes that cause this shrinking in trade, like the
processes that cause an increase in times of revival, are cumulative in their effects. The more workmen discharged, the
smaller becomes consumers' demand. Every reduction in consumers' demand causes a further decline in the business demand for the materials from which consumers' goods are made.
On the one hand, the latter decline causes more workmen to
be discharged, and on the other hand it discourages managers
from making the repairs and renewals they have in mind, and
discourages capitalists from putting their new projects under
contract. The longer these plans for improving and extending
the industrial equipment are deferred, the less grows employment in the enterprises that provide materials. And the longer
men remain wholly or partly idle, the more are their families
forced to scrimp expenditures, so that consumers' demand
shrinks still further, and this shrinkage further intensifies the
influences that are constricting business.

Nevertheless, the lowest ebb in the physical volume of industrial production usually comes in either the first or second
year after a severe crisis. The statistics presented in Part II,
Chapter V, and the index numbers of trade compiled by Kemmerer and Irving Fisher, all point to this conclusion.[4] Agricultural production, of course, is more erratic, increasing during
depression quite as often as it decreases. What forces counter-

act the cumulative shrinkage in the physical volume of trade within two or three years after a crisis is a question that must be deferred to the concluding section of this chapter. (See pp. 139–147, especially pp. 142–146, below.)

B. The Fall in Prices

As a crisis subsides, the confusion that reigns in the markets for commodities (Ch. 3, ii, 4) gradually disappears. But, while the extremely low prices made in a few forced sales may not be matched again, the trend of fluctuations continues downward for a considerable period. Thus the fall in wholesale prices after the crisis of 1890 lasted at least four years in Germany and at least six years in England and France; that after the crisis of 1893 lasted four years in America; that after the crisis of 1900 lasted three years in England and four years in Germany and France; that after the crisis of 1907 lasted from one to two years in different places.[5] So far as the evidence of recorded quotations goes, then, the lowest level of commodity prices is reached, not during the crisis, but toward the close of the subsequent depression, or even early in the final revival of business activity (cf. Ch. 1, ii, 4).

The chief cause of this fall is the shrinkage in the demand for consumers' goods, raw materials, producers' supplies, and construction work analyzed in the preceding section. On the other side of the market stands a reserve army of capital and labor capable of producing the much larger supplies of commodities for which there was call during the recent expansion. The eagerness of these enterprises now standing idle or working below their capacity to get more business intensifies competition in those branches of trade where it already exists, and often extends competition into branches of trade whence it had been banished by agreements to sustain prices. Pools, working agreements, and combinations of other kinds become far more difficult to sustain in the face of a buyers' market, and many of them go to pieces because their members begin to suspect one another of secret undercutting of rates. Moreover, enterprises verging on bankruptcy and enterprises in the hands of receivers are peculiarly dangerous competitors for solvent firms. They often disregard supplementary charges altogether and seek to defray their operating costs by taking work at prices that rivals who are keeping up interest on their bonds find it hard to match. Finally, the fall in prices is cumulative. It spreads from one part of the system of prices to other parts along the various lines of interconnection traced in the sketch of economic organization in Part I, and then spreads back again from the parts that are slow to be affected to the parts in which the decline began.

As on the rise, so on the fall, there are marked differences in the promptness with which different classes of commodity prices begin to change and in the degree to which the change extends. Retail prices lag behind wholesale prices of the same goods; consumers' goods lag behind producers' goods; manufactured commodities lag behind the raw materials from which they are made; farm and forest products are less regular in their fluctuations than mineral products. These differences arise partly from the differences in the shrinkage of demand pointed out above, partly from technical circumstances affecting the possibility of adjusting current production to current consumption, and partly from the effort to adjust selling prices to the total costs incurred by business enterprises rather than to the buying prices of particular wares.[6]

For reasons sufficiently explained, the prices of labor fall less rapidly than the prices of commodities at wholesale.[7] Interest rates on long-time loans behave like wage rates in that they decline at a slow pace, but unlike wage rates in that they fall for a longer time.[8] Short-time interest rates, on the contrary, fall faster and further than commodity prices.[9] There is less hesitation to lend funds freely at low rates for three months than for ten years, and large sums which the owners will later invest in more permanent ways are transferred during depressions from the bond to the money market, checking the fall of rates in the first and accelerating the fall in the second.

As for the prices of securities, high-grade bonds rise because of the decline in long-time interest rates, while, at the other end of the scale, common stocks fall under the combined influence of diminished earnings and dull prospects. Securities that stand between these extremes, like speculative bonds, stocks with a good dividend-paying record, and preferred stocks, rise or fall according as they partake more of the character of gild-edged bonds or of common stocks. Usually, their relation to common stocks is closer and prices decline, though less than the prices of ordinary shares.[10]

C. Savings and Investments

What is known concerning changes in money incomes during depressions suggests that the amount saved declines heavily—a conclusion that receives at least a measure of statistical support from data on deposits in savings banks.[11] That the funds required for current investments in the extension of old or the construction of new concerns also shrink seriously is attested by abundant evidence.[12] Finally, the often noted change in the preference of investors—their neglect of speculative shares which were the favorites of flush days and their taste for ultraconservative bonds—is also demonstrated.[13]

All this corresponds to expectations. But the investment market presents one peculiar feature. The first year of depression often brings an exceedingly heavy issue of securities by large corporations.[14] The apparent anomaly, however, has a simple explanation. During the high tide of prosperity preceding a crisis, many great enterprises provide for their most pressing financial needs by selling short-time notes or by borrowing directly from banks (see Ch. 2, ii, 3, and iii, 1). After the crisis when interest rates have begun to relax, they seek the first opportunity to fund these floating debts into long-time bonds. Of course, large issues of securities made for such purposes represent neither extensions of new equipment nor investments of fresh capital, but at most a shifting from one form of obligation to another, and from one set of lenders to another.

D. The Currency and the Banks

Upon the production of gold, the proportion of the output applied to monetary uses, and the international movements of the existing monetary stock, depression exercises a complicated set of influences which need not be described in detail because they are the precise opposites of the influence exercised by prosperity (see Ch. 2, iii, 4). The net outcome of all the factors involved differs from one depression to the next. In the United States, the one country for which we have adequate data, the stock of gold currency declined in the dull months January to July 1891, February to November 1894, July to September 1895, April to July 1896, March to May 1908, and July 1909 to April 1910; but it rose during the dull months January to May 1897, May to November 1908, April 1910 to May 1911, and during the dull years 1903–04.[15] Thus the belief that the quantity of gold currency contracts regularly with the pecuniary volume of business is not supported by the available evidence.

As for other kinds of money, bank notes alone possess pretensions to elasticity that merit serious consideration. But a survey of the records for England, France, and Germany, as well as for the United States, shows that the amount outstanding has seldom shrunk in years of business depression.[16]

Much more decided than its influence upon the volume of the currency is the influence of depression upon the distribution of the money in circulation between the banks and the public. As soon as the strain of a severe crisis relaxes, current deposits of cash in the banks begin to exceed current withdrawals, so that presently the banks hold a decidedly larger proportion of the monetary stock than in seasons of active trade.[17]

Of course, this process increases the deposits of the banks so far as deposits represent actual cash. In addition, the large reserves increase the ability of the banks to lend their own credit, and therefore to extend the deposits that result from discounts. Nevertheless, deposit currency usually shrinks when prosperity merges into depression. The elasticity of this element in the circulating medium, indeed, is decidedly greater than that of money. As a result, the ratio between deposits subject to check and money in circulation falls in dull years.[18]

One other fact concerning the effect of depression on the currency is brought out in Part II, Chapter VI. The velocity of the circulation of money, and in higher degree the velocity of the circulation of checks, declines with the activity of trade.[19]

By these changes in the quantity of money and of deposit currency and in the velocities at which both money and checks circulate, the volume of payments is reduced in harmony with the fall of prices and the shrinkage in the physical volume of trade. In this complicated series of readjustments the causative influences, however, are not all on the side of the business situation. The failure of the quantity of money to contract promptly when a crisis turns into depression results in monetary redundancy, of which the visible sign is the accumulation of idle cash in the banks. This accumulation, we have seen, does not produce the expansion in loans and deposits that would occur if the prospects of profits were bright.[20] But it does increase the competition among banks for such business as is to be had, and aids in producing that fall in the discount rates which we have seen to be more rapid than the fall of prices at wholesale (sec. B). In so far, the quantity of money is a factor in accelerating the readjustment of costs to selling prices that ultimately restores the prospects of profits and ushers in a period of expanding trade and rising prices (sec. ii). Hence such an increase in the world's production of gold as has been going on in recent years tends to cut short and to mitigate depressions as well as to prolong and to intensify prosperity. By thus altering somewhat both the intensity and the relative duration of these two phases of business cycles, it tends to give an upward direction to those long-period movements of the price curve in which the years of depression and of prosperity are averaged.

II. How Depression Breeds Prosperity

1. READJUSTMENT OF PRIME COSTS

The shrinkage in orders that depression brings and the accompanying decline in selling prices put severe pressure upon the managers of business enterprises to reduce their expenses within the narrowest feasible limits. Certain of the price phenomena mentioned in section i, 2, B indicate that the resulting efforts are successful at least in part.

That wholesale prices fall faster than retail prices, that the prices of producers' goods fall faster than those of consumers' goods, and that the prices of raw materials fall faster than the prices of manufactured products means, of course, that in these cases buying prices are reduced more than the corresponding selling prices.[21] Further, since short-time interest rates fall much faster than wholesale prices, the cost of loans declines in proportion to the prices of products.[22] Wages also are reduced in seasons of severe depression, but in this case the reduction is less than that in commodity prices.[23] It does not necessarily follow, however, that the cost of labor increases in proportion to the selling prices of what labor produces. For there is strong evidence that the efficiency of labor becomes much greater in dull years than it is in brisk years. Overtime ceases, and with it ceases not only the payment of extra rates but also the weariness of long hours. When working forces are reduced in size they are raised in quality by weeding out the less desirable hands. Most important of all, the fear of being discharged at a time when thousands of men are already looking in vain for work disposes every man who is kept to do his best—to keep any pace that may be set, even at grave danger of overtaxing his strength (cf. Ch. 2, i, 3). The heightening of the physical productivity of labor that results from these changes does more than the fall of wages to diminish the ratio between money cost of labor and money value of products.

When selling prices have been materially reduced, enterprises that are poorly equipped, disadvantageously located, or inefficiently managed are often compelled to close altogether, because they cannot get back even their prime costs on an output sold at current rates. Within the stronger enterprises the poorer portions of the equipment are allowed to stand idle for the same reason. Consequently producers who remain in the race during depressions can 'figure' on the basis of prime costs considerably lower than the average that prevails during prosperity.

Finally, depression checks the numerous small wastes that grow up within most business enterprises during years of intense activity. There is not only a strong incentive but also sufficient leisure to economize materials, to make the most of by-products, to supervise the work of every employee, to adjust each successive step of each process accurately to the other steps, and to change the organization in any ways that promise a saving of cost without entailing a heavy investment of fresh capital.

2. READJUSTMENT OF SUPPLEMENTARY COSTS

Reductions in prime costs begin promptly upon the passing of prosperity. But, for a while at least, they are accompanied by an increase of supplementary costs per unit of product, arising from the distribution of the existing fixed charges over a declining volume of sales. To determine the average net effect of these opposing changes upon total cost per unit is impossible for lack of information, detailed in character and extensive in scope, regarding the quantitative importance of the numerous factors involved. But, whatever these net effects, it is certain that the policy of making selling prices cover total costs is perforce abandoned by many enterprises when business enters upon the phase of depression. Competition for what business is to be had often results in a temporary disregard of supplementary costs and the basing of quotations upon estimates that include little beyond the prices of materials, freight, and labor.

Obviously such a disregard of supplementary costs in fixing selling prices cannot continue long without threatening insolvency. Unless the coupons of bondholders and the rents of lessors are met, the creditors will insist on the appointment of a receiver to manage the property in their interest. But, under the modern form of business organization, insolvency does not necessarily involve suspension of operations. When a considerable sum has been invested in real estate, plant, machinery, or good will, so specialized in form that it cannot be diverted to other uses without serious loss, then an insolvent concern is usually kept running as long as it can pay even a slight margin above the indispensable current expenses. The financial obligations of the enterprise, however, are so reorganized as to turn the temporary disregard of supplementary costs into a permanent reduction of fixed charges. The bondholders may be forced to concede a reduction in the rate of interest or in the nominal value of their principal, lessors may be compelled to scale down their rents, preferred shares may be turned into common, outsiders may buy the whole company under foreclosure at a price that leaves little for the common stockholders, or some other plan of reorganization may be arranged among the various parties at interest that enables the enterprise to continue its business with some prospect of meeting all its obligations.[24]

Such forced reductions of supplementary costs are a common feature not only of the months succeeding a crisis but also of the years of depression that follow. For many enterprises that weather the violent storm are so weakened that they cannot withstand the prolonged strain of low prices and meager business. And both the weak enterprises still struggling desperately to avoid receiverships and the enterprises that have been reorganized are especially dangerous competitors for solvent concerns, and make it difficult for the latter to avoid a similar compromise with their creditors. But just as fast as the process of reorganization is carried through, the prospects of profits are improved by the scaling down of costs.

A somewhat similar, but less drastic, reduction of supplementary costs is gradually effected in many enterprises that never pass through the hands of receivers. Reluctantly managers write down the book value of plants and equipment that are not paying their way. New men buy into old enterprises and estimate the selling prices they must charge on the basis of the moderate sums they have invested. As old leases run out they may well be renewed at lower rents, and as old bonds mature they may well be replaced at lower rates of interest. More in general, businessmen are constrained to admit to themselves and to their bankers that the capitalized values of their enterprises have suffered somewhat the same decline that the stock exchange records for listed securities. While these reduced capitalizations arise primarily from the reduction of profits, they also become the basis for reduced expectations of return, and justify a smaller capital charge in fixing selling prices.

Finally, such new enterprises as may be set on foot during depression have the advantage not only of low prime costs, conferred by improved processes and machinery, but also of low supplementary costs, conferred by the low prices for construction work and the low interest on bonds.

3. INCREASE IN THE PHYSICAL VOLUME OF BUSINESS

In section i, 2, A, evidence is cited that the physical volume of business reaches its lowest ebb within the first or second year after a crisis. In other words, the second or third year of depression usually ushers in an expansion in the quantity of goods turned out by factories, transported by railways, and handled by merchants. What are the processes that bring about this result in the face of the many discouraging circumstances of dull times?

First, the accumulated stocks of goods carried over from the preceding period of prosperity are gradually disposed of. Even when current consumption is small, manufacturers and merchants can reduce their stocks of raw materials and finished wares by filling orders chiefly from what is on hand and confining purchases to the small quantities needed to keep full assortments. But when these stocks have once been reduced to the smallest dimensions allowed by the regular filling of orders, then current purchases and current production are perforce increased, even though current consumption does not grow larger.

In somewhat similar fashion, families can get on for a time with the clothing and furnishings purchased in the later days of prosperity, and business enterprises with their old equipment—not, however, indefinitely. As these articles are gradually worn out and discarded, it becomes necessary to buy new ones, if money can be found for the purpose. Then the demand for both consumers' and producers' goods begins to pick up.

Third, aggregate consumers' demand depends in large part upon the population, and the number has been shown to increase at almost the same rate in depression as in good times.[25] This factor counts for nothing in France, but for much in Germany, and for something in England. Its importance in the United States is uncertain, because we have no adequate statistics comparing the excess of births over deaths with the excess of emigrants over immigrants.

Once more, the development of new tastes among consumers, the appearance of new materials, and the introduction of new processes do not come to a standstill even during depressions. While changes in demand may restrict the market for commodities that are being superseded, the losses of their producers are gradually written off and the stimulating effect of activity among producers of the novelties remains.

Finally, and most important of all, demand for new construction increases markedly during the later stages of depression. While the amount saved each year by the people of any country probably declines in hard times, certainly saving never ceases.[26] For a time, however, the fresh accumulations of capital are not accompanied by a corresponding volume of fresh investments in business ventures. Refunding operations constitute a large proportion of the business done in the investment market, for governments and business enterprises alike are keen to take advantage of the low interest rates that then prevail.[27] Of the money seeking fresh investments, whether it is the product of current savings or of refunding, much goes into the purchase of property that embarrassed holders are forced to sell. That is, certainly a considerable and probably an extremely large share of the liquid capital provided by certain individuals during depressions is used merely to cancel part of the losses incurred by other individuals. Such investments represent a redistribution of ownership, but no new creations of industrial equipment.[28] Finally, a part of the funds that in the prosperous phase of the business cycle seek the investment market are left during the earlier stages of depression on deposit in the banks, and used, so far as a use can be found, in making short-time loans (see sec. i, 2, B).

Changes in the business situation that in the later stages of depression direct investment funds once more to the construction of new equipment are numerous. (1) When most of the weaker owners of business enterprises have once been squeezed out and forced to sell their holdings, and when the necessary corporate reorganizations have been largely completed, the opportunities to buy into old enterprises on favorable terms become less numerous. Thereafter more of the men seeking business openings build for themselves. (2) The timidity inspired among investors by the crisis gradually wears off, and capitalists large and small become more ready to risk their funds in business ventures. (3) The low rate of interest at which money can be borrowed on long time, provided good security is offered, means that the more enterprising spirits can borrow whatever funds they require in addition to their own means on terms that will keep the fixed charges moderate for years to come. (4) Even more important in most cases in its bearing on fixed charges is the low initial cost at which contracts for construction can be let when labor is efficient and materials are cheap. (5) Under the influence of systematic research in recent times the progress of industrial technique has become fairly steady and continuous. Hence, the longer the period during which new construction is checked by business depression the greater becomes the accumulation of technical improvements of which new plants can take advantage, and therefore the greater becomes the inducement to invest in new equipment. (6) The gradual growth of the current demand for consumers' and producers' goods, brought about in the manner already explained, stimulates the investment demand with which we are now dealing. When current orders begin to increase, the managers of existing enterprises are encouraged to begin the improvements in their facilities that perhaps have been planned for several years, and the organizers of new ventures are encouraged to let their contracts. Both sets of investors are eager to make their bargains for construction before the cost of building advances and to have their new plants ready for operation by the time a revival of activity becomes pronounced.

Under the combined pressure of these various business forces, then, a marked increase in demand for all the innumerable kinds of commodities and labor required for construction occurs in the later stages of depression. Of course this increase in the volume of demand from investors causes fuller employment of labor and assures more orders to the existing producers of producers' goods. A new expansion in consumers' and producers' demand follows, which reacts in the way suggested to enhance investment demand. Thus the increase in business is cumulative. Unless the processes we have traced are checked by some untoward event such as a serious failure of crops, within a year or two they carry the physical volume of business to higher levels than those reached at the close of the preceding period of prosperity.[20]

4. THE END OF LIQUIDATION

The various processes just described combine reductions in both prime costs and fixed charges with an expansion in the physical volume of business. In this fashion depression ultimately brings about revival. For of course these changes increase prospective profits, and in the money economy prospective profits are the great incentive to activity.

But for many months the processes by which depression works its own ending are kept down to a slow pace by the continued fall of prices. For the data in Part II, Chapters IV and V, indicate that the price level and even the pecuniary volume of business usually continue to fall for some time after the physical volume of business has begun to rise. The rate at which prices fall, however, is slower in the later than in the earlier stages of depression. And the effect of the fall in reducing profits is mitigated, if not wholly offset, by increasing sales. For to the various factors already mentioned as reducing supplementary costs per unit another factor is added when fixed charges begin to be distributed over an increasing output.

The business situation into which depression evolves, then, differs radically from the situation in which it began. Most of the heavy stocks of goods that hung menacingly over the market at the close of the crisis have been disposed of, so that every increase of consumption leads to an equivalent increase of production. The floating debts and the heavy fixed charges that threatened widespread insolvency have been paid off, written down, or otherwise readjusted, so that the enterprises can once more live within their incomes. Even the great mass of business enterprises that did not change hands and that did not compromise with their creditors are now assigned a lower capitalized value corresponding to their moderate expectations of profit. Outstanding credits are well within the limits mercantile houses and banks can support. Investors have ceased to be foolishly timid, and they have not yet become recklessly bold. Prices are still declining, but at a slackening pace. Costs of doing business have been so reduced as to leave a narrow margin of profit despite the low scale of selling prices. The demand for goods of many kinds—though not such as to tax the existing equipment to its utmost—is already large and growing steadily larger.[80]

In fine, this business situation is that described in the first section of Chapter 1—the situation out of which a revival of activity presently develops. Having thus come round again to its point of departure, after tracing the processes of cumulative change by which prosperity breeds crisis, crisis evolves into depression, and depression paves the way for a return of prosperity, the present theory of business cycles has reached its appointed end.

CHAPTER 5

WIDER ASPECTS OF BUSINESS CYCLES

I. Summary of the Preceding Theory of Business Cycles

THE THEORY of business cycles presented in Chapters 1–4 is a descriptive analysis of the processes of cumulative change by which a revival of activity develops into intense prosperity, by which this prosperity engenders a crisis, by which crisis turns into depression, and by which depression, after growing more severe for a time, finally leads to such a revival of activity as that with which the cycle began.

This analysis rests primarily upon an elaborate statistical inquiry into the phenomena of recent cycles in the United States, Great Britain, France, and Germany. The statistical line of attack was chosen because the problem is essentially quantitative, involving the relative importance of divers forces that are themselves the net resultants of innumerable business decisions. The selection of statistical data, the methods of presentation, and the coördination of the results were determined in large part by ideas borrowed from theoretical writers or from financial journals. But all the tables and all the borrowed ideas were fitted into a framework provided by a study of the economic organization of today, which showed that the industrial process of making and the commercial process of distributing goods are both thoroughly subordinated to the business process of making money.

The theory derived from these materials has filled so many pages that a summary may prove serviceable. There is always danger, however, that a plausible summary may carry too much weight. Readers who are familiar with theories of business cycles will appreciate how easy it is to make many dissimilar explanations of crises sound convincing when attention is confined to a restricted range of phenomena. Only by putting any theory to the practical test of accounting for actual business experience can its value be determined. The case for the present theory, therefore, and also the case against it, is to be found not in the easy summary that follows, but in the difficult chapters that precede, including Parts I and II, or better still in an independent effort to use it in interpreting the ceaseless ebb and flow of economic activity.

1. CUMULATION OF PROSPERITY

With whatever phase of the business cycle analysis begins, it must take for granted the conditions brought about by the preceding phase, postponing explanation of these assumptions until it has worked around the cycle and come again to its starting point.

A revival of activity, then, starts with this legacy from depression: a level of prices low in comparison with the prices of prosperity, drastic reductions in the costs of doing business, narrow margins of profit, liberal bank reserves, a conservative policy in capitalizing business enterprises and in granting credits, moderate stocks of goods, and cautious buying.

For reasons that will appear in the sequel, such conditions are accompanied by an expansion in the physical volume of trade. Though slow at first, this expansion is cumulative. Now it is only a question of time when an increase in the amount of business transacted that grows more rapid as it proceeds will turn dullness into activity. Left to itself, this transformation is effected by slow degrees; but it is often hastened by some propitious event arising from other than domestic business sources, such as exceptionally profitable harvests, heavy purchases of supplies by government, or a marked increase in the export demand for the products of home industry.

Even when a revival of activity is confined at first within a narrow range of industries or within some single section of the country, it soon spreads to other parts of the business field. For the active enterprises must buy more materials, wares, and current supplies from other enterprises, the latter from still others, and so on without assignable limits. Meanwhile all enterprises that become busier employ more labor, use more borrowed money, and make higher profits. Family incomes increase and consumers' demand expands, likewise in ever widening circles. Shopkeepers pass on larger orders for consumers' goods to wholesale merchants, manufacturers, importers, and producers of raw materials. All these enterprises require more supplies of various kinds for handling their growing trade, and increase the sums they pay out to employees, lenders, and proprietors—thus stimulating afresh the demand for both producers' and consumers' goods. Soon or late this expansion of orders reaches back to the enterprises from which the impetus to greater activity was first received, and then this whole complicated series of reactions begins afresh at a higher pitch of intensity. All this while, the revival of activity is instilling a feeling of optimism among businessmen, and this feeling both justifies itself and heightens the forces that engendered it by making everyone readier to buy freely.

While the price level is often sagging slowly when a revival begins, the cumulative expansion in the physical volume of trade presently stops the fall and starts a rise. For, when enterprises have in sight as much business as they can handle with their existing facilities of standard efficiency, they stand out for higher prices on additional orders. This policy prevails even in the most keenly competitive trades, because additional orders can be executed only by breaking in new hands, starting old machinery, buying new equipment, or some other change that entails increased expense. The expectation of its coming accelerates the advance. Buyers are eager to obtain or to contract for large supplies while the low level of quotations continues, and the first definite signs of an upward trend of quotations bring a sudden rush of orders.

Like the increase in the physical volume of business, the rise in prices spreads rapidly; for every advance of quotations puts pressure upon someone to recoup himself by making a compensatory advance in the prices of what he has to sell. The resulting changes in prices are far from even, not only as among different commodities, but also as among different parts of the system of prices. Retail prices lag behind wholesale, the prices of staple consumers' behind the prices of staple producers' goods, and the prices of finished products behind the prices of their raw materials. Among raw materials, the prices of mineral products reflect the changed business conditions more regularly than do the prices of raw animal, farm, or forest products. Wages rise often more promptly, but always less than wholesale prices; discount rates rise sometimes more slowly than commodities and sometimes more rapidly; interest rates on long loans always move sluggishly in the early stages of revival, while the prices of stocks—particularly of common stocks—both precede and exceed commodity prices on the rise. The causes of these differences in the promptness and the energy with which various classes of prices respond to the stimulus of business activity are found partly in differences of organization in the markets for commodities, labor, loans, and securities; partly in the technical circumstances affecting the relative demand for and supply of these several classes of goods; and partly in the adjusting of selling prices to changes in the aggregate of buying prices a business enterprise pays, rather than to changes in the prices of the particular goods bought for resale.

In the great majority of enterprises, larger profits result from these divergent price fluctuations combined with larger sales. For, while the prices of raw materials and of wares bought for resale usually, and the prices of bank loans often, rise faster than selling prices, the prices of labor lag far behind, and the prices that make up supplementary costs are mainly stereotyped for a time by old agreements concerning salaries, leases, and bonds.

This increase in profits, combined with the prevalence of business optimism, leads to a marked expansion of investments. Of course the heavy orders for machinery, the large contracts for new construction, and so forth, that result swell still further the physical volume of business, and render yet stronger the forces that are driving prices upward.

Indeed, the salient characteristic of this phase of the business cycle is the cumulative working of the various processes that are converting a revival of trade into intense prosperity. Not only does every increase in trade cause other increases, every convert to optimism make new converts, and every advance in prices furnish an incentive for fresh advances; but the growth of trade also helps to spread optimism and to raise prices, while optimism and rising prices both support each other and stimulate the growth of trade. Finally, as just said, the changes going forward in these three factors swell profits and encourage investments, while high profits and heavy investments react by augmenting trade, justifying optimism, and raising prices.

2. HOW PROSPERITY BREEDS CRISIS

While the processes sketched work cumulatively for a time to enhance prosperity, they also cause a slow accumulation of stresses within the balanced system of business—stresses that ultimately undermine the conditions upon which prosperity rests. Among them is the gradual increase in the costs of doing business. The decline in supplementary costs per unit of output ceases when enterprises have once booked all the business they can handle with their standard equipment, and a slow increase in these costs begins when the expiration of old con-

tracts forces renewals at the high rates of interest, rent, and salaries that prevail in prosperity. Meanwhile prime costs rise at a
relatively rapid rate. Antiquated equipment and plants that
are ill-located or otherwise work at some disadvantage are
brought again into operation. The price of labor rises, not only
because standard rates of wages go up, but also because pay for
overtime is higher. More serious still is the decline in the efficiency of labor, because overtime brings weariness, because of
the employment of 'undesirables,' and because crews cannot be
driven at top speed when jobs are more numerous than men
to fill them. The prices of raw materials continue to rise faster
on the average than the selling prices of products. Finally, the
numerous small wastes, incident to the conduct of business enterprises, creep up when managers are hurried by a press of
orders demanding prompt delivery.

A second stress is the accumulating tension in the investment and money markets. The supply of funds available at
the former rates of interest for the purchase of bonds, for lending on mortgages, and the like fails to keep pace with the rapidly swelling demand. It becomes difficult to negotiate new
issues of securities except on onerous terms, and men of affairs
complain of the 'scarcity of capital.' Nor does the supply of
bank loans grow fast enough to keep up with the demand. For
the supply is limited by the reserves that bankers hold against
their expanding demand liabilities. Full employment and active retail trade cause so much money to remain suspended in
active circulation that the cash left in the banks increases
rather slowly, even when the gold output is rising most rapidly. On the other hand, the demand for bank loans grows not
only with the physical volume of trade, but also with the rise
of prices, and with the desire of men of affairs to use their own
funds for controlling as many business ventures as possible.
Moreover, this demand is relatively inelastic, since many borrowers think they can pay high rates of discount for a few
months and still make profits on their turnover, and since the

corporations that are unwilling to sell long-time bonds at the hard terms that have come to prevail try to raise part of the funds they require by discounting one- or two-year notes.

Tension in the bond and money markets is unfavorable to the continuance of prosperity, not only because high rates of interest reduce the prospective margins of profit, but also because they check the expansion in trade out of which prosperity developed. Many projected ventures are relinquished or postponed, either because borrowers conclude that the interest would absorb too much of their profits or because lenders refuse to extend their commitments farther.

One important group of enterprises suffers an especially severe check from this cause in conjunction with high prices—the group that depends primarily upon the demand for industrial equipment. In the earlier stages of prosperity, this group usually enjoys a season of exceptionally intense activity. But when the market for bonds becomes stringent, and—what is often more important—when the cost of construction has become high, business enterprises and individual capitalists alike defer the execution of many plans for extending old and erecting new plants. As a result, contracts for this kind of work become less numerous as the climax of prosperity approaches. Then the steel mills, foundries, machine factories, copper smelters, quarries, lumber mills, cement plants, construction companies, general contractors, and the like find their orders for future delivery falling off. While for the time being they may be working at high pressure to complete old contracts within the stipulated period, they face a serious restriction of trade in the near future.

The imposing fabric of prosperity is built with a liberal factor of safety; but the larger grows the structure the more severe become these internal stresses. The only effective means of preventing disaster while continuing to build is to raise selling prices time after time high enough to offset the encroachments of costs upon profits, to cancel the advancing rates of interest, and to keep investors willing to contract for fresh industrial equipment.

But it is impossible to keep selling prices rising indefinitely. In default of other checks, the inadequacy of cash reserves would ultimately compel the banks to refuse a further expansion of loans upon any terms. But before this stage has been reached, the rise of prices is stopped by the consequences of its own inevitable inequalities. These inequalities become more glaring the higher the general level is forced; after a time they threaten serious reduction of profits to certain business enterprises, and the troubles of these victims dissolve that confidence in the security of credits with which the whole towering structure of prosperity has been cemented.

What, then, are the lines of business in which selling prices cannot be raised sufficiently to prevent a reduction of profits? In certain lines selling prices are stereotyped by law, by public commissions, by contracts of long term, by custom, or by business policy, and in these no advance, or but meager advances can be made. In other lines prices are always subject to the incalculable chances of the harvests; in these the market value of all accumulated stocks of materials and finished goods wavers with the crop reports. In some lines recent construction of new equipment has increased the capacity for production faster than the demand for their wares has expanded under the repressing influence of the high prices that must be charged to prevent a reduction in profits. The unwillingness of investors to let fresh contracts threatens loss not only to contracting firms of all sorts, but also to all the enterprises from whom they buy materials and supplies. The high rates of interest not only check the current demand for wares of various kinds, but also clog the effort to maintain prices by keeping large stocks of goods off the market until they can be sold to better advantage. Finally, the very success of other enterprises in raising selling prices fast enough to defend their profits aggravates the difficulties of the men who are in trouble. For to the latter every further rise in the prices of the products they buy means a further strain upon their already stretched resources.

As prosperity approaches its height, then, a sharp contrast develops among the business prospects of different enterprises. Many, probably the majority, are making more money than at any previous stage of the business cycle. But an important minority, at least, face the prospect of declining profits. The more intense prosperity becomes, the larger grows this threatened group. It is only a question of time when these conditions, begotten by prosperity, will force some radical readjustment.

Now such a decline in profits threatens graver consequences than the failure to realize expected dividends. For it arouses doubt concerning the security of outstanding credits. Business credit is based primarily upon the capitalized value of present and prospective profits, and the credit outstanding at the zenith of prosperity is adjusted to the great expectations that prevail when trade is enormous, prices are high, and men of affairs optimistic. The rise in interest rates has already narrowed the margins of security behind credits by reducing the capitalized value of given profits. When profits themselves begin to waver the outlook becomes worse. Cautious creditors fear that the shrinkage in the market rating of the business enterprises that owe them money will leave no adequate security for repayment. Hence they begin to refuse renewals of old loans to the enterprises that cannot stave off a decline in profits, and to press for a settlement of outstanding accounts.

Thus prosperity ultimately brings on conditions that start a liquidation of the huge credits it has piled up. And in the course of this liquidation prosperity merges into crisis.

3. CRISES

Once begun, the process of liquidation extends rapidly, partly because most enterprises that are called upon to settle their maturing obligations in turn put similar pressure upon their own debtors, and partly because, despite all efforts to keep secret what is going forward, news presently leaks out and other creditors take alarm.

While this financial readjustment is in progress the problem of making profits on current transactions is subordinated to the more vital problem of maintaining solvency. Business managers concentrate their energies upon providing for their outstanding liabilities and upon nursing their financial resources, instead of upon pushing their sales. In consequence, the volume of new orders falls off rapidly. That is, the factors that were already dimming the prospects of profits in certain lines of business are reinforced and extended. Even though the overwhelming majority of enterprises succeed in meeting the demand for payment, the tenor of business changes. Expansion gives place to contraction, though without a violent wrench. Discount rates rise higher than usual, securities and commodities fall in price, and as old orders are completed working forces are reduced; but there is no epidemic of bankruptcies, no run upon banks, and no spasmodic interruption of the ordinary business processes.

At the opposite extreme from crises of this mild order stand the crises that degenerate into panics. When the process of liquidation reaches a weak link in the chain of interlocking credits and the bankruptcy of some conspicuous enterprise spreads unreasoning alarm among the business public, then the banks are suddenly forced to meet a double strain—a sharp increase in the demand for loans and in the demand for repayment of deposits. If the banks prove able to honor both demands without flinching, the alarm quickly subsides. But if, as has happened twice in America since 1890, many solvent businessmen are refused accommodation at any price, and if depositors are refused payment in full, the alarm turns into panic. A restriction of payments by the banks gives rise to a premium upon currency, to hoarding of cash, and to the use of various unlawful substitutes for money. A refusal by the banks to expand their loans, still more a policy of contraction, sends interest rates up to three or four times their usual figures, and causes forced suspensions and bankruptcies. The government is appealed to for extraordinary aid, frantic efforts are made to import gold, clearing-house loan certificates are issued, and bank-note circulation increases as rapidly as is possible under the existing system. Collections fall into arrears, domestic exchange rates are dislocated, workmen are discharged because employers cannot get money for pay rolls or fear they will not be paid for goods when delivered, stocks fall to extremely low levels, even the best bonds decline somewhat in price, commodity markets are disorganized by sacrifice sales, and business is violently contracted.

That occasionally crises still degenerate into panics in America, but not in Great Britain, France, or Germany, arises primarily from differences in banking organization and practice. In each of the three European countries the prevalence of branch banking and the existence of a central bank so organizes the banking system as a whole that reserves can be applied when and where needed although they constitute only a small percentage of aggregate demand liabilities of all the branches. In marked contrast to the policy of American banks, the central bank not only carries a reserve far in excess of immediate requirements in ordinary times, but also uses it boldly in times of stress. As a result, European businessmen need fear neither a refusal to lend nor a restriction of payments by the banks on which they depend. And when the depositor can get his money at need and the solvent businessman can borrow, there is small chance of panic.

4. DEPRESSION

The close of a panic is usually followed by the reopening of numerous enterprises that have been shut during the weeks of severest pressure. But based, as it is, chiefly upon the finishing of orders received but not completely executed during the preceding prosperity, or upon the effort to work up and market large stocks of materials already on hand or contracted for, this prompt revival of activity is partial and shortlived. It comes to an end as this work is gradually finished, because new orders are not forthcoming in sufficient number to keep the mills and factories busy.

A period follows during which depression spreads over the whole field of business and grows more severe. Consumers' demand declines in consequence of wholesale discharges of wage earners, the gradual exhaustion of savings, and reductions in other classes of family incomes. With consumers' demand falls business demand for raw materials, current supplies, and equipment used in making consumers' goods. Still more severe is the shrinkage in investors' demand for construction work of all kinds, since few individuals or enterprises care to sink money in new business ventures as long as trade remains depressed and the price level is declining. The contraction of business that results from these several shrinkages in demand is cumulative, since every reduction in employment causes a reduction in consumers' demand, and every decline in consumers' demand depresses current business demand and discourages investment, thereby causing further discharges of employees and reducing consumers' demand once more.

With the contraction of trade goes a fall in prices. For, when current orders are insufficient to employ the existing equipment, competition for what business is to be had becomes keener. This decline spreads through the regular commercial channels that connect one enterprise with another, and is cumulative, since every reduction in price facilitates, if it does not force, reductions in other prices, and the latter reductions react in their turn to cause fresh reductions at the starting point.

As the rise in prices that accompanied revival, so the fall that accompanies depression is characterized by certain regularly recurring differences in degree. Wholesale prices fall faster than retail, the prices of producers' goods faster than those of consumers' goods, and the prices of raw materials faster than those of manufactured products. The prices of raw mineral products follow a more regular course than those of raw forest, farm, or animal products. As compared with general index numbers of commodity prices at wholesale, index numbers of wages and interest on long-time loans decline less, while index numbers of discount rates and of stocks decline more. The only important group of prices to rise in the face of depression is that of high-grade bonds.

Of course the contraction of trade and the fall in prices reduce the margin of present and prospective profits, spread discouragement among businessmen, and check enterprise. But they also set in motion certain processes of readjustment by which depression is gradually overcome.

The prime costs of doing business are reduced by the rapid fall in the prices of raw materials and of bank loans, by the marked increase in the efficiency of labor that comes when employment is scarce and men are anxious to hold their jobs, and by closer economy on the part of managers. Supplementary costs also are reduced by reorganizing enterprises that have actually become or that threaten to become insolvent, by the sale of other enterprises at low figures, by reduction in rentals and refunding of loans, by charging off bad debts and writing down depreciated properties, and by admitting that a recapitalization of business enterprises—corresponding to the lower prices of stocks—has been effected on the basis of lower profits.

While costs are thus still being reduced, demand for goods ceases to shrink and then begins slowly to expand—a change that usually comes in the second or third year of depression. Accumulated stocks left over from prosperity are gradually exhausted, and current consumption requires current production. Clothing, furniture, machinery and other moderately durable articles that have been used as long as possible are finally discarded and replaced. Population continues to increase at a fairly uniform rate: the new mouths must be fed and the new backs clothed. New tastes appear among consumers and new methods among producers, giving rise to demand for novel products. Most important of all, investment demand for industrial equipment revives; for though saving may slacken it does not cease, with the cessation of foreclosure sales and corporate reorganizations the opportunities to buy into old enterprises at bargain prices become fewer, capitalists become less timid as the crisis recedes into the past, the low rates of interest on long-term bonds encourage borrowing, the accumulated technical improvements of several years may be utilized, and contracts can be let on highly favorable conditions as to cost and prompt execution.

Once these various forces have set trade to expanding again, the increase proves cumulative, though for a time the pace of growth is kept slow by the continued sagging of prices. But while the latter maintains the pressure upon businessmen and prevents the increase in orders from producing a rapid rise in profits, still business prospects become gradually brighter. Old debts have been paid, accumulated stocks of commodities absorbed, weak enterprises reorganized, the banks are strong— all the clouds upon the financial horizon have disappeared. Everything is ready for a revival of activity, which will begin whenever some fortunate circumstance gives a sudden fillip to demand, or, in the absence of such an event, when the slow growth of business has filled order books and paved the way for a new rise in prices. Such is the stage of the business cycle with which the analysis began, and, having accounted for its own beginning, the analysis ends.

NOTE

RELATION OF THE PRECEDING THEORY OF BUSINESS CYCLES TO
OTHER THEORIES CURRENT IN 1913

When considered in relation to the preceding analysis, none of the theories of business cycles summarized in Part I, Chapter I, seems to be demonstrably wrong, but neither does any one seem to be wholly adequate. Perhaps an effort to suggest the limitations of each theory may throw additional light upon a problem that is dark at best—certainly such an effort will reveal how much the present discussion has borrowed from its predecessors.

Beveridge's theory, that the competitive effort of each producer to engross as much of the market as possible for his own wares necessarily leads to gluts, puts all the emphasis upon a single feature in a set of processes that have been shown to be exceedingly complex. But to do Beveridge justice, he is far from professing to advance an adequate theory of crises. And the one factor he does emphasize certainly counts in the sense that the whole course of business cycles would be profoundly altered were competition among producers suppressed. But the claims freely made some decades ago, in both America and Germany, that the development of trusts and cartels would put an end to crises, have not been sustained by business history. The industries in which combination has made greatest strides toward regulating competition still feel the stress caused by the increasing cost of labor and by tension in the investment and money markets. Nor have the managers of these great combinations been able to avoid the reduction in profits caused by waning demand for their products when prosperity has passed its zenith.

The various forms of the underconsumption theory have already been criticized. Their value lies in bringing out one of the possible obstacles to preventing encroachments of costs upon profits. But it has never been demonstrated that consumers' demand falls behind supply before a crisis has begun. And whatever the facts, there is evidence that the strains that have actually precipitated the crises of recent years have appeared earlier in other branches of trade than those which cater to the wants of consumers (see Ch. 2, iv, 2, D).

Spiethoff's theory of the ill-balanced production of industrial equipment and of complementary goods supplies two elements in the preceding discussion. But here these elements have been given a somewhat different setting. The underproduction of complementary goods appears in the guise of an increase in the costs of materials, labor, and the like, so rapid that it threatens to reduce prospective profits. The overproduction of industrial equipment is presented as one of the reasons why it is difficult to advance selling prices sufficiently to offset this increase in costs. If this setting helps to make the bearing of Spiethoff's analysis clearer, it also serves to indicate that elements besides those upon which he enlarges must be taken into account.

Hull's theory that the high cost of construction work in periods of intense prosperity causes a severe decline in investment demand and hence a crisis, which spreads from such industries as steel to all branches of business, has been incorporated into the preceding analysis. But there it is combined with numerous other ideas Mr. Hull has neglected.

Lescure's theory of variations in prospective profits combined with Veblen's theory of the discrepancy between prospective profits and current capitalization affords the general framework of Chapter 2. But the analysis of these two writers has been developed by the aid of suggestions drawn from other sources, and an attempt has been made to test certain of their assumptions by the use of statistical materials.

Among the suggestions thus utilized are those of Sombart, Carver, and Irving Fisher. While all three suggestions belong in an analysis of how prosperity brings about a decline in prospective profits and thus undermines the basis of credit, no one of them can properly stand alone.

Stresses within the system of prices may well arise, as Sombart holds, because the supply of organic goods does not keep the same pace as the supply of minerals and the like; but, unless the preceding analysis is sheer imagination, other factors are at work, more regular in their operation than the uncertainties of the harvests, and not less potent in encroaching upon profits.

Carver's theory of the dissimilar price fluctuations of producers' and consumers' goods is another way of explaining that prosperity brings on a rapid increase of industrial equipment and a crisis occurs when the increasing supply of goods cannot be sold at a profit. Of course this feature has been considered; but it is far from standing alone—a conclusion Mr. Carver would be prompt to recognize were he dealing with the problem on a more extended scale.

Likewise, the lagging adjustment of interest rates to fluctuations in the price level, utilized by Mr. Fisher to explain the occurrence of crises, is only one among several factors that widen the margins of profit in the early stages of prosperity and narrow them at a later stage.

Finally, Mr. Johannsen's theory of 'impair savings' has been used incidentally: that is, in Chapter 4 it is recognized that investments in refunding bonds, in the securities of companies being reorganized, and in properties sold under foreclosure, have no such stimulating effect upon business as investments in new industrial equipment. It is in part—but only in part— because investments of the former type predominate in the months succeeding a crisis that current production falls off.

While the proofs of this chapter were in my hands, Mrs. Minnie Throop England's preliminary sketch of her projected theory of crises appeared ("Economic Crises," *Journal of Political Economy,* April 1913). Mrs. England seems to have formulated the problem in much the same way as I have done, to have employed like methods, and to have reached broadly similar conclusions.

II. Diversities among Business Cycles and Their Causes

Any analysis that traces the general course of the processes bringing about prosperity, crisis, and depression inevitably leaves a misleading impression of uniformity among business cycles. As a matter of fact these cycles differ widely in duration, in intensity, in the relative prominence of their various phenomena, and in the sequence of their phases.

1. THE DIVERSITIES

If the years between one crisis and the next are taken as the length of a business cycle, the British, French, and German cycles beginning in 1890 lasted ten years, and those beginning in 1900 lasted seven years. The contemporaneous American cycles have wider variations: three years from 1890 to 1893; ten years from 1893 to 1903; and four years from 1903 to 1907. In view of these diversities, the notion that crises have a regular period of recurrence is plainly mistaken.

American experience in 1893–1903 refutes the idea that business cycles always consist of unruffled prosperity, followed by a well-defined crisis, and uninterrupted depression. Depression was broken by the revival in 1895, and then aggravated by the extreme monetary stringency of 1896. The revival that began in 1897 was checked for a brief time by the outbreak of war with Spain in spring 1898. The succeeding prosperous period was marred by the stock-exchange troubles of 1899 and 1901 and the temporary slackening of general business in 1900.

Of examples of differences in intensity, the contrast between French and American cycles is the most striking. But even within the limits of one country, successive cycles bring relatively mild crises like those of 1890 and 1903 in America and severe panics like those of 1893 and 1907; relatively brief and moderate periods of depression like those of 1891 and 1904, and relatively long and drastic ones like that of 1894–96; relatively transient periods of prosperity like those of 1892 and 1909, and relatively long periods of intense prosperity like those of 1898–1902, and 1905–07.

Finally, no two periods of prosperity, crisis, or depression have just the same combination of elements. Speculation is sometimes rampant during prosperity, as in America in 1901, and sometimes held firmly in check, as in Great Britain in 1906–07. A contraction of credit is often the most conspicuous feature of crises, as in the American panics of 1893 and 1907; while at other times it plays a minor rôle in comparison with the declining volume of new business, as in the British crisis of 1907. Different branches of trade and different sections of the country are found to be the chief seats of activity, the chief sources of stress, and the chief sufferers from depression in successive cycles. Indeed, dissimilarities of this type are so numerous and so obvious that it is not worth while to cite more than the few examples given in the foregoing discussion.

2. THEIR CAUSES

Many of these divergences among business cycles are due to events that arise from other than business sources. For the mechanism of the money economy is so delicate that someone's prospects of profits are affected by every day's news. Most important of all these extraneous factors in the long run are the chances of the weather which make crops good or bad, and so affect the prices of farm products, the purchasing power of agricultural communities, the earnings of "granger" railways, etc., etc. The making of war or of peace, disturbances of domestic order, earthquakes, conflagrations, epidemics, changes in monetary standards, tariff revisions, governmental policies concerning corporations, alterations in the gold output, improvements in industrial technique, the opening of new lands to settlement, the depletion of natural resources, the shifting of trade routes—these and a thousand other things can scarcely fail to help or hamper some business venture. If the circle they reach is large and their effects pronounced, they doubtless give a peculiar twist to the business cycle within which they fall. Particularly in times of transition from one phase of the cycle to another, when the set of the current is uncertain, the influence of such events is often marked. But in the midst of prosperity, crisis, or depression, it often seems as though the business community pays no heed to news that does not accord with the tenor of the time.

Less obvious but more persisting in their effect upon the course and character of business cycles are the changes continually occurring in business organization and practice, and in the relative importance of different industries. For example, both the extravagance of 'booms' and the violence of panics have been tempered by closer organization, wider knowledge, and firmer policies among banks. Again, the rapid development of manufacturing and the decline of railway building in rank among American industries have helped to make the business cycles of 1900–10 different from those of 1880–90. Once more, the increasing dominance of large corporations that rely upon the investing public for their funds gives greater influence to the markets for bonds and stocks than these markets exercised in the days of family enterprises. The broad contrast between French and American cycles shows how powerfully the relative development of thrift or of enterprise affects the intensity of both prosperity and depression. Other changes that react upon business cycles are the extension of monopoly control, the integration of industry, the organization of labor with its standardization of wage rates, and in general the readjustment of business to meet changes in the material, political, or social environment.

The reaction of such contemporary changes in economic organization upon the character of successive business cycles may be difficult to trace. But each new change accomplished becomes the basis upon which further change proceeds. That is, the broad changes of economic organization are cumulative, like the lesser changes that cause each phase of every business cycle to evolve into its successor. And, being cumulative, their dominating influence upon the phenomena of business cycles stands out clearly in the lapse of years. Hence economists of each generation will probably see reason to recast the theory of business cycles they learned in their youth.

III. Business Cycles in Economic History

1. GENESIS OF BUSINESS CYCLES

If the term economic crisis is made to cover any serious disturbance of the usual processes of producing and distributing goods, then such crises are at least as old as economic records. Destructive 'acts of God' and the wasteful wrath of man often brought acute distress upon communities of industrious people long before economic organization assumed its present form and business cycles began to run a regular course.

More modern in their character were the disturbances that followed the organization of credit. By the sixteenth century, for example, the public debts of France, Spain, Austria, and other countries had grown so important that royal repudiations became a prolific source of financial crises in centers like Antwerp and Lyons.[1] The rise of banking exposed mercantile circles to still other dangers. The goldsmith bankers in London, to cite specific instances, were subjected to runs and their patrons to panics when the Dutch burned the English fleet at Chatham on the Thames in 1667, and again in 1672 when Charles II stopped payments from the Exchequer. But, though such episodes may fairly be called financial crises, they differ from their recent counterparts both in affecting only a few trades and in depending directly upon war or the fiscal embarrassments of government.

Even in the eighteenth century most English crises arose from other than business sources—though by this time England had definitely assumed the leadership in economic organization. In 1708 the goldsmith bankers took advantage of reports of Jacobite plots and of preparations in France for a descent upon Scotland to attack the credit of the Bank of England. In 1720 the South Sea Bubble burst, ending an almost incredible mania of speculation in stocks. The next crisis occurred in 1745, when the Pretender with his Highlanders penetrated within 120 miles of London. The end of the Seven Years' War was followed in 1763 by lively speculation and collapse upon the Stock Exchange. Again in 1771–73 the making of peace led to speculation and a crash. Five or six years later losses brought on by the war with the American Colonies caused serious business difficulties. When this war ended, in 1783, peace once more gave rise to a sudden expansion of business and the expansion ended in a crisis. Finally, in 1793, came what the historian of these events calls the first of England's great industrial crises, followed by depression in general business.[2]

This brief recital indicates that business cycles are much later in appearing than economic, or even strictly financial crises. In England itself they seem not to have begun before the close of the eighteenth century. But when they did appear, it was in the form of an extension over all branches of industry of difficulties not unlike those which had been suffered for more than a hundred years by large capitalists, bankers, and speculators in stocks. With this extension in scope came a shift in the relative importance of the causes. In the past, the undermining of credit had usually been caused by war, by the making of peace, or by some violation of financial obligations on the part of government. In the future, it was to be caused more frequently by stresses engendered within the world of business itself.

The reason for both changes lay in the gradual extension of the highly organized business enterprise from its earlier centers of foreign commerce, mining, finance, and banking over the wide field of manufacturing and domestic trade—an extension that accompanied the Industrial Revolution. As handicraft gave place to factories managed on business principles, catering to a wide and uncertain market, entering freely into long-term contracts, requiring a heavy investment of fixed capital, and using borrowed money on a liberal scale, the circle of enterprises affected by financial difficulties grew steadily larger, and the danger that financial difficulties would arise from the conduct of business affairs grew steadily greater.

Moreover, as manufacturing and domestic trade became dependent upon the money and investment markets, crises began regularly to be followed by periods of liquidation in manufacturing and mercantile circles. But since the financial difficulties now arose largely from the embarrassment of manufacturers and merchants, a thoroughgoing liquidation on the part of the latter ended the conditions that had caused the crisis and paved the way for a resumption of business activity. And since both the accumulation and the relaxing of these stresses came about regularly as a byproduct of business processes, the irregular, unpredictable crises of the past turned gradually into the cycles of prosperity, crisis, and depression upon which men have come to count and which they are beginning to forecast.

In proportion as the Industrial Revolution and its concomitant changes in the organization of commerce and transportation spread to other countries, the latter began to develop the phenomena of business cycles already familiar in England. And in proportion as the business enterprise completed its domination of manufacturing, wholesale trade, finance, transportation, mining, and lumbering, and began to invade retail trade, the professions, and agriculture, the cyclical oscillations of expansion and contraction brought more and more men under their immediate sway.

2. MAN'S MASTERY OVER THE WORKINGS OF THE MONEY ECONOMY

Business cycles, then, appear at that stage of economic history when the process of making and distributing goods is organized chiefly in the form of business enterprises conducted for profit.

This form of economic organization has been gradually developed out of earlier forms by successive generations of men who have thought to gain some advantage from each successive step. But the complicated machinery and the working of the system are not fully mastered even by the present generation of businessmen, and recurrently the financial machinery inflicts grave suffering upon us who use it. Because we have not learned how to prevent costs from encroaching upon profits and stringency from accumulating in the money markets, how to keep steady the construction of new industrial equipment, how to control the market capitalization of business enterprises, and how to avoid spasmodic expansions and contractions of credits—because our theoretical knowledge and our practical skill are deficient concerning these technical matters, we cannot maintain prosperity for more than a few years at a time.

Nevertheless, within the past century, we have progressed toward mastery over the processes of the money economy. The Tulip Mania in Holland, the South Sea Scheme in England, and the Mississippi Bubble in France have no worthy rivals in recent decades. Even the speculative excitement that preceded the crisis of 1873 in the German states and in America has scarcely been equaled since 1890. By a combination of various agencies such as public regulation of the prospectuses of new companies, legislation supported by efficient administration against fraudulent promotion, more rigid requirements on the part of stock exchanges concerning the securities admitted to official lists, more efficient agencies for giving investors information, and more conservative policy on the part of the banks toward speculative booms, we have learned to avoid certain of the rashest errors committed by earlier generations. Again, from hard experience, European banks at least have learned methods of controlling a crisis and preventing it from turning into a panic. The 'integration of industry' has also done something, though less than is often claimed, toward steadying the course of business both by concentrating power in the hands of experienced officials and by moderating the extreme fluctuations of prices.

3. PROPOSALS FOR CONTROLLING BUSINESS CYCLES

What has already been accomplished in these directions toward controlling our business machinery may well be the earnest of greater achievements. Three promising lines of effort are suggested by the proposals to reorganize the American banking system, to use governmental and railway purchases as a business balance wheel, and to 'stabilize the dollar.'

The first proposal aims primarily at preventing crises from becoming panics. Its feasibility has been demonstrated by European and Canadian experience, and practical plans have been worked out in detail by the Monetary Commission, congressional committees, bankers' associations, and private investigators. Indeed, banking reform is both the most needed and the easiest among all the changes that promise to increase our control over the workings of the money economy. But the literature upon this subject is so large and so accessible that there is no need to go into detail in this book.

The second proposal, to use governmental and railway purchases as a balance wheel to steady the business mechanism, aims primarily at mitigating the severity of depressions. It has been formulated most definitely in France and in England. In 1907 the French Minister of Public Works directed that inquiry be made concerning the effect of crises upon railways. The report argued that it is feasible for the great railway systems to distribute their orders for rolling stock, and so forth, systematically over the full period of a business cycle in such fashion as to reduce the orders now placed in busy years and to increase the volume in dull years. This change would be to the financial advantage of the railways in that equipment is cheaper to build in years of depression, to the advantage of shippers in that a more timely provision of rolling stock would diminish the frequency of freight blockades and car famines, and to the advantage of the public in that employment would be steadied in an important industry. By way of applying these ideas the Minister of Public Works in May 1907 invited the railways to submit a definite program for the purchase of rolling stock covering the years 1907–10.[8]

More ambitious in scope and different in emphasis is the scheme worked out by Mr. and Mrs. Sidney Webb. As part of a comprehensive plan for the prevention of destitution, they propose that a portion of government contracts be held back in years of intense activity and let out in slack years. Dr. A. L. Bowley's figures, on which they rely, indicate that if only 3 or 4 per cent of the government's orders were treated in this fashion, a very large part of the unemployment now caused by cyclical depressions might be counterbalanced. Among the items that could be relegated to a ten-year program, and put to contract only when trade gave signs of falling off, they mention: " . . . one-half of the yearly appropriation for rebuilding and multiplying . . . government buildings . . . ; one-half of the normal annual provision for such stores as blankets, canvas, and khaki cloth, of which there is always a large stock; the whole (or one-half) of the sum allocated annually to the gradual placing of telegraph wires underground, and the gradual extension of the telephone into every little village; the whole of such print-ing as the reports of the Historical Manuscripts Commission, and the official history of the South African War; at least one-half of the annual expenditure on developing the Government forests . . . ; a considerable proportion of the Board of Educa-tion grants for the building of new training colleges and sec-ondary schools; some part of the year's normal shipbuilding . . . ; at least one-half of the annual appropriation for new rifle ranges and drill halls for the Territorial Force; most of the capital expenditure of the Congested Districts Board in Ire-land, and so on. And to this should be added the whole of the sums, amounting to more than a million a year, already placed at the disposal of the Development Commissioners and the Road Board. It is very clear [they conclude] that there is, in the aggregate, a very large amount—out of which the total of four millions a year could easily be selected—and a very considerable variety of expenditure which could, without any appreciable inconvenience, be rearranged within the decade.'"[4]

Finally, if Professor Irving Fisher's ingenious plan of 'stabil-izing the dollar' were adopted, and if it succeeded in keeping fluctuations of the price level within narrow limits, the course of business cycles would doubtless become more even than at present. For if every rise or fall in commodity prices were checked promptly, one of the chief factors now causing changes in the prospects of profits would be virtually removed. Of course there might still occur unequal changes in the relative prices of raw materials and finished products, of consumers' goods at wholesale and retail, or of labor and loans, which would affect profit margins without disturbing in equivalent degree the general index number used as a basis for compensating the dollar. Profits would also be subject to changes arising from variations in the volume of business, in the efficiency of labor, and so forth. But since the magnitude of the effects now produced by these factors results from their cumulative action in heightening one another's intensity, the paralyzing of one potent factor would render the others also less potent.

The feasibility of carrying out these proposals, aside from banking reform, has not been demonstrated on a large scale. Certainly all three plans merit careful consideration. They are brought forward here, however, merely to suggest possible ways in which man's control over the workings of the money economy may be increased.

Apart from such specific reforms in economic organization, progress lies in the direction of bettering our forecasts of business conditions. For when coming troubles are foreseen they may often be mitigated, and sometimes averted.

IV. Forecasting Business Conditions

The uncertainty attending forecasts arises chiefly from the imperfections of our knowledge concerning business conditions in the immediate past and in the present. For, since business cycles result from processes of cumulative change, the main factors in shaping tomorrow are the factors that were at work yesterday and are at work today.

Now the money economy affords most unequal insight into its own workings to different classes of businessmen. These inequalities open a rich source of profit to the favored class, and their efforts to make the most of their chances may increase the violence of crises. One way of increasing social control over economic activity is therefore to democratize the knowledge of current business conditions already possessed by a few. But the ways and means to this end can be discussed better after the present inequalities of knowledge and their consequences have been set forth.

1. EXCEPTIONAL OPPORTUNITIES OF CERTAIN FINANCIERS

Concerning the business condition of crucial importance— fluctuations in profits—it is especially difficult to obtain prompt, reliable, and wide information. Certain men are so placed in the business world, however, that they have a wide outlook over profits, and so trained that they can draw fairly safe conclusions concerning the trend of the changes going forward. The greater capitalists who are actively participating in many enterprises and who have intimate personal relations with other captains of industry are in this position of vantage, as are also the managers of the largest banks. Doubtless the information at the disposal of even these men at the center of the financial system leaves much to be desired in scope and accuracy. Doubtless the inferences they draw are warped by their personal equations and their forecasts diverge appreciably. But could these gentlemen be induced to publish frankly what they know concerning the present and what they really expect in the near future, it is probable that the consensus of their opinions would seldom prove far wrong.

However, this superior foresight is a business asset of too much value to be given away. The man of large means who can forecast the coming of a crisis is able to shift his holdings in such fashion as to avoid losses that will fall upon the unwary and to profit by having funds in hand for buying property at bargain prices. Not until his own affairs have been thus arranged is he likely to take the public into his confidence. When he does speak it may well be with a view toward influencing the trend of sentiment among lesser businessmen and investors to his own advantage. The public, therefore, has good reason to read in a highly critical spirit the interviews prominent financiers occasionally give out.

The advantage enjoyed by this small group of major financiers is not limited to superior opportunities for foreseeing approaching changes. In a measure they can control the events they forecast. This ability arises chiefly from the increasing centralization of power to grant or withhold credits. On the one hand, the rise of the great corporation has made the business enterprises of strategic importance dependent upon the metropolitan markets for loans and securities, rather than upon local banks and investors. On the other hand, the great banks, insurance companies, and investment houses that dominate the financial markets of New York, London, Paris, and Berlin have developed intimate relations and can be controlled by a few small coteries of financiers. To these men is therefore given a large measure of power over the granting of bank loans, the floating of new securities, and the prices of outstanding stocks and bonds. This power they can use, if they choose, to increase the stresses prosperity breeds. If they lock up large sums, for example, they reduce the reserves of banks and precipitate the downward revision of credits with which a crisis begins. If they block corporations from raising loans needed to meet maturing obligations, they force the appointment of receivers, beat down the price of stocks, and create a sentiment of distrust that produces further consequences of its own.

What little is known of the "inside workings of high finance" indicates that this power has not yet been exercised with ruthless efficiency. Doubtless many businessmen would recoil from the idea of deliberately aggravating a crisis for their own gain. Moreover, the financiers who have most power over credit are often heavily interested in industrial enterprises, and fear to lose dividends in the depression that would follow a crisis. A third deterrent is the obsession that the dollar is a stable measure of value. So accustomed do businessmen become to treating the dollar as constant, and imputing all changes in prices to fluctuations in the value of the goods quoted, that they do not readily grasp the money profit to be made out of changes in the general level of prices. Finally, even in the highest circles of finance, centralization of power has not yet gone far enough to guarantee unanimity of action.[5]

Among these deterrents from the effort to aggravate the fluctuations of business conditions, two at least seem to be losing their force. The increasing mobility of investments is making it easier for financiers to extricate their funds from industrial entanglements and put them into such form that a depression can bring no serious loss. And the continual fluctuations in the price level are ever demonstrating that dollars are shifting units, out of whose fluctuations profits might be realized. It is therefore quite possible that financiers may exploit their opportunities of aggravating crises with greater energy in the immediate future than they have in the recent past.[6]

If their efforts in this direction become more energetic, it may be expected that the old-fashioned capitalists who are interested primarily in the uninterrupted conduct of industrial operations will join with the great number of smaller businessmen to safeguard themselves from raids upon credit. Probably the demand for government regulation, which is directed at present chiefly toward regulation of railway and industrial corporations, would then be extended to regulation of all the financial operations concerned with the granting of loans. But it is not yet clear precisely how government could intervene to prevent powerful groups of financiers from locking up money when they saw fit, from refusing banking accommodation when they chose, or from declining to underwrite new issues of securities for corporations out of favor.

Indeed, the increase of governmental regulation in industry may make the most aggressive capitalists more eager to interest themselves primarily in finance and to exploit to the utmost their opportunities of manipulating credit. In that case a second line of defense may be followed by many whose business prospects are jeopardized. If reliable information concerning profits and credits, such as now exists in partial form and in few hands, were collected and published, the strategic advantage of the great financiers in forecasting crises would be materially reduced. For then everyone interested could take such precautions when prosperity was seen to be breeding a crisis as his affairs required and his judgment suggested. Indeed, everyone within the measure allowed by his pecuniary resources might endeavor to turn the coming crisis to his own profit— a condition that would result in few being caught at a disadvantage. The field left open for predatory exploitation by financiers would be reduced to the production of sudden contractions of credit of which the statistics of profits and credits had given no warning. That is to say, these campaigns would run counter to the general trend of business developments and would therefore be far less destructive than campaigns reinforced by the stresses accumulated by prosperity.

But all this concerns a problematical future. How do matters stand with the business public at present?

2. BUSINESS BAROMETERS AVAILABLE TO THE PUBLIC

The American man of affairs who seeks to keep informed about the trend of business conditions at large relies upon the financial columns of his daily paper, supplemented perhaps by one or two financial weeklies and a special trade journal. The data he can compile from these sources cover a considerable range.

Commodity prices at wholesale are represented both by actual quotations for the great staples of commerce and by index numbers like Bradstreet's. The prices of loans on call and on time for thirty days to six months are reported for New York, together with the market and bank rates in London, Paris, and Berlin. The prices of securities dealt in on the New York exchange are published in detail, and for the general trend of the market there are convenient records such as the *Wall Street Journal's* average actual prices of twenty railway and twelve industrial stocks.

Fluctuations in business must be estimated from various sources: bank clearings, railway gross earnings, number of idle cars, imports and exports, coal, copper, pig iron, and steel output, shipments of grain, cotton, livestock, etc. Government crop reports help to forecast the probable state of trade in various agricultural sections. Less systematic but often helpful are the numerous reviews of business conditions in different trades and cities published at regular intervals by several weekly papers.

Information about the currency is supplied by the official estimates of the monetary stock, by reports of gold imports and exports, by the recorded movements of money into and out of the New York banks, and by the figures concerning production and industrial consumption of gold, and the distribution of money between the banks and the public—though these last three statements come but once a year. Regarding the banks there are telegraphic statements from the central institutions of Europe, weekly reports from the clearing-houses of New York, Boston, and Philadelphia, five reports a year from the national banks, and a variety of official and private reports of banks organized under state laws.

Some idea of the amount of investment and speculation going on may be obtained from the transactions of the New York Stock Exchange, the number of building permits granted, the mileage of railway under construction, and from the less systematic news items concerning fresh contracts let, security issues offered to the public, and the like.

Last and most important are the prospects of profits for the railways, whose gross and net earnings are published and commented upon with unfailing interest. The earnings of the United States Steel Corporation probably stand second in general esteem. Then comes a miscellaneous mass of information supplied by such reports as the large corporations engaged in various branches of mining, manufacturing, and banking choose to make public. The other side of the shield is reflected by the statistics of bankruptcy compiled weekly by two great mercantile agencies.

Though far from complete, this list of materials for gauging the trend of business conditions is long. In fact, it is all too long for the average businessman. To compile and to analyze the available data requires more time, more effort, more statistical skill, or more analytic ability than most men have to spend on the task. Hence the typical man of affairs skips the bewildering evidence and reads only the summary conclusions drawn by the editor of his financial paper or by the forecasting agency to which he subscribes. That the studying of business barometers and the forecasting of business weather has itself become a profitable business affords convincing proof at once of the need and the difficulty of using effectively materials published to all. It is from such specialists, rather than from the average merchant and manufacturer, that we may expect the improving and disseminating of the information required as a basis for perfecting social control over the workings of the money economy.

Now, these professional forecasters attached to the staffs of financial papers, investment houses, and the like do not find the data already at hand too elaborate. They have the time and the patience, they will acquire whatever they now lack of statistical technique and analytical skill to extract the essence from large masses of data. What they most need to improve their forecasts is more extensive and more reliable materials to work upon. But it is also quite possible to better the use they make of data already available.

In the next section certain suggestions are offered for constructing new and improving old business barometers. Since they have grown out of an effort to understand recent cycles, these suggestions may be of service to professional business forecasters if not to the business public.

3. SUGGESTIONS FOR BETTERING BUSINESS BAROMETERS
A. New Barometers Needed

Among the most needed additions to the list of American business barometers are the following:

A general index number of the physical volume of trade could be made from data on the production of certain staples, the shipments or receipts of others, the records of foreign commerce, and similar sources. In the Appendix of his *Purchasing Power of Money* Irving Fisher has shown that much material for this purpose is already incidentally provided in official documents, and doubtless much more could be had for an inquiry that did not go back of 1900 or 1905. Separate averages should be struck for the great departments of industry, since the differences between the relative activity in different lines would often be not less significant than the computed changes in the total. So far as feasible these subdivisions of the index number of the physical volume of trade should be made to correspond with those of the wholesale price index.

Mr. Hull's plan for obtaining reports on contracts let for construction work and the percentage of work performed upon old contracts merits careful consideration.[7] Since it comes from a man intimately acquainted with the business, the feasibility of the plan cannot be lightly denied. Few sets of figures would give more insight into business conditions when prosperity was verging toward a crisis or when depression was paving the way for prosperity.

An index number of the relative prices of bonds, and corresponding figures giving changes in interest rates upon long-term loans, would not be difficult to prepare.[8] Even if standing alone, these two series would possess great value as reflecting the attitude of investors; but they would be still more useful if accompanied by data on the amount of bonds and short-term notes put on the market by business enterprises and by governments, whether central or local.

Certain states—notably New York and Massachusetts—have begun to compile statistics of unemployment on a modest scale. But we have no comprehensive data of this kind comparable with those for Great Britain, France, and Germany. Their value, as an index not only of welfare among wage earners, but also of changes in activity within important industries and changes in the demand for consumers' goods is such as to make this deficiency of American statistics of grave concern.

Most to be desired of all are statistics depicting the relative fluctuations of costs and profits. Unhappily, the difficulties both theoretical and practical in the way of obtaining such figures are especially great. But certainly every extension of public authority over corporate activity should be utilized to require such uniform methods of accounting as have been imposed upon the interstate railways, and the reports obtained by the government should be made available in some significant form for the information of the business public.

Finally, the information practically available in forecasting business conditions could be materially increased by prompter publication of many of the data supplied by the government. In numerous cases extremely valuable figures are not given to the press until they have become matters of historical interest rather than current news.

B. Improvement of Old Barometers

The index numbers of commodity prices at wholesale would be more useful were separate series computed for raw materials and for the articles manufactured from them, and were raw materials subdivided into farm, animal, forest, and mineral products. Differences in the fluctuations of these several groups would be of great assistance in determining the causes, and therefore the significance, of changes in the grand total. Further, an index number of identical commodities in the United States, Great Britain, France, and Germany would facilitate the effort to follow the concomitant courses of business cycles in different countries and to anticipate the reaction of foreign upon domestic conditions.

Stock prices should be computed upon the index-number plan instead of in the current form of average actual prices of shares in a selected list of corporations or the aggregate market values of certain issues of securities. To facilitate comparisons the basis chosen for the index number of stocks should agree with that chosen for commodity prices. The distinctively investment stocks should be separated from the speculative favorites, and averages should be struck for railways, industrials, and public utilities. By proper selection of data fluctuations in the average relative prices of the industrial stocks might be made to reflect the fortunes of enterprises especially concerned with the providing of industrial equipment. In contrast, the public-utility stocks would be affected by a relatively steady consumers' demand, and railway stocks by the activity of general business.

The weekly and monthly reports of clearings also would be more useful were they accompanied by index numbers that reflected the relative magnitude of the changes in actual amounts. Separate averages of these relative figures should be provided for the centers in which financial operations, industrial activity, and agricultural conditions are the dominant factors.

Banking statistics would be more instructive were the actual amounts of the leading items supplemented by ratios not only of reserves to deposits, but also of loans to deposits. Another set of relative figures should be made to reflect the amplitude of the fluctuations in the leading items. If the clearing-house associations would require from their members and make public accurate returns of the receipts and shipments of currency the activity of business in various sections could be followed with greater certainty. Finally, one of the darkest points of current business conditions in America could be cleared up if the rates of discount upon first-class commercial paper in these various centers could be regularly ascertained. But perhaps no thoroughly comparable statistics of discount rates can be compiled until the varying qualities of commercial paper now in circulation have been standardized by permitting the national banks to accept drafts after the European fashion.

To extend this list of suggestions for bettering figures of the sorts already published would be easy; but enough has been said to make clear the character of the desirable changes. In general, the need is for more careful discrimination between dissimilar data now often lumped together in a single total, the collecting from new centers of data already published for New York, more uniform methods of compilation to guarantee the comparability of what purport to be similar figures, and the computing of relative fluctuations upon a common basis. In many if not all cases a double set of relative figures is highly desirable—one set referring to average actual amounts in some fixed decade, the other set making comparisons with the corresponding period of the preceding year.

C. Difficulties

When the discussion of how to improve our control over the workings of the money economy is thus brought down to practical details, the complexity of the task becomes patent. Scarcely one of the suggestions for bettering or extending the indices of business conditions but calls to mind various obstacles that hinder the getting of trustworthy data—the reluctance of private interests to divulge information, the diversity of business practices in various trades and sections of the country, the continual changes in business organization, modifications in the relative importance of different raw materials and still more in the kinds and qualities of manufactured products, the technical puzzles of statistical classification and averaging, etc. In view of these difficulties, the prospect of rapid improvement in the data for business forecasting is not so bright as might be desired.

The vigor of the efforts to overcome the difficulties will depend largely upon the demands of businessmen for better service. Today the one class that evinces the clearest sense of the usefulness of a comprehensive statistical survey of the business present as a basis for forecasting the business future is the speculator in stocks. But many men who prefer to call themselves investors, and an increasing number of brokers, bankers, merchants, manufacturers, contractors, and the like are becoming active consumers of such reports. Since these classes can be counted upon to subscribe to those papers and confidential agencies which give them the most satisfactory service, business forecasting will doubtless become a more extensive profession, and make such progress as is possible under private initiative spurred on by competition.

Concerning many lines of business, however, information that is both reliable and comprehensive cannot be obtained by private enterprise. Whether the government will extend the scope of its present activities in this field will probably be determined chiefly by large issues of public policy. For most of the figures compiled by the government are byproducts of measures taken with other ends in view than to increase the knowledge concerning the workings of the money economy. As the railway statistics are an incidental result of the interstate commerce law, the banking statistics of the National Banking Act, etc., so future additions to the government's statistical output will be made or not as public control over business affairs is extended or restricted.

Certainly the community as a whole has a deep interest in developing this branch of the government's work. The businessmen who study financial journals are chiefly concerned to make profits or to avoid losses arising from the ups and downs of the markets. The community, on the contrary, is interested in reducing the disturbances that these market ups and downs cause in the process of producing and distributing useful goods. But so long as this process of producing and distributing useful goods is subordinated to the process of making money, the community's interest in steadying the pace of economic activity can be promoted by giving all businessmen alike the best possible opportunities for knowing the present and forecasting the future. However, a vivid realization of what might be accomplished along this line for the general welfare is not common. More direct efforts to apply governmental agencies to the correction of what are deemed to be ill results of business enterprise appeal more strongly to the majority of voters. Hence it is those who desire to see the present form of economic organization perfected rather than fundamentally changed who are most concerned with pressing the demand for better governmental reporting of business conditions.

V. The 'Money Surface of Things' and What Goes on Beneath

The preceding theory of business cycles is concerned mainly with the pecuniary phases of economic activity. The processes described relate to changes in prices, investments, margins of profit, market capitalization of business enterprises, credits, the maintenance of solvency, and the like—all relating to the making of money, rather than to the making of goods or to the satisfaction of wants. Only two nonpecuniary factors command much attention—changes in the physical volume of trade and in the efficiency of labor—and even these two are treated with reference to their bearing upon present and prospective profits.

The reason for thus staying upon the 'money surface of things' in analyzing business cycles, rather than attempting to penetrate beneath to the motives that actuate economic conduct, is the reason set forth in Part II, Chapter II. Modern economic activity is immediately animated and guided, not by the quest of satisfactions, but by the quest of profits. Therefore business cycles are distinctly phenomena of a pecuniary as opposed to an industrial character. To dip beneath the business considerations relating to profit and loss, to deal with 'psychic income' and 'psychic cost,' even to deal with physical production and consumption in other than their pecuniary bearings, is to distort the problem. For the processes actually involved in bringing about prosperity, crises, and depression are the processes performed by businessmen in endeavoring to make money. Businessmen refuse to complicate their problems by going back of the dollar to that for which the dollar stands, and he who would understand what they are doing must treat their action as it is.

But if the causes of business cycles that are important to trace lie almost wholly within the pecuniary order, the consequences of moment are matters of human well-being. The ways in which business prosperity, crisis, and depression react upon the bodily and mental welfare of the community are so numerous, however, that it is feasible to mention only a few of the most significant.

First, the provision made for satisfying the community's needs—the physical volume of current production—grows more abundant when business is prosperous and more scanty in the earlier stages of business depression. But neither the expansion nor the shrinkage in this supply of useful goods is as great as the expansion and the shrinkage in the corresponding pecuniary values. And the alteration that does occur in the output of industry is distinctly greater with reference to producers' than to stable consumers' goods. That is, the amount of food, clothing, and the like produced by the community for its own current use is steadier than the business barometers suggest.

Upon the distribution of this current supply of useful goods business cycles exert a strong influence, since they produce widespread changes in both money incomes and the purchasing power of dollars. The precarious plight of the wage earner's family in the money economy consists largely in the shrinkage of employment caused by business depression. The physical privations, the anxieties, and the humiliations forced upon this class by inability to find work are not only themselves a grievous evil but also prolific sources of further evils—intemperance, prostitution, chronic idleness, the desertion of families, and the stunting of children. Profits doubtless shrink in larger proportion than wages, and many families that draw their income from this source are forced to adopt painful economies and to endure much anxiety, though they seldom suffer such extreme hardships as those of wage earners out of work. On the other hand, the relatively small class of persons whose incomes really do remain fixed during depression profit by the reduced cost of living; for this material advantage, however, they pay a heavy price in uncertainty and in sympathetic participation in the sufferings of others.

Business cycles also affect material well-being by influencing the selection of business leaders, the centralization of economic power, and the progress of industrial technique.

Prosperity stimulates enterprise and encourages businessmen to set up for themselves. But by making it easier for the unfit managers to survive for a time, it reduces somewhat the community's economic efficiency. Even the abler businessmen, under the press of hurry, relax somewhat their precautions against waste. Meanwhile investors become more inclined toward rash ventures, and an increasing proportion of society's energy is thrown away in unprofitable undertakings. Crisis and depression, on the contrary, serve at least to weed out the less competent managers, to enforce vigilant attention to detail upon all, and to make investors cautious.

The foreclosure sales and reorganizations to which depression gives rise afford the best opportunity for the increase of fortunes already large, and for the rise of business magnates already powerful.[9] In this way depression promotes the centralization of control in the world of business. But, on the contrary, it often weakens or destroys loosely cemented alliances or pools for the regulation of competition. And the promotion of great combinations among business enterprises formerly independent is usually undertaken in the middle stages of prosperity, when investors are optimistically inclined and before the money and bond markets have become stringent.

For the progress of industrial technique, in the sense of the practical application of improvements already invented, the most favorable phase of the business cycle is the revival. Depression forces men to cast about for any feasible method of reducing cost; but it offers little inducement for the immediate expenditure of large sums upon improvements. It is the season when alterations are planned; revival is the season when they are executed on the largest scale. Prosperity is less favorable, not for lack of funds, but for lack of time and attention.

In general, prosperity is a season of strenuous activity, recompensed by material comfort and enlivened by high hopes. Its chief social drawbacks are the waste incidental to hurry, the extravagance bred by affluence and optimism, the obsession of attention by business interests, and the anxieties that cloud its later days. A crisis intensifies these anxieties, particularly for businessmen and investors. The turmoil subsides in depression; but the subsidence brings despondency upon those whose fears have been realized, and leaves others with a dull outlook at best. To workingmen it is the season of most suffering—of overdriving when at work and of privation when on the street. For these disadvantages its repression of waste, stimulation of plans for technical improvements, and enforcement of caution concerning investments are but partial compensation.

Brief as it is, this statement of how business cycles react upon social well-being suffices to suggest the double personality acquired by citizens of the money economy. Money making for the individual, business prosperity for the nation, are artificial ends of endeavor imposed by pecuniary institutions. Beneath one lie the individual's impulsive activities—his maze of instinctive reactions partly systematized into conscious wants, definite knowledge, and purposeful efforts. Beneath the other lie the vague and conflicting ideals of social welfare that members of each generation refashion after their own images. In this dim inner world lie the ultimate motives and meanings of action, and from it emerge the wavering standards by which men judge what is for them worth while.

The money economy has not supplanted, but it has harnessed these forces. Upon human activity and human ideals it has stamped its own pattern. How it has facilitated the division of labor, how it has given a pecuniary twist to the desire for distinction, how it has shifted the basis of political power and given rise to new social classes—these results of the money economy are widely recognized. How it has taught men to think in terms of its own formal logic, efficient within certain limits but arid when pushed to extremes, has been partly worked out by writers like Simmel, Sombart, and Veblen. How its technical exigencies subject economic activity to continual alternations of expansion and contraction this book has aimed to describe in detail.

Subject as men are to the sway of pecuniary concepts and ideals, they can still judge the workings of the money economy by more intimate and more vital standards. To make these latter standards clear, to show in what definite ways the quest of profits transgresses them, and to devise feasible methods of remedying these ill results, is a large part of the task of social reform. Economic theory will not prove of much use in this work unless it grasps the relations among the pecuniary institutions civilized man is perfecting, the human nature he inherits from savage ancestors, and the new forces science lends him. To treat money as an empty symbol that 'makes no difference save one of convenience' is a habit exceeded in superficiality only by the habit against which it protests—that of treating money-making as the ultimate goal of effort.

NOTES

Chapter 1. The Cumulation of Prosperity

[1] The quickening of activity in the autumn of 1900 hardly deserves to be included in this list, because the preceding slackening of activity had been so mild, so restricted, and so brief.

[2] See the relevant sections of Part II, Chapter III, in my *Business Cycles*, Vol. 3 of *Memoirs of the University of California*, 1913.

[3] Again see the relevant sections of Part II, Chapter III.

[4] See Part I, Chapter III, section iii, 1 and 5.

[5] Compare Part II, Chapter V, section vi.

[6] Compare Part II, Chapter II, ii, 1.

[7] This statement is based upon a comparison between the leading indices of the volume of business presented in Part II, Chapter V, and the revivals in business activity pointed out in Part I, Chapter III. For further discussion of the increase in business during depressions see Chapter 4, ii, 3.

[8] Though the recovery of business from the depression that followed the crisis of 1890 is dated from the year 1895 in England and France, the English and French index numbers in Part II, table 11, indicate not only that prices failed to rise in 1895 but that they continued to decline in 1896, and advanced merely a trifle in 1897. On the contrary, English index numbers show a slight rise in 1904, though the revival of business can scarcely be said to have begun before 1905. Therefore the failure of index numbers to rise does not justify the inference that business has not improved, and the occurrence of a rise does not justify the inference that depression is past.

[9] See the tables in Part II relating to these various subjects and note the fluctuations in the years of revival and the years immediately preceding.

[10] See section i, and for a more thorough analysis, Chapter 4, ii, 1 and 2.

[11] Certainly the advance of prices in this country was more rapid than in foreign countries where the revival was sustained. See the index numbers for identical lists of commodities in the United States and other countries, Part II, table 12, and the confirmatory evidence borne by table 11.

A. D. Noyes, *Forty Years of American Finance* (New York, 1909), pp. 245, 246, expresses the opinion that an overrapid advance of prices contributed also to checking the revival of 1895. While the above mentioned tables do not show a marked difference between the course of prices in America, where the revival was short lived, and in Europe, where it developed into full-blown prosperity, the accompanying detailed comparisons by months lend a rather equivocal support to Noyes's opinion.

RELATIVE PRICES AT WHOLESALE IN THE UNITED STATES, ENGLAND, AND GERMANY, BY MONTHS, 1895-96

Month	United States		England	Germany
	Falkner	Bradstreet	Sauerbeck	Schmitz
1895—April	84.7	5.97	61.7	83.47
July	85.2	6.42	62.8	84.30
October	86.3	6.52	63.3	84.70
1896—January	85.2	6.31	61.4	83.82

[12] See Part II, Chapter IV, i, 7.

[13] See Part II, Chapter IV, i, 8.

[14] See Part II, tables 9 and 10, and the discussion appended to each—Chapter IV, i, 8.

[15] See Part II, Chapter IV, i, 3-6.

[16] Of course rent, wages, and interest charges are themselves aggregates of prices paid for certain business adjuncts. What happens, then, is that certain prices that enter into the cost of retailing rise less rapidly than wholesale prices of wares. Hence the lagging of retail behind wholesale prices may be described as an adjustment of retail prices to the *aggregate* of the prices the shopkeeper must pay.

[17] After this chapter was written, Professor E. S. Meade published an index number of the prices of 18 commodities produced by trusts and of 18 commodities produced under competitive conditions. His data were obtained from the Bureau of Labor and his relative prices were computed on the basis of actual prices in January 1897. The articles selected and the results obtained are as follows:

Non-trust	Trust
Manila rope	Anthracite coal
Bituminous coal (Youghiogheny)	American cement
New Orleans molasses	Refined petroleum
Pig-iron (Bessemer, Pittsburgh)	Cotton-seed oil
Bleached sheetings	Glucose
Corn meal	Newsprint
Yellow pine	Proof spirits
Plain white oak	Leather
Print cloth	Wire nails
Glass tumblers	Steel rails
Vici kid shoes	Raw linseed oil
Sheet zinc	Pig lead
Flour (New York)	American fine salt
Cotton	Plug tobacco
Bare copper wire	Sulphuric acid
Wilton carpet	Granulated sugar
Earthenware plates	Cotton thread
Bleached shirtings	Domestic parlor matches

	Non-Trust	Trust	Non-Trust	Trust	Non-Trust	Trust
	1897		1898		1899	
January	100.0	100.0	98.7	104.9	102.7	105.9
February	99.8	98.3	98.7	104.9	104.5	108.1
March	99.8	100.2	94.6	105.4	108.3	110.5
April	99.4	99.9	100.2	104.1	110.8	113.7
May	99.2	99.9	102.2	106.5	112.2	113.9
June	98.2	100.8	104.4	107.1	114.4	114.6
July	98.2	100.9	104.3	107.1	113.6	116.1
August	99.3	105.7	103.8	107.2	115.5	116.8
September	100.9	108.3	103.5	104.5	119.9	119.0
October	99.9	107.2	101.9	103.2	121.3	122.0
November	98.5	104.0	102.6	104.8	121.4	124.0
December	98.7	104.0	102.2	104.1	127.3	127.2
	1900		1901		1902	
January	131.6	130.1	119.2	126.5	123.7	126.2
February	132.1	133.3	119.1	128.7	124.3	129.1
March	134.0	133.4	118.7	128.6	125.2	130.2
April	134.1	133.6	119.5	128.8	125.2	129.8
May	131.9	130.5	117.3	127.5	128.0	128.8
June	128.3	131.3	117.5	126.9	128.0	128.3
July	136.9	131.0	117.0	131.3	128.0	130.4
August	123.5	128.8	118.2	131.1	127.3	129.6
September	121.2	128.9	120.1	126.8	127.3	127.7
October	121.2	128.8	121.3	128.3	128.6	125.2
November	119.7	131.0	123.3	127.4	129.5	123.1
December	119.1	128.0	124.4	125.9	128.3	125.4
	1903		1904		1905	
January	127.8	124.4	127.1	122.3	125.1	122.9
February	127.8	124.5	130.5	124.5	124.0	120.4
March	127.9	127.2	130.7	124.7	124.4	121.7
April	128.8	127.8	131.5	125.2	124.5	120.9
May	128.9	126.4	128.2	123.3	124.5	121.8
June	131.3	126.3	130.4	122.0	125.5	122.8
July	131.3	125.8	124.2	122.8	128.3	121.0
August	132.4	125.2	122.9	121.4	130.5	121.8
September	131.5	124.6	119.0	121.5	130.7	123.8
October	128.2	125.4	123.9	121.6	130.5	121.5
November	127.4	122.5	126.8	114.8	133.7	122.2
December	126.5	123.7	129.3	123.3	135.5	123.0
	1906		1907		1908	
January	135.9	124.5	142.1	130.2	142.7	130.1
February	135.2	126.3	143.8	130.2	142.2	130.0
March	133.7	122.7	147.2	131.7	138.5	131.8
April	136.5	126.1	147.5	131.4	136.0	130.1
May	136.7	124.4	147.7	131.8	135.9	129.8
June	136.8	124.2	153.8	135.3	132.0	131.2
July	136.8	123.9	154.5	132.9	131.8	129.8
August	136.6	125.7	152.3	133.1	131.5	131.0
September	136.6	125.3	146.5	133.3	130.1	131.4
October	137.6	126.3	148.3	133.1	131.7	132.0
November	141.1	126.8	146.9	130.4	132.1	130.3
December	142.8	130.0	142.1	130.1	133.3	131.5

	Non-Trust	Trust	Non-Trust	Trust		
	1909		1910			
January.........	133.3	129.2	144.4	136.7		
February........	133.2	130.8	143.9	135.2		
March...........	133.1	130.8	143.8	137.2		
April...........	133.0	128.0	142.9	135.6		
May.............	134.0	128.2	139.2	133.8		
June............	135.4	128.5	138.6	134.0		
July............	137.3	129.0	138.6	132.4		
August..........	138.9	128.5	138.6	138.4		
September........	138.9	130.4	137.4	141.4		
October.........	138.9	130.8	137.4	133.7		
November........	142.2	135.4	135.1	133.3		
December........	142.4	133.7	135.2	138.3		

From these figures Meade concludes (1) that in the years 1897–1900, while the trusts were in process of formation, the two series of relative prices ran nearly parallel; (2) that since 1900 the trust-made products have had lower relative prices than those made under conditions of competition; and (3) that the trust-made products have been decidedly more stable in price than the others, so far as concerns large fluctuations.—"The Economies of Combination," *Journal of Political Economy,* April, 1912. Professor Meade has kindly provided me with a revised version of his table, in which an error or two has been corrected.

[18] See Part II, Chapter V, i.

[19] Compare Part II, Chapter IV, i, 6.

[20] Table 28 (Part II) shows, for example, that in London and Paris both the market and the bank rates were lower in 1895 than in 1894, and that in these markets and in Berlin also the rates were lower in 1905 than in 1904. The more detailed data for New York, when averaged by phases of the business cycle, give similar results (Part II, table 26). Almost every time business conditions have improved discount rates have dropped. If the examination is pushed back into the monthly figures of table 22 (Part II), the situation is found to be complicated by the regularly recurring seasonal fluctuations in rates. But, when this factor has been allowed for, the conclusion remains that in their earlier stages business revivals are characterized by low and often by declining discount rates.

[21] Compare the ratios of cash on hand to demand liabilities in Part II, tables 82, 83, 89, 97, 100, and 104.

[22] Compare Part II, table 90, and the context.

[23] See Part II, tables 18–28.

[24] T. F. Woodlock, "The Stock Exchange and the Money Market," in *The Currency Problem and the Present Financial Situation, a Series of Lectures Delivered at Columbia University, 1907–08* (New York, 1908), p. 37; cf. Part II, Chapter VII, i.

[25] See Part II, Chapter IV, iii.

[26] See Part II, Chapter VIII, i.

[27] See Part II, Chapter IX, i.

[28] See Part II, chart 25.

[29] Compare Part II, Chapter IV, iv, 6.

[30] The accompanying figures compare the index number for 40 common stocks with the index numbers of prices at wholesale that are available by months for each period of revival in America since 1890.

	January	April	July	October	January
1891–92:					
Falkner's index..........	.....	.....	97.7	97.9	96.5
Railway stocks..........	.....	.....	102.5	125.0	128.0
1895–96:					
Falkner's index..........	84.7	84.7	85.2	86.3	85.2
Railway stocks..........	74.0	80.0	93.0	93.0	77.0
1897:					
Falkner's index..........	82.0	80.9	79.9	83.6	.....
Railway stocks..........	79.5	72.0	83.0	95.5	.....
1900–09:					
Bureau of Labor index...	111.4	112.9	109.3	108.7	108.3
Railway stocks..........	128.0	140.0	128.0	131.5	169.0
1904–05:					
Bureau of Labor index...	113.2	114.0	112.0	111.8	114.0
Railway stocks..........	184.0	172.5	177.5	217.5	236.5
1908–09:					
Bureau of Labor index...	125.7	124.0	121.7	122.1	124.0
Railway stocks..........	174.5	181.0	206.0	217.0	259.0

It would be a mistake to conclude from these figures that whenever stock prices rise commodity prices will presently follow. Table 44 (Part II) shows several instances in which the stock market turned upward and then relapsed again while commodity prices were falling.

[31] The deciles for the relative prices of 40 common stocks cover a wider range than the deciles for 145 commodities; see Part II, tables 33 and 8.

[32] See Part II, tables 34, 37, and 42, together with the accompanying text.

[33] An anomaly in the tables of applications for loans that may trouble readers at this point is explained in Chapter 4, i, 1, C.

Chapter 2. How Prosperity Breeds Crisis

[1] The accompanying figures from Part II, tables 9, 11, 15, and 17, compare the index of wages in manufacturing enterprises with the index of prices at wholesale in the United States and England during two cyclical expansions. The minus sign indicates a fall.

Year	United States				England			
	Wages	Prices	Advance during the year		Wages	Prices	Advance during the year	
			Wages	Prices			Wages	Prices
1897	99	89	−1	0	100	93	1	1
1898	100	93	1	4	102	97	2	4
1899	102	103	2	10	105	104	3	7
1900	105	111	3	8	111	115	6	9
1904	116	114	1	0	106	108	0	2
1905	118	116	2	2	106	111	0	3
1906	123	122	5	6	108	119	2	8
1907	129	130	6	8	113	123	5	4

In each of these four expansions the margin by which the rise in prices exceeds the rise in wages declines toward the end of the prosperous period; but in only one does the rise in prices in the culminating year fail to exceed the rise in wages.

[2] See Part II, table 68; compare A. de Lavergne and L. Paul Henry, *Le Chomage* (Paris, 1910), pp. 66–68.

[3] Compare W. H. Beveridge, *Unemployment* (London, 1909), pp. 21, 22.

[4] See Part II, p. 271.

[5] Compare Josephine Goldmark, *Fatigue and Efficiency* (New York, 1912), Chapter VI.

[6] P. 113. Similar statements from many sources may be found on pp. 21, 22, 146, 148, 159, 160, 164, 165, 168, 222, 273, 285, 327, 380, 382, 442, 711, 712, 810, 832, 884, and 910.

[7] The following figures relate to the 'operating roads' in the year ending June 30, 1909:

	Actual amounts in millions of dollars	Percentages of the total
Salaries	86	3.8
Wages	902	39.5
Other operating expenses	662	29.0
Taxes	85	3.7
Rents for leases of other roads	120	5.2
Interest	354	15.5
Miscellaneous	75	3.3
Total	2,284	100.0

Compiled from *Statistics of Railways in the United States for the Year Ending June 30, 1909.*

[8] Part II, Chapter IV, i, 3, 5, 6, and 9.

[9] The evidence, based on Part II, tables 3, 5, 6, 7, and 13, may be summarized as follows. Minus signs indicate that prices fell.

NUMBER OF POINTS BY WHICH RELATIVE PRICES ROSE

	1896–1900	1904–07	1908–09
25 foods at wholesale in the United States	17	9	..
25 foods at retail in the United States	6	11	..
23 foods at wholesale in England	10	6	2
19 foods at retail in England	8	1	0
23 foods at wholesale in France	11	12	0
36 foods at retail in France	−2	7	−5
20 raw materials	33	22	9
20 manufactured products	23	20	4
5 raw materials	30	10	16
5 partly manufactured products	20	5	10
5 finished commodities	11	12	1
45 raw producers' goods	30	22	9
28 manufactured producers' goods	24	18	−1
18 raw mineral products	27	24	2
23 manufactured mineral products	20	9	0
10 raw forest products	17	27	13
9 manufactured forest products	15	19	−1
9 raw animal products	29	21	20
18 manufactured animal products	20	13	8
18 raw farm products	35	9	7
40 manufactured farm products	16	15	−2

[10] Part II, Chapter IV, i, 6.

[11] The sources of raw materials are given as follows:

From farms	$1,941,000,000
From forests	119,000,000
From mines	320,000,000
From the sea	10,000,000
From all sources	$2,390,000,000

Twelfth Census of the United States, Manufactures, Part I, p. cxxxv. The "farm" products of this classification include both the animal and vegetable products of the tables in Part II, Chapter IV.

[12] "Rent of offices, insurance, interest, etc." all put together made only 6.4 per cent of the total manufacturing cost in 1900.—*Ibid.,* compare the data in Tables XLIX and I.

[13] A conspectus of the evidence obtained by comparing figures from Part II, tables 11 and 28, follows. To avoid the effect of crises in raising interest rates, the levels in the last year of depression and in the last year before the crisis are compared. The minus sign indicates a fall.

NUMBER OF POINTS BY WHICH RELATIVE PRICES AND RELATIVE DISCOUNT RATES ROSE

	1896–99	1904–06
Wholesale prices in America	14	8
Discount rates in New York	−38	31
Wholesale prices in England	12	11
Market discount rates in London	85	66
Wholesale prices in France	15	11
Market discount rates in Paris	53	27
Wholesale prices in Germany	14	16
Market discount rates in Berlin	47	30

The one exception to the rule that discount rates rise faster than prices cannot be wholly explained away by the tension in the New York money market caused by the free-silver campaign of 1896. If 1897 is compared with 1899 wholesale prices are found to have risen 14 points and discount rates only 10 points.

[14] The production of pig iron, for example, undergoes much wider fluctuations between seasons of prosperity and depression than the production of coal, as the following figures from Part II, tables 50 and 51, show.

RELATIVE PRODUCTION OF PIG IRON AND COAL IN THE UNITED STATES, UNITED KINGDOM, FRANCE, AND GERMANY, 1890–1910

Average actual production in 1890–99 = 100

Year	United States		United Kingdom		France		Germany	
	Pig iron	Coal	Pig iron	Coal	Pig iron	Coal	Pig iron	Coal
1890	98	82	99	95	88	93	79	83
1891	89	88	93	97	88	93	79	88
1892	98	93	84	95	93	93	84	86
1893	76	95	88	86	93	89	84	89
1894	72	89	93	98	93	96	91	92
1895	100	100	97	99	93	100	93	97
1896	92	100	109	102	107	103	109	105

(*Table continued on next page*)

RELATIVE PRODUCTION OF PIG IRON AND COAL IN THE UNITED STATES, UNITED KINGDOM, FRANCE, AND GERMANY, 1890–1910—(*Continued*)

Average actual production in 1890–99 = 100

Year	United States		United Kingdom		France		Germany	
	Pig iron	Coal	Pig iron	Coal	Pig iron	Coal	Pig iron	Coal
1897	104	105	111	106	112	107	117	113
1898	126	114	108	106	116	114	124	119
1899	145	133	118	115	116	114	138	127
1900	147	141	113	118	126	117	145	139
1901	170	153	99	115	112	114	134	143
1902	190	157	109	119	112	107	145	140
1903	192	186	112	120	130	121	171	152
1904	176	183	109	121	135	121	171	158
1905	246	205	121	124	140	125	185	162
1906	270	216	127	131	153	121	209	180
1907	276	251	127	140	163	128	219	192
1908	170	217	114	137	158	132	200	201
1909	276	240	121	138	163	132	214	203
1910	292	262	126	138	186	135	252	208
				Averages				
1890–99	100	100	100	100	100	100	100	100
1900–09	211	195	115	126	139	122	179	167

[15] They may, but they are far from doing so always. In the interests of symmetry, certain writers like Spiethoff have tried to show that this group of trades is regularly the chief seat of overinvestment during prosperity and the chief seat of weakness in the subsequent crises. But less partial examination of the very evidence on which Spiethoff mainly relies indicates that the lead in the German 'boom' of 1896–99 and in the collapse of 1900–01 was not held by industries that are most largely devoted to the production of means of production. See, for example, W. Sombart, *Schriften des Vereins für Socialpolitik*, CXIII, 130; J. Lescure, *Des Crises générales et périodiques de surproduction* (Paris, 1907), p. 516.

[16] See Part II, Chapter VIII, ii, 5.

[17] Part II, Chapter VIII, ii, 2 and 3; Chapter IV, iii, 1, 2, and 4.

[18] An interesting exception is afforded by the experience of the United States in 1897–1902; see Part II, Chapter IV, iv, 7.

[19] Compare Part II, Chapter VIII, ii, 2, and footnote 20, below.

[20] The following figures, compiled from Part II, table 113, show the total amount of securities newly listed each year on the New York Stock Exchange, and the proportions borne to the total by bonds and by stocks.

Year	Amount in millions of dollars	Percentage of	
		Stocks	Bonds
1890	359	44.8	55.2
1891	288	33.7	66.3
1892	275	36.4	63.6
1893	233	40.3	59.7
1894	222	16.7	83.3
1895	244	31.6	68.4
1896	224	34.4	65.6
1897	141	37.6	62.4

Year	Amount in millions of dollars	Percentage of	
		Stocks	Bonds
1898	315	22.2	77.8
1899	467	66.6	33.4
1900	445	66.7	33.3
1901	650	66.2	33.8
1902	449	55.9	44.1
1903	365	47.4	52.6
1904	551	22.0	78.0
1905	694	18.0	82.0
1906	540	43.9	56.1
1907	406	39.2	60.8
1908	773	16.0	84.0
1909	1,010	29.4	70.6
1910	877	34.8	65.2

It will be noticed that the proportion of bonds rises in the years of depression and declines rapidly in the years of full prosperity.

The substitution of short-term notes for bonds was particularly prominent in the tight money markets of 1903 and 1907. See the current issues of the financial journals, and for summaries the *Financial Review*, 1904, p. 27; 1908, p. 32.

[21] Compare Mr. Hull's theory of industrial depressions, summarized in Part I, Chapter I, ii, 8.

[22] See, for example, the weekly reports of *Iron Age* during the summer of 1907. The following figures of unfilled orders on the books of the United States Steel Corporation at the end of the month are significant of the general trend:

Year	Month	Tons
1906	December	8,500,000
1907	March	8,000,000
	June	7,600,000
	September	6,400,000
	December	4,600,000

[23] Compare the relative rates of discount in Part II, table 28, with the relative rates of bond yields in table 27.

[24] Discount houses and bill brokers do a banking business themselves, depend largely upon banks for their funds, or act merely as middlemen between the borrower and a lending bank. Even the credits extended to their customers by American mercantile houses are scarcely an exception; because the lenders usually have recourse to banks for aid in carrying such accounts.

[25] Compare the tables in Part II, Chapter VII, showing the concomitant fluctuations of bank loans and deposits, or bank loans and total demand liabilities.

[26] The validity of this statement is not affected by such long-standing differences in banking organization and practice as, for example, enable British banks to sustain a far greater volume of demand liabilities with a given reserve than American.

[27] See Part II, tables 82, 83, 85, and 86.

[28] See Part II, Chapter VI, iv, and Chapter 4, i, 2, D, below.

[29] Concerning the New York banks, see Part II, Chapter VII, i. The reserve ratios from Part II, table 89, are for all national banks (see p. 202, top).

Month		Depression (percentage)	Prosperity (percentage)	Month
February	1894	26.9	19.6	September 1895
March	1897	24.7	18.7	September 1899
June	1904	18.1	14.8	November 1906
May	1908	18.6	15.1	March 1910

The tables for national banks in country and city districts show that a similar policy is followed in all parts of the United States. The foreign statistics, though scanty, yield similar results. See the various sections of Part II, Chapter VII.

[30] See Part II, Chapter VI, i.

[31] *Ibid.*, ii.

[32] See Part II, Chapter V, v.

[33] See Part II, Chapter VI, iii.

[34] *Ibid.*, v.

[35] *Ibid.*, vi.

[36] How a decline of prospective profits puts a close to prosperity is explained in the closing section of this chapter.

[37] See Part I, Chapter II, iv, 2 and 3.

[38] See Part I, Chapter I, ii, 3 and 5.

[39] Some light is shed upon the theory of underconsumption by figures that represent the purchasing power of wage earners' incomes. The federal Bureau of Labor has computed the average changes in the purchasing power of factory hands by combining its index numbers of wages per hour, hours per week, and retail prices of food. The results, reproduced herewith, indicate a slight decline between the early and the late stages of prosperity in the amount of food a wage earner can buy. Thus the statistics seem to bear out the contention that consumers' demand does not expand rapidly. But several factors of moment have been omitted from the computation. (1) The number of employees in the establishments investigated by the Bureau increases rapidly during prosperity. To show the effect of this factor upon market demand for food, a final column has been added to the table as published by the Bureau. It is made by multiplying the relative purchasing power of full-time weekly earnings by the relative number of employees. A rapid expansion in purchasing power appears in the results, though the rate of growth becomes somewhat slower as the climax of prosperity is approached. (2) The increase of money incomes arising both from the greater steadiness of employment and the greater frequency of 'overtime' in active periods is unrepresented. (3) The proportion of money income spent on consumers' goods may change. If extravagance does become as widespread as popular moralists assert, the rate of savings may shrink somewhat in comparison with the early days of prosperity—shrink to the detriment of would-be borrowers, but to the advantage of purveyors of consumers' goods.

RELATIVE NUMBER OF EMPLOYEES, HOURS PER WEEK, WAGES PER HOUR, FULL-TIME WEEKLY
EARNINGS PER EMPLOYEE, RETAIL PRICES OF FOOD, AND PURCHASING POWER OF
HOURLY WAGES AND OF FULL-TIME WEEKLY EARNINGS PER EMPLOYEE,
MEASURED BY RETAIL PRICES OF FOOD, 1890–1907

(Relative numbers computed on basis of averages for 1890–99=100)

Year	Number of employees	Hours per week	Wages per hour	Full-time weekly earnings per employee	Retail prices of food, weighted according to family consumption	Purchasing power measured by retail prices of food of		
						Full time		Weekly earnings multiplied by number of employees
						Hourly wages	Weekly earnings per employee	
1890	94.8	100.7	100.3	101.0	102.4	97.9	98.6	93.5
1891	97.3	100.5	100.3	100.8	103.8	96.6	97.1	94.5
1892	99.2	100.5	100.8	101.3	101.9	98.9	99.4	98.6
1893	99.4	100.3	100.9	101.2	104.4	96.6	96.9	96.3
1894	94.1	99.8	97.9	97.7	99.7	98.2	98.0	92.2
1895	96.4	100.1	98.3	98.4	97.8	100.5	100.6	97.0
1896	98.6	99.8	99.7	99.5	95.5	104.4	104.2	102.8
1897	100.9	99.6	99.6	99.2	96.3	103.4	103.0	103.9
1898	106.4	99.7	100.2	99.9	98.7	101.5	101.2	107.7
1899	112.1	99.2	102.0	101.2	99.5	102.5	101.7	114.0
1900	115.6	98.7	105.5	104.1	101.1	104.4	103.0	119.1
1901	119.1	98.1	108.0	105.9	105.2	102.7	100.7	119.9
1902	123.6	97.3	112.2	109.2	110.9	101.2	98.5	121.7
1903	126.5	96.6	116.3	112.3	110.3	105.4	101.8	128.8
1904	125.7	95.9	117.0	112.2	111.7	104.7	100.4	126.2
1905	133.6	95.9	118.9	114.0	112.4	105.8	101.4	135.5
1906	142.9	95.4	124.2	118.5	115.7	107.3	102.4	146.3
1907	144.4	95.0	128.8	122.4	120.6	106.8	101.5	146.6

Mr. George H. Wood's British figures ("Real Wages and the Standard of Comfort since 1850," *Journal of the Royal Statistical Society*, March 1909, Vol. 72, p. 103) seek to cover some of these omitted items. His series for retail prices includes other articles than food. He has estimated the variations in working-class rents, and combined the data for unemployment with the data for wages. Further, Mr. Wood points out that in England there has been a steady shifting away from the ill-paid toward the well-paid occupations. Hence the "average workman" has improved his position more rapidly than the "workman of unchanged grade." The final results of his investigation, converted from English into American money and shifted from the basis actual amounts in 1850=100 to the basis average actual amounts in 1890–99 = 100, are summed up in the accompanying table.

Estimated Changes in the Real Wages of English Workmen, 1890-1902

	1890	1891	1892	1893	1894	1895	1896	1897	1898	1899	1900	1901	1902
Relative money wages................	99	99	99	99	99	99	99	101	102	105	109	109	107
Relative retail prices...............	104	105	105	101	99	96	95	98	99	98	101	103	104
Percentage unemployed...............	2.1	3.5	6.3	7.5	6.9	5.8	3.4	3.5	3.0	2.4	2.9	3.8	4.4
Money cost of:													
Commodities (1850 = 10s).......	$3.55	$3.58	$3.58	$3.46	$3.38	$3.26	$3.24	$3.33	$3.41	$3.33	$3.46	$3.50	$3.55
Rent (1880 = 20s).............	1.22	1.24	1.24	1.24	1.24	1.27	1.27	1.27	1.27	1.29	1.29	1.29	1.29
Rent and Commodities (1850 = 20s)....	4.77	4.82	4.82	4.70	4.62	4.53	4.50	4.60	4.67	4.62	4.75	4.79	4.84
Money wages, assuming 20s in 1850:													
Full work...................	7.91	7.91	7.86	8.10	7.86	7.86	7.91	8.08	8.13	8.35	8.69	8.69	8.57
Allowing for unemployment......	7.74	7.64	7.37	7.28	7.32	7.40	7.64	7.79	7.88	8.15	8.42	8.35	8.18
Relative real wages:													
Full work (1890-99 = 100).....	97	96	95	98	99	102	103	103	102	105	107	106	104
Allowing for unemployment......	99	97	94	95	97	100	104	103	103	108	108	106	103
Relative figures for workmen of unchanged grade:													
Money wages:													
Full work.................	100	100	100	99	99	98	99	100	102	104	108	107	105
Allowing for unemployment....	103	101	98	96	97	96	100	101	103	106	109	108	106
Real wages...............	98	97	96	98	100	100	102	102	102	104	106	104	102

They show a definite increase in the purchasing power of money wages up to the very end of the prosperous period 1896–1900. If these figures could be multiplied by the relative number of employees, the total purchasing power represented would doubtless increase much more rapidly.

Walter T. Layton (*Introduction to the Study of Prices*, London, 1912, p. 150) has extended to 1910 Mr. Wood's relative figures for money wages, retail prices, unemployment, and real wages of men in full work, allowing for unemployment. The last-mentioned series, shifted to the basis 1890–99 = 100, runs as follows:

RELATIVE REAL WAGES IN ENGLAND, ALLOWING FOR UNEMPLOYMENT

1890	99	1897	104	1904	98
1891	97	1898	103	1905	100
1892	94	1899	108	1906	103
1893	95	1900	109	1907	104
1894	97	1901	107	1908	97
1895	100	1902	104	1909	96
1896	104	1903	100	1910	98

These figures, like the others, indicate a gain in the purchasing power of wage earners' incomes up to the years of the crises—even without counting the gain in the number of persons at work. The rate of gain, however, becomes slower in the crisis years. It is noteworthy that real wages did not attain as high a level in 1907 as in 1899–1900.

Interesting as are these estimates, they leave much to be desired. Even if the figures are accepted at their face value, they show merely that, despite the rise of retail prices, one large class of people is able to buy an increasing volume of consumers' goods in periods of prosperity. How matters stand with other classes remains conjectural. The incomes of bondholders must increase rather slowly; indeed, they do not increase at all except so far as these persons have fresh savings to invest at the high rates that become prevalent in prosperity or venture to shift their funds to securities that yield higher returns. If tables 121–28 in Part II and the analysis of Chapter 1 above may be trusted, stockholders and other recipients of profits enjoy a more rapid increase of money income than wage earners. It may also be said with some assurance that the incomes of the landlord and salaried classes grow more slowly on the average than do wages. But concerning the nonsalaried professional men, farmers, and wage earners outside manufacturing industries, there is no substantial basis for even a guess at the average increase of money incomes. And, if the rates of increase were known, there would be no satisfactory data to confirm or disprove Hobson's assertion that the proportion of income saved gains upon the proportion spent. Finally, if we did know at what average rate expenditure upon consumers' goods increases, we would still be unable to complete the demonstration; for we have no satisfactory statistics of the increase in the volume of consumers' goods produced and sent to market.

[40] Compare Thorstein Veblen, *Theory of Business Enterprise,* pp. 92–97.

[41] Additional elements are considered when an enterprise offers the lender of credit some guarantee in support of its promise to pay. If the security consists of endorsements by other business enterprises, or of promissory notes, bills of exchange, etc., owned by the applicant, then the lender estimates the financial standing of the other enterprises on the basis just described. If the security is stocks offered as collateral, their pecuniary value is estimated, and again the factor of chief importance is the present and prospective profits of the business

enterprise concerned. If the security is bonds, it is still necessary to know what profits the issuing corporation makes in order to determine the chances that the interest will be paid promptly. In case the security consists of warehouse receipts, bills of lading, bills of exchange, or similar documents that carry with them the legal title to certain commodities, the prices the latter will command become the matter of prime importance. But even then the business standing of the applicant for credit is taken into account, since lenders do not want the trouble, delay, and uncertainty involved in having to sell the commodities to get their money back.

[42] Compare the rapid increase in bank loans shown by tables 82–104, Part II.

[43] The commodity prices are from the *Bulletin of the Bureau of Labor,* March 1910, p. 398. The other data are all compiled from Part II, tables 22, 25, 32, and 44.

[44] Indeed, the relative prices of bonds can be computed only on the basis of their net yields; see Part II, Chapter IV, iv, 6.

[45] Compare Part II, Chapter IV, iv, 1.

[46] Among the seven industrial groups into which the 103 companies fall, two show a slight average rise between January 1906 and January 1907—the mining and smelting companies and the great iron and steel companies that mine much of their own coal and ore. On the other hand, these two groups suffered a heavier average fall in market valuation between January and September 1907 than did any of the five other groups. These facts accord well with the preceding analysis. The rapid rise in the prices of raw mineral products during prosperity enables the mining company to offset the encroachments of costs upon profits until the falling off in new contracts for construction work begins. But when the cycle has reached that point these same companies experience a peculiarly violent constriction in demand, and their prospective profits drop suddenly.

Among the other groups, which differ widely in the character of their products, the fall of stock prices from January 1906 to January 1907, and again from the latter date to September 1907, presents surprisingly uniform averages.

The data upon which these statements rest are given in the following table. The actual prices are means between the highest and lowest quotations reported by the *Financial Review.*

PRICES OF COMMON SHARES IN 103 BUSINESS ENTERPRISES IN JANUARY 1906, JANUARY 1907, AND SEPTEMBER 1907

Enterprise	Mean actual prices			Mean relative prices (Actual prices in Jan. 1906 = 100)			Rise (+) or fall (−) in relative prices between		
	Jan. 1906 (dollars)	Jan. 1907 (dollars)	Sept. 1907 (dollars)	Jan. 1906	Jan. 1907	Sept. 1907	Jan. 1906 / Jan. 1907	Jan. 1906 / Sept. 1907	Jan. 1907 / Sept. 1907
Mining and Smelting									
Amalgamated Copper Co.	109.69	116.13	65.38	100	106	80	+ 6	−40	−46
American Smelting and Refining Co.	167.75	148.31	93.94	100	88	56	−12	−44	−32
Columbus and Hocking Coal and Iron	22.06	26.06	22.44	100	118	102	+18	+ 2	−16
Federal Mining and Smelting Co.	168.50	161.50	95.50	100	96	57	− 4	−43	−39
Homestake Mining Co.	81.50	85.00a	71.25	100	104	87	+ 4	−13	−17
National Lead Co.	87.69	71.13	49.88	100	81	57	−19	−43	−24
Ontario Silver Mining Co.	3.44	6.56	3.50	100	191	102	+91	+ 2	−89
Pittsburgh Coal Co. of New Jersey	16.06	16.13	9.75	100	100	61	...	−39	−39
U.S. Reduction & Refining Co.	32.00	28.88	13.75	100	90	43	−10	−57	−47
Average, 9 enterprises	....	....	....	100	108	69	+ 8	−31	−39
Iron and Steel									
Colorado Fuel and Iron Co.	69.38	52.19	21.88	100	75	32	−25	−68	−43
Republic Iron and Steel Co.	35.50	37.44	22.38	100	105	63	+ 5	−37	−42
Sloss-Sheffield Steel and Iron Co.	91.50	73.63	46.50	100	80	51	−20	−49	−29
Tennessee Coal and Iron Co.	147.00	158.00	135.00b	100	107	92	+ 7	− 8	−15
U.S. Steel Corporation.	44.13	46.56	29.75	100	106	67	+ 6	−33	−39
Virginia Iron, Coal, and Coke Co.	26.57	43.50	26.25	100	164	99	+64	− 1	−65
Average, 6 enterprises	....	....	....	100	106	67	+ 6	−33	−39

a February 1907.
b August 1907.

PRICES OF COMMON SHARES IN 103 BUSINESS ENTERPRISES IN JANUARY 1906, JANUARY 1907, AND SEPTEMBER 1907—(Continued)

Enterprise	Mean actual prices Jan. 1906 (dollars)	Jan. 1907 (dollars)	Sept. 1907 (dollars)	Mean relative prices (Actual prices in Jan. 1906 = 100) Jan. 1906	Jan. 1907	Sept. 1907	Rise (+) or fall (−) in relative prices between Jan. 1906 / Jan. 1907	Jan. 1906 / Sept. 1907	Jan. 1907 / Sept. 1907
Machinery and Railway Equipment									
Allis Chalmers Co.	24.69	15.19	7.56	100	62	31	−38	−69	−31
American Car and Foundry Co.	43.50	43.19	39.06	100	99	90	−1	−10	−9
American Locomotive Co.	74.62	72.38	52.38	100	97	70	−3	−30	−27
American Steel Foundries	14.44	9.75	6.63	100	68	46	−32	−54	−22
General Electric Co.	176.63	159.13	126.50	100	90	72	−10	−28	−18
International Power Co.	76.50	49.38	40.88	100	65	53	−35	−47	−12
International Steam Pump Co.	32.50	37.63	22.50	100	116	69	+16	−31	−47
New York Air Brake Co.	159.25	137.25	109.00	100	86	68	−14	−32	−18
Pressed Steel Car Co.	59.06	52.00	28.13	100	88	48	−12	−52	−40
Railway Steel Spring Co.	60.75	54.25	28.13	100	89	59	−11	−41	−30
U.S. Cast Iron Pipe and Foundry Co.	49.56	47.38	30.13	100	96	61	−4	−39	−35
Westinghouse Electric Manufacturing Co.	171.00	151.38	138.00	100	89	81	−11	−19	−8
Average, 12 enterprises	.....	.....	.....	100	87	62	−13	−38	−25
Manufacturing, various									
American Agricultural Chemical Co.	29.31	24.19	16.88	100	83	58	−17	−42	−25
American Beet Sugar Co.	30.50	21.50	12.50	100	70	41	−30	−59	−29
American Cotton Oil Co.	40.63	30.88	32.50	100	76	80	−24	−20	+4
American Grass Twine Co.	10.75	7.38	4.63	100	69	43	−31	−57	−26
American Hide and Leather Co.	9.31	5.88	3.94	100	63	42	−37	−58	−21
American Ice Securities Co.	40.88	86.50	42.88	100	212	105	+112	+5	−107
American Linseed Co.	24.63	17.63	8.50	100	72	35	−28	−65	−37
American Sugar Refining Co.	150.69	132.81	112.38	100	88	75	−12	−25	−13
American Woolen Co.	44.31	33.63	22.44	100	76	51	−24	−49	−25
Butterick Co.	57.44	49.06	31.25	100	85	54	−15	−46	−31
Central Leather Co.	47.06	36.38	17.88	100	77	38	−23	−62	−39
Distillers Securities Corp.	52.56	72.25	54.38	100	137	103	+37	+3	−34
General Chemical Co.	79.50	75.13	63.00[a]	100	95	79	−5	−21	−16
International Paper Co.	24.18	16.88	14.00	100	70	58	−30	−42	−12
Knickerbocker Ice Co. (Chicago)	64.88	54.75	50.75	100	84	78	−16	−22	−6
National Biscuit Co.	69.00	81.63	73.50	100	118	107	+18	+7	−11
National Enameling and Stamping Co.	17.25	14.25	10.94	100	83	63	−17	−37	−20
U.S. Rubber Co.	54.75	50.13	30.25	100	92	55	−8	−45	−37
Union Bag and Paper Co.	14.31	7.56	5.38	100	53	38	−47	−62	−15
Virginia-Carolina Chemical Co.	51.00	35.94	19.75	100	70	39	−30	−61	−31
Average, 20 enterprises	.....	.....	.....	100	89	62	−11	−38	−27

[a] February 1907.

PRICES OF COMMON SHARES IN 103 BUSINESS ENTERPRISES IN JANUARY 1906, JANUARY 1907, AND SEPTEMBER 1907—(Continued)

Enterprise	Mean actual prices			Mean relative prices (Actual prices in Jan. 1906 = 100)			Rise (+) or fall (−) in relative prices between		
	Jan. 1906 (dollars)	Jan. 1907 (dollars)	Sept. 1907 (dollars)	Jan. 1906	Jan. 1907	Sept. 1907	Jan. 1906 / Jan. 1907	Jan. 1906 / Sept. 1907	Jan. 1907 / Sept. 1907
Public Utilities									
American Telephone and Telegraph Co.	141.44	130.50	109.75*	100	92	78	− 8	− 22	− 14
Brooklyn Rapid Transit Co.	89.69	77.75	45.81	100	87	51	− 13	− 49	− 36
Brooklyn Union Gas Co.	171.50	110.50	102.31	100	64	60	− 36	− 40	− 4
Chicago Union Traction Co.	11.38	5.31	3.00	100	47	26	− 53	− 74	− 21
Consolidated Gas Co.	174.88	136.00	101.63	100	78	58	− 22	− 42	− 20
Detroit United Railways	97.06	79.56	63.00	100	82	65	− 18	− 35	− 17
Metropolitan Street Railways	123.50	105.50	40.81	100	85	33	− 15	− 67	− 52
N. Y. and N. J. Telephone Co.	154.75	113.00	105.00	100	73	68	− 27	− 32	− 5
North American Co. (new stock)	102.50	85.00	59.88	100	83	58	− 17	− 42	− 25
Peoples Gas, Light, and Coke Co. (Chicago).	100.50	96.44	88.88	100	96	86	− 4	− 14	− 10
Third Avenue Railway Co.	137.25	120.25	50.50	100	88	37	− 12	− 63	− 51
Toledo Railways and Light Co.	34.13	28.50	21.50	100	84	63	− 16	− 37	− 21
Twin City Rapid Transit Co.	119.63	105.31	93.31	100	88	78	− 12	− 22	− 10
Average, 13 enterprises.	....	....	....	100	81	59	− 19	− 41	− 22
Miscellaneous									
Brunswick Dock and City Improvement Co.	19.00	14.00	10.00	100	74	53	− 26	− 47	− 21
Pullman Co.	244.88	175.56	156.75	100	72	64	− 28	− 36	− 8
U.S. Realty and Improvement Co.	91.25	83.75	50.00	100	92	55	− 8	− 45	− 37
Average, 3 enterprises.	....	....	....	100	79	57	− 21	− 43	− 22
Average, 63 industrial enterprises.	....	....	....	100	91	63	− 9	− 37	− 28
Transportation Companies									
New York, New Haven, and Hartford.	200.94	186.63	150.25	100	93	75	− 7	− 25	− 18
New York, Ontario, and Western.	54.25	45.44	33.31	100	84	61	− 16	− 39	− 23
New York Central.	152.06	129.88	104.25	100	85	69	− 15	− 31	− 16
Pennsylvania.	144.25	135.44	119.88	100	94	83	− 6	− 17	− 11
Erie.	48.75	38.94	20.81	100	80	43	− 20	− 57	− 37
Central of New Jersey.	226.75	215.00	173.00	100	95	76	− 5	− 24	− 19
Delaware and Hudson.	223.63	217.75	158.50	100	97	71	− 3	− 29	− 26
Delaware, Lackawanna, and Western.	465.75	495.00	469.00	100	106	101	+ 6	+ 1	− 5
Philadelphia and Reading.	149.13	129.19	94.44	100	87	63	− 13	− 37	− 24
Cleveland, Cincinnati, Chicago, and St. Louis.	107.44	90.00	62.25	100	84	58	− 16	− 42	− 26

* July 1907.

Prices of Common Shares in 103 Business Enterprises in January 1906, January 1907, and September 1907—(*Concluded*)

Enterprise	Mean actual prices			Mean relative prices (Actual prices in Jan. 1906 = 100)			Rise (+) or fall (−) in relative prices between		
	Jan. 1906 (dollars)	Jan. 1907 (dollars)	Sept. 1907 (dollars)	Jan. 1906	Jan. 1907	Sept. 1907	Jan. 1906 / Jan. 1907	Jan. 1906 / Sept. 1907	Jan. 1907 / Sept. 1907
Transportation Companies—(Continued)									
Wheeling and Lake Erie	19.19	14.75	9.69	100	77	50	−23	−50	−27
New York, Chicago, and St. Louis	69.50	60.75	35.89	100	87	52	−13	−48	−35
Wabash	23.38	17.31	11.69	100	74	50	−26	−50	−24
Pittsburgh, Cincinnati, Chicago, and St. Louis	85.25	75.69	66.50	100	89	78	−11	−22	−11
Canada Southern	69.94	64.63	60.88	100	92	87	−8	−13	−5
Lake Erie and Western	41.44	27.75	16.56[a]	100	67	40	−33	−60	−27
Illinois Central	178.00	165.00	138.00	100	93	78	−7	−22	−15
Chicago, Milwaukee, and St. Paul	186.38	151.31	120.19	100	81	64	−19	−36	−17
Chicago and Northwestern	230.00	192.38	145.50	100	84	63	−16	−37	−21
Chicago, St. Paul, Minneapolis, and Omaha	194.00	165.00	127.00	100	85	65	−15	−35	−20
Duluth, South Shore, and Atlantic	21.00	18.00	9.50	100	86	45	−14	−55	−41
Iowa Central	32.19	26.44	15.94	100	82	50	−18	−50	−32
Minneapolis and St. Louis	82.13	57.88	39.63	100	70	48	−30	−52	−22
Wisconsin Central	30.50	24.19	15.13	100	79	50	−21	−50	−29
Chesapeake and Ohio	58.56	52.50	33.69	100	90	58	−10	−42	−32
Norfolk and Western	89.13	88.38	70.88	100	99	80	−1	−20	−19
Louisville and Nashville	152.50	139.50	107.81	100	91	71	−9	−29	−20
Missouri Pacific	103.13	89.38	69.44	100	87	67	−13	−33	−20
Missouri, Kansas, and Texas	38.31	38.63	35.00	100	101	91	+1	−9	−10
Texas and Pacific	36.06	34.19	27.38	100	95	76	−5	−24	−19
Atchison, Topeka, and Santa Fe	92.94	103.31	86.88	100	111	93	+11	−7	−18
Denver and Rio Grande	44.94	39.13	23.69	100	87	53	−13	−47	−34
Southern Pacific	69.25	93.25	85.44	100	135	123	+35	+23	−12
Union Pacific	154.25	175.94	129.69	100	114	84	+14	−16	−30
Canadian Pacific	173.38	187.50	164.00	100	108	95	+8	−5	−13
American Express Co.	235.75	241.00	202.00	100	102	86	+2	−14	−16
United States Express Co.	131.25	113.50	89.47[a]	100	86	68	−14	−32	−18
Wells-Fargo Express Co.	244.00	285.00	280.00	100	117	115	+17	+15	−2
Pacific Mail Steamship Co.	48.75	37.50	24.38	100	77	50	−23	−50	−27
Western Union Telegraph Co.	93.63	83.63	75.50	100	89	81	−11	−19	−8
Average, 40 enterprises	......	......	......	100	91	70	−9	−30	−21
Grand average, 103 enterprises	......	......	......	100	91	66	−9	−34	−25

a Interpolated.

Chapter 3. Crises

[1] Especially when the banking system has such a rudimentary organization as in the United States at present; compare section v, below.

[2] On the panic of 1893 see Part I, Chapter III, iii, 6; A. C. Stevens, "Analysis of the Phenomena of the Panic in the United States in 1893," *Quarterly Journal of Economics,* January 1894; O. M. W. Sprague, *History of Crises under the National Banking System* (Publications of the National Monetary Commission), Chapter IV; W. J. Lauck, *The Causes of the Panic of 1893* (Boston and New York, 1907). The panic of 1907 is described very briefly in Part I, Chapter III, viii, 4.

[3] Compare Sprague, *History of Crises under the National Banking System* (Publications of the National Monetary Commission), pp. 251, 252. Mr. Edmond Kelly says that the Knickerbocker Trust Company had become "an independent financial power" of which the "Wall Street Group" was jealous, and that this group took advantage of the institution's temporary financial embarrassment to get rid of its efficient president, Mr. Charles J. Barney. Subsequent events proved that the company was solvent; and might have been saved from passing into the hands of receivers (*Twentieth Century Socialism,* New York, pp. 182–84). Interesting personal details concerning this incident and its consequences are given by Carl Hovey, *The Life Story of J. Pierpont Morgan* (New York, 1919), Ch. XIV.

[4] Sprague regards this delay as "the most serious error made" in managing the panic of 1907; *op. cit.,* p. 257.

[5] A. P. Andrew, "Hoarding in the Panic of 1907," *Quarterly Journal of Economics,* February 1908.

[6] For the importation of gold see table 3. The volume of national-bank notes outstanding was as follows:

Date	Dollars	Date	Dollars
October 1	603,900,000	December 1	656,200,000
October 15	607,100,000	December 15	676,900,000
November 1	611,800,000	December 31	690,100,000
November 15	631,300,000	January 18	695,900,000

Response of the Secretary of the Treasury to Senate Resolution No. 33 of December 12, 1907 (60th Cong., 1st Sess., Sen. Doc. 208), pp. 11, 126.

To provide lawful security for this increase of notes and for further government deposits, on November 17 the Secretary of the Treasury offered to receive subscriptions for $50,000,000 in Panama Canal bonds and $100,000,000 in 3 per cent certificates of indebtedness, and to permit 90 per cent of the proceeds of the bonds and 75 per cent of the proceeds of the certificates to remain in the national banks as government deposits. But only $24,631,980 of the bonds and $15,436,500 of the certificates were actually sold. (*Report of the Secretary of the Treasury,* 1908, pp. 21, 22.)

[7] A. P. Andrew, "Substitutes for Cash in the Panic of 1907," *Quarterly Journal of Economics,* August 1908, pp. 501, 502.

[8] *Ibid.,* p. 515. As an additional aid to the banks in restricting payments, the governors of Oklahoma, Nevada, Washington, Oregon, and California declared a succession of legal holidays; Sprague, *op. cit.,* pp. 286, 287.

[9] The average gain (+) or loss (–) to the New York banks by interior movements of cash from October to January during the decade 1899–1908 was, in thousands of dollars:

October—1st week	−3,883	December—2nd week	− 836
October—2nd week	−2,543	December—3rd week	+ 515
October—3rd week	−3,014	December—4th week	+ 60
October—4th week	−3,685	December—5th week	+2,188
November—1st week	−2,700	January—1st week	+6,684
November—2nd week	−2,666	January—2nd week	+6,621
November—3rd week	−1,530	January—3rd week	+7,773
November—4th week	− 563	January—4th week	+6,895
December—1st week	− 213		

E. W. Kemmerer, *Seasonal Variations in the Demand for Money and Capital in the United States* (Publications of the National Monetary Commission), p. 125.

[10] The Trust Company of America is said to have paid out some $34,000,000 in two weeks; Sprague, *op. cit.*, p. 254.

[11] Compare Sprague, *op. cit.*, pp. 260–77.

[12] Kemmerer, *op. cit.*, p. 118.

[13] Compare Sprague, *op. cit.*, pp. 291–97.

[14] *Ibid.*, pp. 241 and 246.

[15] The imports and exports of merchandise were as follows:

Month	Imports	Exports	Balance
September	$103,400,000	$135,400,000	+$ 32,000,000
October	111,800,000	180,400,000	+ 68,600,000
November	110,900,000	204,500,000	+ 93,600,000
December	92,300,000	207,100,000	+ 114,800,000
January	85,000,000	206,200,000	+ 121,200,000

Compiled from the *Monthly Summary of Commerce and Finance.*

[16] A. Strauss, "Gold Movements and the Foreign Exchanges," in *The Currency Problem and the Present Financial Situation,* a series of addresses delivered at Columbia University 1907–08, pp. 65–67.

[17] *Financial Review,* 1908, p. 59.

[18] *Bradstreet's,* indeed, publishes the nominal rates of discount in several cities; but table 8 shows that nominal rates are not trustworthy indices of money-market conditions during a panic. For that reason it would be vain to compile the figures for other towns.

[19] The statement in the table that the banks and trust companies were out of the call-loan market from the last week of October to the end of the year does not mean that they lent no money on call. They did lend perforce at the "money post" on the Stock Exchange, though not over their own counters. Compare Mr. T. F. Woodlock's excellent paper on "The Stock Exchange and the Money Market," in *The Currency Problem and the Present Financial Situation,* a series of addresses delivered at Columbia University, 1907–08.

[20] Probably the 60- and 90-day loans made at 12 per cent and over in November went largely to stockbrokers, who usually carry half or more of their loans on time, and depend on call money for the balance. Some of these time loans to brokers had to be renewed during the panic, as part of the plan to forestall worse things on the Stock Exchange.

[21] Sprague, *op. cit.*, p. 300; compare Part II, Chapter VII, i.

[22] See table 5, and compare Sprague, *op. cit.*, pp. 303–13.

[23] Though it is difficult to discover and classify the causes of all bankruptcies, *Bradstreet's* figures possess great interest as a pioneering effort in an important field of enquiry. Rearranged for convenience, the data for 1904–08 are:

	Percentage of number of failures					Percentage of liabilities				
	1908	1907	1906	1905	1904	1908	1907	1906	1905	1904
Faults of those failing:										
Lack of capital	34.2	37.1	35.9	33.4	32.2	27.2	18.4	30.9	33.0	32.0
Incompetence	21.6	22.6	22.3	24.4	23.1	16.0	8.9	15.5	21.6	14.1
Fraud	11.5	10.1	10.0	9.2	8.6	6.9	5.1	16.2	8.2	6.4
Inexperience	4.0	4.9	4.9	4.8	5.1	1.8	3.2	2.2	2.1	3.2
Unwise credits	2.0	2.3	2.6	3.5	3.4	3.7	3.1	2.1	4.2	4.8
Neglect	2.2	2.5	2.2	2.9	3.1	.8	.5	1.5	1.1	1.6
Extravagance	1.0	.9	1.0	1.1	.8	.9	.5	.9	1.2	.7
Speculation	1.0	.7	.8	.7	.8	4.7	4.9	3.6	7.7	5.3
Total	77.5	81.1	79.7	80.0	77.1	62.0	44.6	72.9	79.1	68.1
Not faults of those failing:										
Specific conditions	18.9	16.3	17.3	16.3	19.1	31.3	51.7	17.9	15.5	22.7
Failure of others	1.8	1.4	2.0	2.2	2.5	5.0	3.3	8.8	4.5	8.2
Competition	1.8	1.2	1.0	1.5	1.3	1.7	.4	.4	.9	1.0
Total	22.5	18.9	20.3	20.0	22.9	38.0	55.4	27.1	20.9	31.9

[24] For animal products, however, this maximum was less than that of the preceding February.

[25] The changes in the general index numbers which include many commodities of different classes are less illuminating than these detailed figures. For the points of time such series as those published by the Bureau of Labor, *Bradstreet's*, and Sauerbeck mark as the beginning of recession clearly depend upon the proportionate representation allowed to consumers' and producers' goods, to manufactured articles and raw materials, and to the raw products of the mines, forests, and farms. Thus the Bureau of Labor's index number puts the maximum price in October 1907, and *Bradstreet's* index number in March, primarily because the former includes relatively more manufactured goods than the latter.

[26] The exceptional gain of clearings in March enforces this opinion; for this was the only month in the year when the number of shares sold in 1907 was greater than in 1906. See the table in the *Financial Review*, 1908, p. 35.

[27] The slight excess of the July clearings in 1907 occurred in the face of a decline in the number of shares sold from 16.3 to 12.8 millions.

[28] See the London *Economist*, Vol. 65, pp. 1144, 1192, 1328.

[29] *Ibid.*, p. 1284. The failure of the Manchurian railway loan attracted especial attention because of the attractiveness of the terms offered—interest 5 per cent, subscription price 97, amount of issue £4,000,000. The underwriters included some of the strongest British banks, and the guarantee of principal and interest by the Japanese government seemed to afford good security.

[30] *Ibid.*, p. 1261.

[31] *Ibid.*, pp. 1138–39.

[32] *Ibid.*, p. 1583.

[33] *Ibid.*, p. 1502.

[34] The *Economist's* "Commercial History and Review of 1907," p. 1.

[35] *Economist*, Vol. 65, p. 1499.

[36] In Great Britain as in the United States metropolitan clearings are a less

faithful guide to the volume of business than country clearings. Even the town clearings in London show no decline if the figures for stock-exchange pay days and consols settling days be excluded; see the *Economist's* "Commercial History and Review of 1907," p. 3; for statistics of clearings and exports see tables 19–21.

[37] *Economist*, Vol. 65, pp. 1138, 1583, 1755–56, 1814–15, 1977, 2083–84, and 2171.

[38] *Ibid.*, pp. 1840, 1886.

[39] See Part II, tables 101 and 104.

[40] See the money article of the *Economist*, October 26 and November 2.

[41] See the weekly money article of the *Economist* in November and December.

[42] This institution received in return long dated bills at 4¾ per cent discount, charged 1 per cent premium for the gold, and stipulated that the reimbursement should be in sovereigns. See the French correspondence of the *Economist*, November 9.

[43] See the money articles of the *Economist*, November 30, December 14 and 21.

[44] Doubtless the gold received from the Bank of France is counted among the imports.

[45] *Economist*, Vol. 65, pp. 1863, 1945.

[46] This so-called index number gives the aggregate 'values' of 387 representative issues of securities, including both stocks and bonds. For 1907–08 they are, in millions of dollars:

1907—January	18,702	1907—August	17,023
February	18,571	September	17,188
March	17,962	October	17,062
April	17,972	November	16,823
May	17,792	December	17,033
June	17,461	1908—January	17,334
July	17,685	February	17,320

[47] *Economist*, Vol. 65, p. 2031, and "Commercial History and Review of 1907," pp. 3, 4.

[48] *Ibid.*, pp. 2022, 2071–72.

[49] Whether the provisions for the issue of emergency currency made by the Aldrich-Vreeland Act, passed after the panic of 1907, afford an adequate remedy for this long-standing defect in the American currency system cannot be told until the new machinery has been tested in practice. And this law seems likely to expire by limitation before occasion has arisen for its application.

[50] Part II, Chapter VII, i and ii.

[51] Compare F. S. Mead, "Bank Reserves in the United States, Canada, and England," *Quarterly Journal of Economics*, May 1907.

[52] Sprague, *History of Crises under the National Banking System* (Publications of the National Monetary Commission), especially the chapters dealing with the crises of 1884, 1893, and 1907.

[53] Sprague's suggestion that institutions that make a business of holding banker's deposits should be required by law to keep larger reserves than institutions that do a purely local business merits careful consideration. See his *Banking Reform in the United States* (Cambridge, Mass., 1911), pp. 94 ff.

Chapter 4. Business Depression

[1] In 1908 several businessmen in St. Louis, inspired by sentiments of this sort, organized a "National Prosperity Association," which sought to establish branches in all parts of the country. The chief effort of the association was directed toward inducing producers and manufacturers to agree upon a general resumption of operations on June 1. *Financial Review*, 1909, p. 22.

[2] These reports of fresh suspensions are seldom given as much prominence as the more cheerful news of earlier weeks. Indeed, the newspapers sometimes report the opening of a conspicuous establishment several times within a few months, without referring to its intermittent suspensions. Such cases usually mean that the managers let their small current orders accumulate for a few weeks until enough work is on hand to justify starting the machinery, execute the work rapidly, and then close once more. Compare *Iron Age*, July 30, 1908, Vol. 82, p. 324.

[3] This restriction of demand and the patent misery from which it arises are ordinarily more severe in large cities and industrial towns than in country districts. Farmers may have abundant crops and remunerative prices at the very time mills are idle and their hands are walking the streets. Even when, as in 1894–96, the agricultural interest also suffers from bad seasons or low prices, there is less acute privation in the country than in the towns. Agricultural depression, however, renders the depression in the industrial centers still more intense; for the slackening of the farmers' demand for goods ruins the market for many manufacturing and mercantile enterprises.

[4] Part II, Chapter V, iii; E. W. Kemmerer, *Money and Credit Instruments in their Relation to General Prices* (ed. 2, New York, 1909), p. 131; Irving Fisher, *The Purchasing Power of Money* (New York, 1911), pp. 478–86.

[5] Part II, tables 9, 11, and 12.

[6] For index numbers of the various classes of prices referred to see Part II, Chapter IV, i, 2, 3, 4, 5, 6, and 9; for a fuller analysis of the causes of the differences in range of fluctuation see Chapter 1, iii, 1, D, above.

[7] For index numbers see Part II, Chapter IV, ii; for analysis see Chapter 1, iii, 2, above.

[8] For index numbers see Part II, Chapter IV, iii; for analysis see the next section in the text.

[9] For index numbers see Part II, Chapter IV, iii, 1, 3, and 4.

[10] See Part II, Chapter IV, iv. As the tables in that section show, there is usually a reaction from the lowest prices touched during a crisis, particularly if the crisis has degenerated into a panic; but when the subsequent depression is severe and prolonged prices begin to sag again, and sometimes reach a lower point than that recorded in the time of most intense strain.

[11] See Part II, Chapter VIII, i, and ii, 1.

[12] *Ibid.*, ii, 3–6.

[13] *Ibid.*, 2.

[14] *Ibid.*, 3.

[15] See the monthly figures for the stock of gold money in the appendices to the annual *Reports of the Treasurer of the United States*.

[16] Part II, Chapter VI, iii.

[17] *Ibid.*, iv.

[18] *Ibid.*, v.

[19] *Ibid.*, vi.

[20] New York often presents an apparent exception. In 1908, for example, bank loans were larger in this city than in 1907, chiefly because country banks were sending to New York idle funds they could not use at home, and were depositing in the banks at 2 per cent interest funds they had formerly lent on their own account at call on the Stock Exchange. The demand that absorbed the increased supply of loans arose largely because money could be had for 1 per cent or even less at call and invested in securities that yielded interest or dividends of 4 per

cent or more. The national banks as a whole, and the great foreign banks for which we have statistics, usually show a decline in loans when prosperity is succeeded by depression. See Part II, tables 82–104.

[21] The statistical evidence given in Part II, tables 2–13, is summarized here.

	Number of points by which relative prices fell		
	1893–96	1902–04	
25 foods at wholesale in the United States	31	7	..
25 foods at retail in the United States	10	0	..
	1891–96	1900–03	1907–08
23 foods at wholesale in England	21	5	0
19 foods at retail in England	12	+4	+3
	1891–96	1900–04	1907–08
23 foods at wholesale in France	25	1	8
36 foods at retail in France	8	+1	+2
	1890–96	1902–04	1907–08
20 raw materials in the United States	27	4	12
20 manufactured products in the United States	22	7	9
5 raw materials in the United States	41	+7	7
5 partly manufactured products in the United States	23	+12	6
5 finished commodities in the United States	14	+6	5
45 raw producers' goods in the United States	28	0	15
28 manufactured producers' goods in the United States	22	0	14
18 raw mineral products in the United States	27	5	20
23 manufactured mineral products in the United States	22	2	10
10 raw forest products in the United States	13	+19	18
9 manufactured forest products in the United States	20	+5	13
9 raw animal products in the United States	22	16	7
18 manufactured animal products in the United States	18	1	3
18 raw farm products in the United States	43	+2	2
40 manufactured farm products in the United States	27	+2	7

[22] A similar summary follows of the evidence from Part II, Chapter IV, i and iii, relating to wholesale prices and discount rates during depressions.

	Number of points by which relative prices and relative rates of interest fell		
	1893–97	1903–04	1907–08
Wholesale prices in America	16	0	9
Discount rates in New York, 60–90 days	72	25	41
	1890–95	1900–04	1907–08
Wholesale prices in England	15	7	11
Market discount rates in London	153	46	107
Wholesale prices in France	15	8	14
Market discount rates in Paris	47	43	59
Wholesale prices in Germany	21	8	8
Market discount rates in Berlin	59	43	54

[23] The evidence of Part II, tables 2–17, is as follows:

	Number of points by which relative prices and relative wages fell		
	1893–95	1903–04	
Wholesale prices in America...................................	12	0	..
Relative wages in America....................................	3	+1	..
	1891–95	1900–04	1907–09
Wholesale prices in England..................................	15	7	9
Relative wages in England....................................	3	5	3

[24] Compare, for example, Stuart Daggett's detailed study of *Railroad Reorganization* (Harvard Economic Studies, Vol. IV, Boston, 1908).

[25] See Part II, Chapter V, i.

[26] See Part II, Chapter VIII, i.

[27] Compare Part II, tables 108–13.

[28] Compare the digest of Johannsen's theory of 'impair savings' in Part I, Chapter I, ii, 14.

[29] Compare the various indices of the volume of business presented in Part II, Chapter V.

[30] Alone among the writers reviewed in Part I, Chapter I, Veblen held that the business conditions of depression tend to become chronic rather than to breed prosperity (sec. ii, 10). The basis for this view is that the continual improvements in industrial technique give new plants such an advantage in cost over their older competitors as to keep the majority of existing enterprises always in difficulties. The one remedy Veblen saw for this condition, apart from the favorable accidents that occasionally interrupt the downward trend of prices, is an ever more thorough coalition or combination among businessmen to restrain competition.

The reason business history has not yet answered this expectation is that other price-making factors have proved more potent than technical improvements in methods of production. Among these other factors, the one on which Veblen laid stress—extension of combinations in restraint of competition—certainly requires attention. But the factors mentioned above—particularly the reduction in the operating and supplementary costs of the old enterprises themselves, and the increase of demand for construction work—have so far exercised a powerful influence in restoring conditions that promise a fair margin of profit.

To forecast the future relative force of the numerous factors involved is far from easy. Of course depressions bred prosperity in the days before competition had been severely shackled by combination; but in those days the progress of technique was seemingly less steady than it is now. Should the further progress of combination be checked, however, it is still probable that the changes depression brings about in the efficiency of labor, in the policy of investors, in the capitalization of corporations, in the relative prices of finished products and raw materials, etc., would continue to overbalance the depressing influence exercised by the introduction of improved processes and machinery.

Chapter 5. Wider Aspects of Business Cycles

[1] See the second volume of R. Ehrenberg's *Das Zeitalter der Fugger* (Jena, 1896).

[2] Mentor Bouniatian, *Studien zur Theorie und Geschichte der Wirtschaftskrisen*, Vol. II; *Geschichte der Handelskrisen in England, 1640–1840* (Munich, 1908), chapters 3–6.

[3] *Notice sur la périodicité des crises économiques et ses rapports avec l'exploitation des chemins de fer français;* Ministère des Travaux Publics (Paris, December 1907). Quite independently, Mr. Carl Snyder has suggested the financial advisability of much the same policy for the American railways; New York *Globe and Financial Advertiser*, January 3, 1913.

[4] *The Prevention of Destitution* (London, 1912), pp. 118, 119, and the references given on p. 157; compare B. S. Rowntree and B. Lasker, *Unemployment* (London, 1911), pp. 306–08.

[5] In New York, for example, there seem to be several groups of powerful financiers, each group more or less firmly cemented together by family ties and business interests, but changing from time to time in personnel, in relative prestige, and especially in their relations with other similar groups. Ordinarily each group acts more or less independently, and frequently one group engages in a bitter contest with some rival. Sometimes such contests bring about grave disturbances in the business world, as when the fight between the Hill and Harriman interests for the control of the Burlington railroad led to the Northern Pacific corner of May 1901. But at other times the lack of concerted action is a factor of safety in that it lessens the control any single power can exercise over the financial markets.

[6] Compare Veblen, *Theory of Business Enterprise*, pp. 206–09; Edmond Kelly, *Twentieth Century Socialism* (New York, 1910), Book II, Chapter VI.

[7] George N. Hull, *Industrial Depressions* (New York, 1911).

[8] Compare Part II, Chapter IV, iii, 1, and iv, 6. Since this chapter was written the *New York Times Annalist* has started such compilations.

[9] See Anna Youngman, *The Economic Causes of Great Fortunes* (New York, 1909).

INDEX